Library of
Davidson College

Village Water Supply

*Economics and Policy
in the
Developing World*

A WORLD BANK RESEARCH PUBLICATION

The photograph on the cover and dust jacket was taken in Upper Volta by Ray Witlin for the World Bank.

ROBERT J. SAUNDERS

JEREMY J. WARFORD

Village Water Supply

*Economics and Policy
in the
Developing World*

PUBLISHED FOR THE WORLD BANK

THE JOHNS HOPKINS UNIVERSITY PRESS
Baltimore and London

333.9
S257v

Copyright © 1976 by the International Bank
for Reconstruction and Development

THE WORLD BANK
1818 H STREET, N.W.
WASHINGTON, D.C. 20433
U.S.A.

All rights reserved

The views and interpretations in this book are those of the authors and should not be ascribed to the World Bank, to its affiliated organizations, or to any individual acting in their behalf.

Library of Congress Cataloging in Publication Data

Saunders, Robert J
    Village water supply.

    Bibliography: p. 239
    Includes index.
    1. Underdeveloped areas—Water resources development. 2. Underdeveloped areas—Water supply. I. Warford, Jeremy J., joint author. II. International Bank for Reconstruction and Development. III. Title.
HD1702.S28   333.9′1′091724   76-11758
ISBN 0–8018–1876–1
ISBN 0–8018–1877–X pbk. 77-10188

Contents

Preface ∫ xi

**Part One
Introduction**

1 The Nature of the Problem ∫ 3

    The Current Situation in Developing Countries
        and 1980 Goals ∫ 5
    The Implications of Increasing Emphasis on Rural
        Water Supply and Sanitation Programs ∫ 13
    The Definition of a Rural Program ∫ 20
    Overview of the Study ∫ 26

**Part Two
Goals and Benefits**

2 The Goal of Improved Health ∫ 31

    Water-Related Diseases and
        Their Link with Man ∫ 33
    Multiple Disease Sources and
        Disease Control Factors ∫ 35
    The Empirical Evidence ∫ 36
    The Water-Use Link ∫ 43
    Placing a Value on Better Health ∫ 46
    Indexing and Cost Effectiveness ∫ 52

3 Economic Effects of Investments in Rural Water Supply and Sanitation ∫ 56

Macroeconomic Implications ∫ 56
Direct Effects on Health and Output ∫ 31
Improved Health and Labor Productivity ∫ 66
Increased Time for Productive Work ∫ 71
Effects of Increases in Population
 on per Capita Incomes ∫ 73
Averted Costs ∫ 77
Rural to Urban Drift and Population Location ∫ 78
Summary ∫ 84

Part Three
Program Planning

4 The Determination of Investment Priorities ∫ 89

Costs, Economies of Scale, and Quality of Service ∫ 89
Growth-Point Strategies ∫ 102
Income Redistribution and "Worst-First" Strategies ∫ 103
Financial Contribution and Community Enthusiasm ∫ 108
Conclusions ∫ 110

5 Special Problems of Program Planning ∫ 112

Tradeoffs between Health and Project Costs ∫ 112
System Design and Quality of Service ∫ 118
Population Acceptance ∫ 128
Estimating the Monetary Value of Village Labor ∫ 130
Shadow Pricing ∫ 131
Level of Technology ∫ 134
Complementary Programs ∫ 135
The Time Frame for Investment ∫ 138

6 Administration of Rural Water Supply Programs ∫ 141

Construction Phase ∫ 141
Operation and Maintenance ∫ 142
Centralization versus Decentralization ∫ 144
Agency Responsibility ∫ 147
Training and Incentives ∫ 153
Financial and Income Distribution Considerations ∫ 158

7 Water Charges and Project Evaluation ∫ 164

Some Basic Principles ∫ 165
Relevance of Pricing Theory for Village Water Supply ∫ 171
The Willingness- and Ability-to-Pay Criterion ∫ 184

Part Four
Summary

8 Conclusions and Recommendations ⟩ 193

Population to Be Served ⟩ 193
Economic Development ⟩ 194
Health-Related Benefits ⟩ 195
Redistribution of Income ⟩ 197
System Design ⟩ 198
Administration and Finance ⟩ 198
Long-Term Strategy ⟩ 200

Appendixes

A Improved Water Supply and Sanitation: Studies of Its Impact on Health ⟩ 205

Studies of Diarrheal Disease ⟩ 205
Studies of Several Diseases Including Skin and Diarrheal Diseases ⟩ 213
Studies Dealing with Cholera ⟩ 214
Studies Dealing with Schistosomiasis (Bilharziasis) ⟩ 217
Studies on Child Mortality ⟩ 220

B The "Health-State" Approach to Project Evaluation ⟩ 223

C Economies of Scale: Regression Analysis of U.S. Waterworks Data ⟩ 227

D The Metering Decision ⟩ 235

Bibliography ⟩ 239

Index ⟩ 265

Tables

1.1 Access to Water Supply in 91 Selected Developing Countries, December 31, 1970 ⟩ 4
1.2 Access to Water Supply in 75 Selected Developing Countries, 1962 and 1970 ⟩ 6
1.3 Urban Population in 61 Selected Developing Countries Served by Sewage Disposal Facilities, by Type of Service, December 31, 1970 ⟩ 8

1.4 Total Urban and Rural Population in 61 Selected Developing Countries Served by Sewage Disposal Facilities, December 31, 1970 § 9

1.5 Annual Investment for Construction of Community Water Supply and Sewage Disposal Facilities, 1970 § 10

1.6 Urban Water Supply Targets for 1980 and Related Estimated Costs, by Type of Service § 11

1.7 Urban and Rural Water Supply Targets for 1980 and Related Estimated Costs § 12

1.8 Total Water Supply Targets for 1980 and Related Estimated Costs § 13

1.9 Urban Sewage Disposal Targets for 1980 and Related Estimated Costs, by Type of Service § 14

1.10 Urban and Rural Sewage Disposal Targets for 1980 and Related Estimated Costs § 15

1.11 Total Sewage Disposal Targets for 1980 and Related Estimated Costs § 16

1.12 Percentage of Yearly Country Investment Needed Each Year, to Meet UNDD Village Water Supply Goals § 16

2.1 Diseases Related to Deficiencies in Water Supply or Sanitation § 32

3.1 External Assistance Received for Community Water Supply Projects, 1966–1970 § 58

3.2 External Assistance Received for Community Sewage Disposal Projects, 1966–1970 § 58

4.1 Specifications and Cost Estimates for Four Village Water Supply Systems in Tanzania § 93

4.2 Hypothetical Capital Cost Implications of Service Levels and Treatment § 96

4.3 Estimated Cost for Sewage Disposal § 100

5.1 Responsibility for Surveillance of Drinking Water Quality § 120

5.2 Extent and Frequency of Bacteriological Examinations of Drinking Water § 120

5.3 Adoption of Standards for Quality of Drinking Water § 122

5.4 Daily Water Consumption from Community Water Supply § *124*

5.5 Rural Water Supply House Connections in Peru, 1969–72 § *127*

5.6 Percentage Cost of Imported Material to Total Construction Cost in Community Water Supply and Sewage Disposal § *136*

6.1 Types of Agencies Responsible for Planning of Community Water Supply § *146*

6.2 Types of Agencies Responsible for Construction of Community Water Supply § *148*

6.3 Types of Agencies Responsible for Operation and Maintenance of Community Water Supply § *149*

6.4 Types of Agencies Responsible for Planning of Sewage Disposal Systems § *150*

6.5 Types of Agencies Responsible for Construction of Sewage Disposal Systems § *151*

6.6 Types of Agencies Responsible for Operation and Maintenance of Sewage Disposal Systems § *152*

6.7 Relation of Number of Professional Water Supply Staff Requiring Training during 1972–1976 to Availability of Adequate In-Country Training Facilities § *154*

6.8 Relation of Number of Subprofessional Water Supply Staff Requiring Training during 1972–1976 to Availability of Adequate In-Country Training Facilities § *156*

7.1 Patterns of User Participation in Covering Cost of Urban Water Supply and Sewers § *186*

7.2 Patterns of User Participation in Covering Costs of Rural Water Supply § *187*

7.3 Estimated Monthly Water Charges as a Percentage of Estimated Monthly Income, by Income Group, Twelve Selected Cities § *188*

A.1 Relation between Sanitation and Cholera in Bacolod City, Philippines, 1968–1972 § *216*

A.2 Frequency of Introduction of Cholera Infection into Four Communities, Bacolod City, Philippines, 1968–1972 § *218*

B.1 Simulated Life Prognosis in Village with Endemic Schistosomiasis and Cholera § 223
B.2 Derivation of Village Water Supply Health Status Index § 226
C.1 Selected Regressions, Examining Cost Economies of Scale in the Provision of Water Supplies, United States, 1960 § 231

| *Figures*

1.1 Relation between Village Population, System Costs, and Ability to Pay and Maintain § 24
5.1 Hypothetical Relations between Village Health and Cost of Water Supply Project § 115

Preface

Aware that benefits of national income growth in many countries of the developing world tend to bypass the poorest elements of society, the World Bank has in recent years given increasing attention to investment programs and policies promising direct benefits to lower-income groups. In this regard, hastening the extension of basic services such as water supply and sanitation to less privileged members of society is felt to be of primary importance. This study focuses on the special problems that must be overcome if rapid improvement in this area is to be achieved.

The majority of the poor are found in the rural areas of most developing countries, a fact clearly reflected in the extent to which urban and rural communities have access to a potable water supply and adequate means of waste disposal. Because the technical issues are fairly straightforward and well understood, this study emphasizes the economic, social, financial and administrative issues characteristic of village water supply and sanitation programs and makes policy recommendations accordingly. Although these recommendations are directed to the special circumstances of rural communities, they are also relevant to provision of adequate water and supply and sanitation facilities to the poor—and not so poor—in urban areas of developing countries.

We have based our findings and recomendations upon a detailed survey of the relevant literature, both published and unpublished; personal observation of the operations of village water supply and sanitation programs in about twenty-five countries; and the benefit of the accumulated experience of numerous colleagues and friends at the World Bank, other international organizations, and academic institutions, as well as the operators of the water supply programs themselves. Given the nature of the exercise, which involved the collection of information by means of personal contact rather than simply the analysis of documents, the number of persons to whom we are indebted is particularly large; the following list mentions only a few. Special acknowledgment is due, for their general support and expert advice, to Mervyn L. Weiner, Walter J. Armstrong, Yves Rovani, Harold Shipman, Visvanathan Rajagopalan, Charles Morse, and Richard Middleton; for help in conducting field surveys, to Arthur Bruestle and David Donaldson; for their help and cooperation in the field work, to A. C. Chaturvedi, Tito Cairo, Gladwin Unrau, Alfonso Zavala, C. E. Ngunya, A. K. Roy, C. K. Annan, and N. Saravanapavanathan; for advice on specific issues, to Abel Wolman, David Bradley, B. Cvjetanović, Charles Pineo, Ian Carruthers, Paul Bierstein, Ian Burton, Daniel Okun, Harris Seidel, Donald Lauria, D. Schliessmann, and Gilbert White; for editorial assistance on early drafts to Celeste Boland; and for secretarial help to Maria del Solar and Pattie Koh. The final manuscript was edited and the index prepared by Julia McGraw.

ROBERT J. SAUNDERS
JEREMY J. WARFORD
Energy, Water, and
Telecommunications Department
The World Bank

Washington, D.C.
Spring 1976

Village Water Supply

*Economics and Policy
in the
Developing World*

Part One | *Introduction*

1 | The Nature of the Problem

THE DIRECTOR GENERAL of the World Health Organization stated recently that the provision of a safe and convenient water supply and basic sanitation services is of paramount importance to the health of people living in developing countries.[1] It is universally accepted that an adequate supply of water for drinking, personal hygiene, and other domestic purposes, and an adequate means of waste disposal are essential to public health and well-being. Unfortunately, vast numbers of people in the developing world, most of them living in rural areas, do not have access to a safe and convenient source of water, and where they do, normally do not have satisfactory sewage disposal facilities. A description of the magnitude and nature of the problem and suggestions for dealing with it are the objectives of this book. Its scope is restricted to problems of supplying water and waste disposal facilities for domestic purposes in rural areas of developing countries. Provision of water primarily for agricultural irrigation, industrial, or commercial use, with human consumption goals secondary, will not be considered in detail.

Our definition of "water supply" encompasses everything from a relatively sophisticated pumping, storage, treatment, and distribution system to a simple protected spring or well with no storage, treatment,

---

1. Halfdan Mahler, "Health Strategies in a Changing World," *WHO Chronicle* 29, no. 6 (1975):212.

Table 1.1. Access to Water Supply in 91 Selected Developing Countries, December 31, 1970

World Health Organization region	Urban population supplied						Rural population with reasonable access		Total urban and rural	
	House connections		Public standposts		Total urban					
	Thousands	Percent	Thousands	Percent	Thousands	Percent	Thousands	Percent	Thousands	Percent
Africa	8,876	29	11,921	39	20,797	68	16,717	11	37,514	21
Central and South America	95,410	60	26,724	17	122,134	76	29,549	24	151,683	54
Eastern Mediterranean	38,093	59	16,726	26	54,819	84	31,255	18	86,074	33
Algeria, Morocco, Turkey	12,406	50	5,426	22	17,832	73	18,400	44	36,232	55
Southeast Asia	56,391	36	26,798	17	83,189	53	61,095	9	144,284	17
Western Pacific	25,107	65	3,668	10	28,775	75	16,067	21	44,842	40
Total	236,283	49	91,263	19	327,546	68	173,083	14	50,629	29

Note: The definitions of "rural" and "urban" are those adopted by each country and, as such, are not uniform.
Source: World Health Organization, "Community Water Supply and Sewage Disposal in Developing Countries (End of 1970)," *Statistics Report*, vol. 26, no. 11, 1973, p. 726.

or extensive distribution system. Sanitation facilities include public sewerage, although this is rarely relevant for rural areas in developing countries, where pit privies, septic tanks, public latrines, cesspools, soak-away pits, and rudimentary drains for the removal of water from the immediate vicinity of private residences and public standposts usually represent the appropriate technology.

The Current Situation in Developing Countries and 1980 Goals

Evidence is periodically collected and presented by the World Health Organization (WHO) that the large majority of people in developing countries do not have what is considered in industrialized countries to be a basic necessity, that is, "reasonable access" to a "safe" water supply and adequate means of waste disposal.[2] As of December 31, 1970, in 91 developing countries, only 68 percent of the urban population and 14 percent of the rural population (a weighted average of 29 percent) were adequately served (Table 1.1). Although the relative mixture of rural and urban supplies differs among regions of the world, rural water supply programs lag behind urban programs in all parts of the developing world, with the percentage lag greatest in the two regions least able to meet their urban water supply needs, Africa and Southeast Asia.

The changes occurring in 75 developing countries in the percentage of population supplied with water have been surveyed by WHO in 1962 and in 1970 (Table 1.2). Progress has been made in all of the regions, although the percentages of population supplied with water in the urban areas of the Americas and the Algeria, Morocco, and Turkey region actually declined over the period. This was partly because of the inability of urban public services to keep up with the rapid migration of population from rural to urban areas.

The situation with regard to sewage disposal is slightly worse than that of water supply. By the end of 1970 only 25 percent of the popu-

---

2. "Reasonable access" to water in an urban area as defined by WHO includes, apart from household connections, a public fountain or standpost located not farther than 200 meters from a house. The definition of reasonable access used for rural areas is much less precise. It states simply that the "housewife or members of the household do not have to spend a disproportionate part of the day in fetching the family's water needs." A "safe" water supply is defined simply as uncontaminated water.

Table 1.2. Access to Water Supply in 75 Selected Developing Countries, 1962 and 1970

World Health Organization region	Urban population supplied						Percent of rural population with reasonable access		Percent of total urban and rural	
	Percent by house connections		Percent by public standposts		Percent of total					
	1962	1970	1962	1970	1962	1970	1962	1970	1962	1970
Africa	12	29	38	38	50	67	n.a.	11	n.a.	21
Central and South America	70	59	27	17	86	76	n.a.	22	n.a.	53
Eastern Mediterranean	43	60	28	26	71	86	n.a.	20	n.a.	39
Algeria, Morocco, Turkey	35	50	39	22	74	73	n.a.	44	n.a.	55
Southeast Asia	12	36	19	17	31	53	n.a.	5	n.a.	14
Western Pacific	16	65	34	10	49	75	n.a.	22	n.a.	39
Total	33	50	26	19	59	69	n.a.	12	n.a.	28

n.a. Not available.
Source: Same as Table 1.1, pp. 726–27.

lation in the 61 countries represented in Tables 1.3 and 1.4 had access to adequate pit privies or sewage collection and disposal facilities. In rural areas an average of only 8 percent had access to adequate disposal facilities, with the Southeast Asia region lowest at 3 percent.

A conservative estimate, in our opinion, of the investment in the construction of community water supplies in 91 developing countries, and sewage disposal facilities in 61 countries in 1970 is presented in Table 1.5. Despite the nearly US$1,000 million invested in water supply and US$200 million in sewage disposal in that one year, only 29 and 25 percent, respectively, of the populations of the countries surveyed were served with safe and accessible water and with adequate sewage disposal. A problem of such magnitude will require the commitment of massive resources if it is to be brought under control in the foreseeable future.

Population service targets for water supply and sewage disposal, to be attained by 1980, have been set for the United Nations Development Decade (UNDD). For water supply in all regions except the Americas the 1980 targets are as follows: the supply of 60 percent of the urban population through house connections; the supply of 40 percent of the urban population through public standposts; and the supply of 25 percent of the rural population with easy access to safe water. For the Americas the minimum goals were set at a conference of health ministers in Santiago in 1972: the reduction in the percentage of population not supplied with safe water in 1970 by 50 percent for city dwellers and by 30 percent for the rural population for every country. The water supply targets and what are probably extremely conservative estimates of the costs of meeting those goals are shown in Tables 1.6 to 1.8. It can be seen that more than US$14 billion (in 1970 dollars) must be invested in water supply between 1970 and 1980 to achieve the objectives.[3]

For all regions except the Americas, the 1980 UNDD targets for sewage disposal facilities are the following: to have 40 percent of the urban population connected to public sewerage systems; 60 percent of the urban population provided with household systems; and 25 percent of the rural population provided with adequate sewage disposal facilities. The minimum target adopted by the Pan American

---

3. Several knowledgeable sanitary engineers have suggested that the cost estimates may be low. Informally, they have estimated that, at 1973 prices, 1980 rural target costs would exceed $6 billion, and the combination of rural and urban costs would be at least equal to $20 billion.

Table 1.3. Urban Population in 61 Selected Developing Countries Served by Sewage Disposal Facilities, by Type of Service, December 31, 1970
(Thousands)

World Health Organization region	Public sewage system					Household systems			
	Conventional treatment	Oxidation ponds	Without treatment	Total	Percent of total population	Pit, privy, septic tank	Buckets	Total	Percent of total population
Africa	696	159	347	1,202	11	3,431	953	4,384	40
Central and South America	2,933	1,614	45,699	50,246	34	46,041	20	46,061	31
Eastern Mediterranean	1,023	164	751	1,938	8	21,274	300	21,574	86
Algeria, Morocco, Turkey	267	20	2,976	3,263	27	1,148	355	1,503	13
Southeast Asia	4,468	500	36,659	41,627	26	31,950	43,220	75,170	48
Western Pacific	1,341	19	8,633	9,993	26	14,182	6,099	20,281	53
Total	10,728	2,476	95,065	108,269	27	118,026	50,947	168,973	42

Source: Same as Table 1.1, p. 738.

Table 1.4. Total Urban and Rural Population in 61 Selected Developing Countries Served by Sewage Disposal Facilities, December 31, 1970

World Health Organization region	Total urban		Rural with adequate disposal		Total	
	Thousands	Percent	Thousands	Percent	Thousands	Percent
Africa	5,586	51	13,534	18	19,120	22
Central and South America	96,307	65	25,595	22	121,902	46
Eastern Mediterranean	23,512	94	14,704	21	38,216	40
Algeria, Morocco, Turkey	4,766	40	848	5	5,614	19
Southeast Asia	116,797	74	23,055	3	139,852	16
Western Pacific	30,274	80	3,870	5	34,144	31
Total	277,242	69	81,606	8	358,848	25

Source: Same as Table 1.1, pp. 732-33.

Health Organization (PAHO) for the Americas was the reduction of the percentage of population not served in 1970 by 30 percent for each country. A summary of the 1980 sewage disposal targets and the estimated investment necessary to reach those targets is found in Tables 1.9 to 1.11. As in the case of the water supply cost estimates, the estimated sewage disposal facility costs seem to be conservative, but still amount to almost US$7 billion.

Although the WHO data presented in the tables (and referred to throughout this book) constitute the most recent and comprehensive information available on the state of water supply and sanitation in the developing world, compilers agree that the estimates are subject to error and are therefore useful only for general purposes. One reason for inaccuracy is the variety of definitions current among countries of the terms "urban" and "rural" (accepted as standard for purposes of the survey). Another difficulty is that estimates of the percentage of population served seem too high, appearing in some cases to be as much as 30 percent in error.

With regard to the overall UNDD population service targets, our own estimates suggest that these targets are in some cases unrealistic when viewed in relation to the investment taking place in developing countries today. For example, Table 1.12 presents, for ten of the more populous developing countries, estimates of the proportion of 1972 or 1973 public sector and total investment which would have

Table 1.5. Annual Investment for Construction of Community Water Supply and Sewage Disposal Facilities, 1970 (Thousands of U.S. dollars)

World Health Organization region	Community water supply construction			Sewage disposal system construction		
	Urban	Rural	Total	Urban	Rural	Total
Africa	72,200	19,890	92,090	7,373	2,150	9,523
Central and South America	262,753	46,172	308,925	65,440	5,299	70,739
Eastern Mediterranean	197,656	36,534	234,190	28,970	100	29,070
Algeria, Morocco, Turkey	27,481	66,816	94,297	21,601	460	22,061
Southeast Asia	141,926	43,618	185,544	29,550	4,280	33,830
Western Pacific	62,540	3,992	66,532	13,260	100	13,360
Total	764,556	217,022	931,578	166,194	12,389	178,583

Note: Annual investment includes external, national, and local capital, material, and labor.
Source: Same as Table 1.1, p. 744.

Table 1.6. Urban Water Supply Targets for 1980 and Related Estimated Costs, by Type of Service

World Health Organization region	House connections			Public standposts			
	Population to be served (thousands)		Cost per consumer (U.S. dollars)	Total cost (millions of U.S. dollars)	Population to be served (thousands)		Cost per consumer (U.S. dollars)	Total cost (millions of U.S. dollars)
	By 1980	Increase over 1970			By 1980	Increase over 1970		

Region	By 1980	Increase over 1970	Cost per consumer	Total cost	By 1980	Increase over 1970	Cost per consumer	Total cost
Africa	31,561	22,685	53	1,196.2	21,041	9,299	28	260.9
Central and South America	186,933	95,963	40	3,861.3	26,074	—[a]	—[a]	—[a]
Eastern Mediterranean	61,927	24,248	30	735.4	40,121	24,558	11	274.4
Algeria, Morocco, Turkey	25,140	12,734	12	1,528.1	16,759	11,333	25	283.3
Southeast Asia	143,948	87,557	16	1,387.0	95,966	69,168	9	618.5
Western Pacific	36,577	11,489	22	253.5	24,384	20,316	20	415.4
Total	486,086	254,676	35	8,961.5	224,345	135,074	14	1,853.5

a. Category not applicable.
Source: Same as Table 1.1, pp. 732–33.

Table 1.7. Urban and Rural Water Supply Targets for 1980 and Related Estimated Costs

World Health Organization region	Total urban			Rural with easy access to safe water			
	Population to be served (thousands)		Total cost (millions of U.S. dollars)	Population to be served (thousands)		Cost per consumer (U.S. dollars)	Total cost (millions of U.S. dollars)
	By 1980	Increase over 1970		By 1980	Increase over 1970		
Africa	52,602	31,984	1,457.1	46,841	30,913	20	631.7
Central and South America	213,007	95,963	3,861.3	59,971	31,378	24	749.3
Eastern Mediterranean	102,048	48,806	1,010.8	54,077	37,165	13	465.6
Algeria, Morocco, Turkey	41,899	24,067	1,811.4	12,029	2,671	20	53.4
Southeast Asia	239,914	156,725	2,605.5	218,458	163,269	8	1,244.2
Western Pacific	60,961	32,205	668.9	22,354	8,405	6	52.1
Total	710,431	389,750	10,815.0	413,730	273,801	12	3,196.3

Source: Same as Table 1.1, pp. 732-33.

Table 1.8. Total Water Supply Targets for 1980 and Estimated Cost

World Health Organization region	Population to be served (thousands) By 1980	Increase over 1970	Total cost (millions of U.S. dollars)
Africa	99,443	62,897	2,088.8
Central and South America	272,978	127,341	4,610.6
Eastern Mediterranean	156,125	85,971	1,476.4
Algeria, Morocco, Turkey	53,928	26,738	1,864.8
Southeast Asia	458,372	319,994	2,249.7
Western Pacific	83,315	40,610	721.0
Total	1,124,161	663,551	14,011.3

Source: Same as Table 1.1, pp. 732–33.

to be allocated to village water supplies and sanitation each year between 1970 and 1980, if countries are to meet the targets that have been established on a global basis for the UNDD. Percentages of resources needed vary widely among countries, because of differences in national wealth and in the distribution of population between urban and rural areas. Given the relatively small proportion of uncommitted public sector investment which a country can reallocate from year to year, meeting the 1980 rural water supply targets would seem in many instances to present an overwhelming absorption and distribution problem and to require a reallocation of country resources on such a large scale as to be unattainable. It should be stressed, however, that the targets are global ones, and that, in establishing them, it was intended to leave to individual countries the setting of their own targets, within their own limitations and needs, using UNDD targets as guidelines.

The Implications of Increasing Emphasis on Rural Water Supply and Sanitation Programs

Despite a general awareness of the cost implications of the UNDD targets, governments throughout the developing world are making serious efforts to achieve those goals, which, among others, give greater attention than ever before to rural water supply and sanitation—both in absolute and, with regard to urban facilities, relative terms. That rural development in general, and village water supply

Table 1.9. Urban Sewage Disposal Targets for 1980 and Related Estimated Costs, by Type of Service

World Health Organization region	Public sewerage systems				Household systems			
	Population to be served (thousands)		Cost per user (U.S. dollars)	Total cost (millions of U.S. dollars)	Population to be served (thousands)		Cost per user (U.S. dollars)	Total cost (millions of U.S. dollars)
	By 1980	Increase Over 1970			By 1980	Increase Over 1970		
Africa	7,831	6,629	35	231.2	11,744	7,360	13	96.3
Central and South America	121,510	71,264	26	1,840.5	46,061	—[a]	—[a]	—[a]
Eastern Mediterranean	15,440	13,502	72	975.9	24,274	2,801	23	64.4
Algeria, Morocco, Turkey	8,221	4,958	29	143.8	12,332	10,829	5	54.1
Southeast Asia	95,652	54,025	16	864.4	143,478	68,308	9	586.2
Western Pacific	24,040	15,066	46	692.9	36,060	15,780	12	191.5
Total	272,694	165,444	29	4,748.7	273,922	106,078	9	992.5

a. Category not applicable.
Source: Same as Table 1.1, pp. 740–41.

Table 1.10. Urban and Rural Sewage Disposal Targets for 1980 and Related Estimated Costs

World Health Organization region	Total urban			Rural with adequate disposal			
	Population to be served (thousands)		Total cost (millions of U.S. dollars)	Population to be served (thousands)		Cost per user (U.S. dollars)	Total cost (millions of U.S. dollars)
	By 1980	Increase over 1970		By 1980	Increase over 1970		
Africa	19,575	13,989	327.5	23,575	15,943	5	84.6
Central and South America	167,571	71,264	1,840.5	57,181	32,192	6	185.2
Eastern Mediterranean	39,687	16,303	1,040.3	21,945	9,220	11	106.0
Algeria, Morocco, Turkey	20,553	15,787	197.9	5,571	4,723	3	14.2
Southeast Asia	239,130	122,333	1,450.6	218,212	196,333	3	561.1
Western Pacific	60,100	30,846	884.4	21,580	19,514	4	81.4
Total	546,616	270,522	5,741.2	348,064	277,925	4	1,032.5

Source: Same as Table 1.1, pp. 740–41.

Table 1.11. Total Sewage Disposal Targets for 1980 and Related Estimated Costs

World Health Organization region	Population to be served (thousands) By 1980	Population to be served (thousands) Increase over 1970	Total cost (millions of U.S. dollars)
Africa	43,150	29,932	412.1
Central and South America	224,752	103,456	2,025.7
Eastern Mediterranean	61,632	25,523	1,146.3
Algeria, Morocco, Turkey	26,124	20,510	212.1
Southeast Asia	457,342	318,666	2,011.7
Western Pacific	81,680	50,360	965.8
Total	894,680	548,447	6,773.7

Source: Same as Table 1.1, pp. 740–41.

and sanitation in particular, are increasingly important objectives in developing countries is reflected in a significant shift in emphasis in the policies of bilateral and international aid agencies.

The many and complex reasons for the increasing attention paid to rural water supply obviously include a reaction to the phenomenon of rural to urban drift, with its problems of absorption and attendant economic, social, and political difficulties. Moreover, improved communications make inhabitants of remote communities aware of the facilities available to those living in towns and other more privileged areas, and they exert pressure on their local representatives to help

Table 1.12. Percentage of Yearly Country Investment Needed Each Year, to Meet UNDD Village Water Supply Goals

Country	Percent public sector investment	Percent total country investment
Iran	0.27	0.15
Philippines	1.70	0.20
Brazil	0.84	0.22
Mexico	1.26	0.44
Thailand	1.42	0.92
Nigeria	2.86	1.10
India	3.33	1.93
Indonesia	3.92	1.96
Pakistan	6.28	3.14
Ethiopia	53.80	14.50

Source: World Bank data on total and public sector investments; UNDD goals, as in Tables 1.6–1.8.

them in the same way. Because the greater proportion of the people in developing countries live in rural areas, it is important to politicians to let it be known that they are doing something for this group, even though the actual dent that can be made in the overall problem may remain quantitatively negligible.

A significant shift in emphasis from urban to rural could have important implications for water supply, relative to both achievement of service targets and to the benefits that result from investments in the sector.

At any one time the basic service target in the water supply and sanitation field is to serve the largest possible population with a given quantity of investment. It is generally accepted that, holding constant the quality of service, geological factors, and climate, it is cheaper per person to provide water in urban areas with relatively high population densities than in rural areas with sparsely settled, spatially separated populations. Provided an adequate water source can be developed, the economies of scale associated with the supply and distribution of water and with the administration of water supply and sewerage systems are an argument often used to justify the traditional emphasis on urban facilities.[4]

Proponents of water supply and sanitation investment in rural areas argue that in many cases, however, it is not necessary to provide to residents of rural areas the same quality of water service as that provided to residents of more densely populated and sometimes more affluent urban areas. Residents of large urban areas generally consider it desirable to have house connections, some houses with multiple taps, or, at the very minimum, convenient neighborhood standposts. On the other hand, the protection of an existing water source, the provision of several protected wells with hand pumps, or the provision of a larger well, an infiltration gallery, or an earth dam with a standpost distribution system may be a relatively major improvement in many rural areas of developing countries. Often this lower quality of service, but quite safe, rural system can be constructed at a lower per capita cost than a higher quality of service urban system.

It is also generally true that lower income consumers using the lower quality of service rural systems consume a smaller amount of water daily. In addition, therefore, to smaller per capita investment

---

4. See J. M. Henderson, *Report on Global Urban Water Supply Program Costs in Developing Nations* (Washington, D.C.: International Cooperation Administration, 1961), and the discussion of economies of scale in Chapter 4.

in the distribution system, investment in the water source will not have to be as large on a per capita basis, because lower income rural users do not generally have water-using appliances, flush toilets, or kitchen sinks. Furthermore, rural dwellers use smaller amounts when they have to carry water to their houses instead of having it piped to the house.[5]

Whereas specific cost figures relating to differences in quality of service between urban and rural areas are difficult to find, some empirical evidence supports the contention that per capita costs (presumably for lower quality of service) in rural areas can be lower.[6] When comparing and interpreting financial cost figures, however, care must be taken to ensure that the figures include all the costs, that is, planning, engineering, central administration, personnel training, and continuing technical assistance. Finally, in some cases, rural construction costs can be lowered because rural populations are supposedly more willing than urban populations to work and contribute free labor (in financial terms) to the project.

In summary, if it is accepted that the quality of service in rural areas can or should be less than in urban areas, the objective of serving the greatest number of people per unit of investment can be realized by concentrating on lower quality service in rural water supply and sanitation investment. There is therefore a tradeoff between

---

5. Gilbert F. White, David J. Bradley, and Anne U. White, *Drawers of Water: Domestic Water Use in East Africa* (Chicago: University of Chicago Press, 1972); R. P. Morfitt & Associates, "A Non-Conventional Mass Approach to Rural Village Water Projects," a report to the Pan American Health Organization (Corvallis, Ore., 1969); Richard J. Frankel and P. Shouvanaberakul, "Demand for Water in Small Communities of Northeast Thailand" (Bangkok: Asian Institute of Technology, n.d.).

6. Somnuek Unakul, "Thailand's Rural Community Water Supply Programme, in *Water Supply and Wastewater Disposal in Developing Countries*, ed. M. B. Pescod and D. A. Okun (Bangkok: Asian Institute of Technology, 1971); Dennis Warner, *The Economics of Rural Water Supply in Tanzania*, Economic Research Bureau Paper no. 70.19 (Dar es Salaam: University College, 1970); Pan American Health Organization, *Community Water Supply and Sewage Disposal Programs in Latin America and Caribbean Countries*, Technical Series no. 5 (Washington, D.C.: Dept. of Engineering and Environmental Sciences, 1969), p. 91; White, *Drawers of Water*, pp. 88–91; World Health Organization, "Strategy of Cholera Control" (abbreviated proceedings of the WHO Seminar on the Organization of Cholera Control, Manila, October 6–9, 1970 [BD/Cholera/71.1], Geneva, 1971), p. 17; David Donaldson, "Progress in the Rural Water Programs of Latin America (1961–1971)" (Washington, D.C.: Pan American Health Organization, January 1973), p. 23.

economies of scale and density in urban areas and a lower quality of service in rural areas.

Investment in rural areas can also be cheaper on a per consumer basis in the short run where readily available sources of water are being used to their fullest capacity around the developing country's big urban areas (long-run marginal cost is rising very steeply). Because a massive investment would be required to increase the available water supply to these areas (a major dam, reservoir, or lengthy aqueduct), it might be cheaper on a per person basis to develop low volume, relatively cheap sources of water supply for the rural population. On this basis, however, water supply investment in rural areas would not generally lead to an efficient resource allocation unless the growth of the urban areas were to be completely stopped, an unlikely and undesirable event in most developing countries.

In a more advanced developing country where all big cities and intermediate size towns have some form of functioning water supply system, it is sometimes argued that greater health and economic benefits would be generated if water were improved in rural "bad water" areas rather than urban ones. Although urban areas may need additional investment to reach WHO water supply standards, the contention is that there would be small change in health and economic activity from urban water supply improvement relative to the change to be expected from setting up a series of new water supply systems in rural areas or smaller villages lacking any potable water systems at all. Additional investment in urban areas may show diminishing returns, while initial investment in rural areas would not immediately do so to a significant extent. Because there is very little empirical evidence available on which to base this argument, any investment allocated on these grounds would have to be carefully thought through on a case-by-case basis.

There are, however, compelling reasons to continue emphasis on improving the water supply systems of big cities. In some cases, it is argued, meeting the demands imposed by the increasing population pressure in larger cities should take precedence; otherwise, intermittent supply and emptying of pipes where there is wastewater infiltration would turn the water distribution system into a transmission vehicle for many of the very diseases water supply systems are designed to prevent.

Furthermore, the water supply and sanitation needs of many rural dwellers are often less severe than those of their urban counterparts.

The rural poor usually have some source of water available to them, even if it is unsafe and at a considerable distance from the house. Residents of densely populated urban squatter areas, on the other hand, usually have no alternative for water supply other than a public system (often with private vendors acting as intermediaries). The hardship of the urban poor in circumstances where public water supply and sanitation assistance are unprovided is inevitably more severe, particularly when coupled with the intensified threat of epidemics as population density increases.

The Definition of a Rural Program

When rural or village water supply systems are discussed, one issue that always arises is what constitutes a "rural" area and what exactly is a "village." For purposes of water supply investment there are many alternative ways to define rural or village target areas but, in practice, a hard and fast line cannot be drawn between a large, rural village system and a small, urban system. Village systems expand into urban systems; and scarce manpower, limited financial resources, and the geography of countries in many cases necessitate the consolidation of effort to deal with the entire water supply and wastes sector rather than separately with each subsector. Discussion of the rural water supply subsector in isolation can lead to a failure in the development of sound economic and social policies and programs for dealing with the nation's water supply as a whole. National water supply and sanitation sector surveys are usually a necessity if plans are to be developed which will permit the establishment of the most feasible programs for coping with a country's total urban and rural needs.

Definition by Population Size

The most common means of identifying water supply programs within countries is to define specific programs as dealing with all villages, towns, cities, and so on, having populations that fall within certain size limits. This kind of program definition is, of course, somewhat arbitrary; and official program-size limits vary widely from country to country, region to region, and sometimes among different program agencies within the same country. Worldwide, rural water supply program limits vary from settlements with only 50 to 100 village inhabitants, to rural cities with populations over 20,000. A few examples include (a) a program administered by the Ministry of Health in Peru which concentrates on villages with a population of less than 2,000; (b) a program administered by the Secretary of Hydraulic Resources in Argentina which concentrates on towns with a population of 3,000 or fewer inhabitants who can be "feasibly" connected to a central water system; (c) a program in Mexico, administered by the Ministry of Health, concentrating on towns with a population of less than 2,500, and a companion program administered by the Secretary of Hydraulic Resources concentrating on towns with a population of 2,500 to 5,000; (d) a program administered by the national water agency (INAPA) in the Dominican Republic which is attempting to serve all localities with a population of 2,000 or less in which there is a concentrated population of at least 500; and (e) a program administered by the Sanitary Engineering Division of the Ministry of Health in Thailand which concentrates on communities with a population between 500 and 5,000.

Other Considerations in Defining Programs

A number of other considerations enter into rural water supply and sanitation program definitions in different countries. Rural water supply programs in Kenya, for example, have essentially been defined on the basis of which international or bilateral aid agencies are interested in financing what kinds of programs. As a result, among Kenya's specific rural water programs are (a) a Minor Urban Water Supply Program, half of whose financing is from a grant from Norwegian Aid (NORAD), which is building or renovating systems in forty so-called growth centers with populations ranging between 1,000 and 20,000, and averaging about 2,500; (b) a Rural Water Supply Program financed partly by loans from the Swedish International Development Authority (SIDA), the first stage of which was to construct 83 water supply systems for areas of population between 300 and 52,000 (a second-stage loan was signed in 1972, and a third-stage loan was negotiated in 1975); and (c) a County Council Water Supply Program, supposed to provide 561 small, rural schemes and promoted and financed primarily as a WHO/UNICEF Demonstration Project. Other countries have simply identified geographic regions and defined regional programs that are primarily rural in nature with the objective of supplying "everyone possible" in those regions with access to potable water.

Additional modifications sometimes noted in official definitions of rural water supply programs are the following:

1. That it is generally too costly to supply sparsely concentrated populations with water. The Dominican Republic definition cited above, in which the localities with a population of 2,000 or less must have a "concentrated" population of at least 500 is an example of such a definition.

2. That low-income populations will probably not be able to pay the total financial costs of their water supply systems. In Ghana, for example, rural systems were, during a recent period, defined as those supplying water to communities with populations of 10,000 and below because a population less than 10,000 was thought to be generally unable to provide the financial support for urban levels of service.

3. That villages included in the program and supplied with water should be able to generate local leadership support and a general population enthusiasm necessary to use and maintain a water supply system properly (investment may easily be wasted without local support). It is common, for example, to find statements about existing rural supply programs such as: "It has been observed that greater numbers of those supposedly served by the wells are not using them during seasons when a nearby pond, canal, or backyard dug well has plenty of water at shorter carrying distance, or are not using the water at all because of taste or high iron content, or prefer a traditional family source." [7] Even the most rudimentary technologies may be too much for some communities to cope with in the absence of appropriate leadership, education, or community enthusiasm. To quote the same source again, in some communities, even "maintenance of hand pumps has so far proved to be an insurmountable problem." [8]

4. That since the heart of rural development rests on agricultural productivity, a community where agriculture, or subsistence agriculture, is the primary employment could be classified as a rural community for purposes of potable water supply and sanitation investment. A rural community definition such as this was suggested by Unesco in 1958 and is in use in the USSR.[9]

5. That population migration to the larger urban areas is creating a problem in most developing countries, and therefore those villages

---

7. Frederick E. McJunkin, *Community Water Supply in Developing Countries,* U.S. Agency for International Development and the U.S. Public Health Service, Office of International Health (Chapel Hill, N.C., 1969), p. 17.
8. Ibid., p. 43.
9. Donaldson, "Progress in the Rural Water Programs," p. 40.

or areas with the most rapid population exodus are the villages or regions which should receive priority water supply.

In practice, it is fairly obvious that, when choosing the types of villages to be served under a particular water supply program, there will be a considerable overlap in the villages or geographic areas which fit under the above definitional considerations. An eligible village with a population between 500 and 4,000 can also be a source of out-migration to urban areas, have a predominantly subsistence agricultural economy and a strong and supportive local government, and be close to several other smaller clusters of population that could also be served efficiently from a central water supply system.

In choosing an exact program definition and focus, the way in which the country's rural population is located on a spatial basis is certainly one of the most important factors to consider. It is generally not feasible, because of high per capita costs, to provide potable water near all dwellings when the target population is relatively dispersed. In the case of a dispersed population, which is not concentrated in clusters or in villages with more than the equivalent of 50 to 100 single-family dwellings, the best that can probably be done is to sponsor a program of occasional protected springs or dug wells with hand pumps, each of which serves a particular geographic area. A more technically complicated system for a dispersed population would generally be very costly on a per consumer basis and would be almost impossible to maintain. A program designed to serve the non-clustered population could simply be called a "dispersed population water supply program," or some similar name describing the target which is the focus of the program. Of course, there are many acceptable ways to define or classify problem-oriented programs for a particular country. One example of a more or less specific classification system is the one proposed by the Pan American Health Organization,[10] in which the possibilities were consolidated into three groups: (a) a community well program for the dispersed population, (b) a rudimentary aqueduct program for semiconcentrated populations, and (c) a rural aqueduct program for the concentrated and village populations.

If differences in the cost of obtaining water from different sources are ignored and only more sophisticated piped water supply systems for clusters of population in rural areas are considered, the average per

10. Ibid., p. 41.

capita cost of systems tends to be less for larger villages (see the discussion of costs and economies of scale in Chapter 4). Larger villages also tend to be better able financially to contribute to the support of a piped system and, in some countries, are more likely to contain a population able to be trained to help maintain a piped system. Figure 1.1 illustrates this general relation.

Experience in several Latin American countries indicates that for a water supply system with storage and distribution facilities, and with a mixture of house connections and public fountains, the minimum size of village which can be served satisfactorily is one with 100 dwellings, or approximately 500 to 700 people. A system may be defined as "satisfactory" if it functions technically as it was designed to do, and if the financial contribution of the local water consumer covers at least operating and maintenance costs. Clearly, however, the minimum satisfactory size of the system will vary from one part of the world to another.

Given these general size-cost guidelines, a rural water supply program designed to do more than dig wells and install hand pumps could actually be defined as a "non-urban concentrated population" water supply program. In fact, further concentration of rural populations may be an objective of such a program. This applies in part to the rural water supply program in Mexico, where in 1971 approxi-

Figure 1.1. Relation between Village Population, System Costs, and Ability to Pay and Maintain

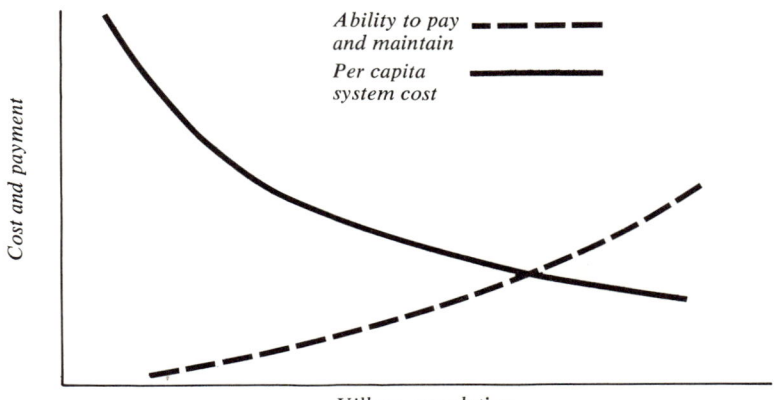

mately 13,600 communities with a population between 500 and 2,500 were targeted as communities which should be served by a rural water supply program. It was hoped that, by providing water to these communities, they would increasingly attract some of the 9.5 million people living in the 87,000 communities with a population of fewer than 500. If so, more people could be served with available resources at a lower average cost.

Even a "dispersed population well program" could serve through time to concentrate population into clusters. In Panama, water supply systems are currently being introduced into communities which grew up around wells with hand pumps installed with UNICEF assistance in the early 1960s. Exact data on the specific reasons for the increased population clustering are not available, but it is reasonable to assume that the protected wells with hand pumps were a contributing factor.

An Appropriate Basis for Definition

The reason for having different sets of conditions for supplying water in urban and rural areas is, then, that there tend to be different problems to be overcome and different goals to be met, necessitating the creation of water supply and sanitation programs having different policies for urban and rural areas.

There clearly are differences: as communities become smaller or more sparsely populated, the nature of the water supply and sanitation problem changes. For a given quality of supply the combination of relatively low incomes and relatively high per capita costs of piped supplies in rural areas are, we believe, dominant factors to consider in defining communities as rural and in establishing appropriate policies to deal with them. The problem of financial feasibility we find also to be absolutely critical in distinguishing urban from village water supply and sanitation operations. Generally, as a proxy for economic feasibility of systems, financial feasibility gives us an idea as to the economic justification of investments, and therefore removes the need to try the impossible: to trace the exact impact of improved facilities on health, or to attempt to enumerate and measure other benefits. Furthermore, the abysmal record on the physical operation and maintenance of rural systems in developing countries appears to be closely associated with inability to collect sufficient revenues from consumers. This deficiency sometimes reflects inability to pay, but more often implies inadequate management and institutional arrangements, and a lack on the part of consumers of appreciation of the value of potable water.

A definition which reflects only low incomes and high costs can lead to apparently absurd conclusions—perhaps that cities with such tremendous economic and social problems as Calcutta should be included in the rural category. The primary issue in all these cases, however, is one, first, of reforming technical and administrative policies in order to reduce costs and improve efficiency, and, second, of finding methods to raise the necessary funds, either by community contribution or by direct payment from consumers. The same general approach might therefore be necessary whether the population of the community concerned is ten million or ten. The issue of whether for policy purposes a community should be included within the group classified as rural can be reduced to the question: After all means of improvement on the cost and efficiency side have been exhausted, does self-generation of sufficient funds remain impossible? Although physical differences between large and small, densely or sparsely populated communities are important for technical purposes, the financial implications of those differences are a far more useful basis for classifying communities.

Overview of the Study

Chapter 2 addresses a fundamental issue: the relation between improved water supply and sanitation, on the one hand, and health, on the other. Although improvement in health is normally cited as the basic justification for investment in this area, the empirical evidence to date (twenty-eight studies are summarized in Appendix A) does not do much to help us predict the impact of a water supply or sanitation project on health in a particular instance. As is shown in Chapter 3, the problem of the prediction of specific benefits of water supply and sanitation investment (economic or social, physical or monetary) is pervasive. This chapter discusses the economic benefits that might obviously be expected to result from investments in rural water supply schemes, but great uncertainty is invariably present.

In the light of these difficulties, the determination of investment priorities becomes as much an art as a science. There are, however, a number of relatively objective tests that can be carried out which will help to ensure that investment priorities are determined in a sensible, if not a scientifically rigorous, fashion. These tests include cost minimization (economies of scale are important), the economic viability of the community, and the probability of financial feasibility of the system. These are analyzed and recommendations are made in Chapter 4.

Chapter 5 discusses a number of the program planning issues that invariably arise; these include tradeoffs between health and project costs, quality of service, population acceptance, self-help schemes, and the appropriate level of technology to be employed. Administrative issues are further amplified in Chapter 6. Determination of the appropriate authority to run a rural water supply program and of policies relating to such diverse areas as training and staff incentives are linked by their relevance for the efficient operation and maintenance of rural water supply installations. Indeed, the poor operation and maintenance of existing systems is widely believed to be the single most important obstacle to rapid improvement in this area.

Chapter 7 contains an analysis of the importance of economic pricing rules for the efficient allocation of resources used in water supply and sanitation projects, showing how general principles may be adapted to suit the special case of rural water supply. The chapter brings together important issues dealt with earlier, such as the problem of benefit measurement, the need to generate revenues, the use of self-help schemes, the general issue of how to determine investment priorities, and so on. Our conclusion is that prediction with an acceptable degree of precision as to the exact effects of improved rural water supply and sanitation is unlikely and that time is wasted in trying to make such predictions. Rather, we shall have to continue to rely upon rule-of-thumb tests for project desirability, at least for investments which provide for the basic needs—necessary to achieve health objectives—of the rural poor. To assist the financial feasibility and continued satisfactory operation of the water supply authority, and to ensure that clearly wasteful use of water and of water supply investment is avoided, one clear message does emerge: that all water in excess of a basic minimum necessary for health purposes should be charged for on the basis of its true economic cost to society. Such a policy must be followed if a good rate of improvement in this area is to be achieved. Chapter 8 summarizes our conclusions and recommendations.

Part Two | Goals and Benefits

2 | The Goal of Improved Health

AN IMPROVEMENT IN WATER SUPPLY and sanitation can generate interrelated improvements in health, income, and social welfare. Although such benefits are used to justify massive investment expenditures, in practice they are hard to identify and harder to measure. While it is possible to make rational decisions about unquantifiable goals or benefits if their economic costs are known, even this information is often unavailable.

There are many possible benefits that might derive from a rural water supply and sanitation program. We need to identify these benefits because, in most rural programs, we cannot—as we can in the case of most urban systems—use financial feasibility or consumers' willingness to pay as a demonstration of the economic worth of investments in this sector.[1] The goal most frequently cited in existing project literature is that of improved health. Some of the major problems inherent in achieving this goal will be noted, as well as some of the difficulties of measuring the extent of its potential benefits.

---

1. We recommend, however, that this is something to aim for over the long run (see Chapter 7).

Table 2.1. Diseases Related to Deficiencies in Water Supply or Sanitation

Group	Diseases	Route leaving man [a]	Route entering man [a]
Waterborne diseases	Cholera	F	O
	Typhoid	F, U	O
	Leptospirosis	U, F	P, O
	Giardiasis	F	O
	Amoebiasis [b]	F	O
	Infectious hepatitis [b]	F	O
Water-washed diseases	Scabies	C	C
	Skin sepsis	C	C
	Yaws	C	C
	Leprosy	N(?)	?
	Lice and typhus	B	B
	Trachoma	C	C
	Conjunctivitis	C	C
	Bacillary dysentery	F	O
	Salmonellosis	F	O
	Enterovirus diarrheas	F	O
	Paratyphoid fever	F	O
	Ascariasis	F	O
	Trichuriasis	F	O
	Whipworm (*Enterobius*)	F	O
	Hookworm (*Ankylostoma*)	F	O, P
Water-based diseases	Urinary schistosomiasis	U	P
	Rectal schistosomiasis	F	P
	Dracunculosis (guinea worm)	C	O
Water-related vectors	Yellow fever	B	B mosquito
	Dengue plus dengue hemorrhagic fever	B	B mosquito
	West-Nile and Rift Valley fever	B	B mosquito
	Arbovirus encephalitides	B	B mosquito
	Bancroftion filariasis	B	B mosquito
	Malaria [c]	B	B mosquito
	Onchocerciasis [c]	B	B *Simulium* fly
	Sleeping sickness [c]	B	B tsetse
Fecal disposal diseases	Hookworm (*Necator*)	F	P
	Clonorchiasis	F	Fish
	Diphyllobothriasis	F	Fish
	Fasciolopsiasis	F	Edible plant
	Paragonimiasis	F, S	Crayfish

a. F = feces; O = oral; U = urine; P = percutaneous; C = cutaneous; B = bite; N = nose; S = sputum.
b. Though sometimes waterborne, more often water washed.
c. Unusual for domestic water to affect these much.

Water-Related Diseases and Their Link with Man

Water-related diseases affecting man's health are relatively widespread and abundant in rural areas of developing countries. The incidence of these diseases depends on local climate, geography, culture, sanitary habits and facilities, and, of course, on the quantity and quality of the local water supply, and methods of waste disposal. Changes in water supply may affect different groups of diseases in different ways: one group may depend on changes in water quality, another on water's availability, and another on indirect effects of standing water.

For example, the installation of a safe water supply piped into the house in a tropical village may protect the family against cholera, previously transmitted through the polluted pond supply, against the skin and diarrheal diseases resulting from their previous inability to wash, against schistosomiasis which infected them when they stood in the pond to collect water, and against the virus fevers spread by the mosquitoes breeding in the old water storage jar.

Some of the important water-related infective diseases are summarized in Table 2.1. They are grouped in five general categories which help to predict the likely effects of changes in water supply upon the health of man.[2] It should be noted that the groups are not necessarily mutually exclusive and that there is some uncertainty over several diarrheal diseases as to which of the first two categories they best occupy. Of the five groups, four are primarily water related, whereas the fifth is determined chiefly by the adequacy of sanitation facilities.

Waterborne diseases Water acts only as a passive vehicle for the infecting agent. All of these diseases depend also on poor sanitation.

---

2. The five-group classification system and the group defintions which follow are derivatives of those originally proposed by David J. Bradley, "Infective Disease and Domestic Water Supplies," in *Water Supply,* ed. G. Tschannerl, BRALUP Research Paper no. 20 (Dar es Salaam: University of Dar es Salaam, 1971, pp. 115–30; and by Gilbert F. White, David J. Bradley, and Anne U. White, *Drawers of Water: Domestic Water Use in East Africa* (Chicago: University of Chicago Press, 1972). David Bradley is the primary source of the disease transmission information presented in Table 2.1, and of the classification system.

Water-washed diseases	Lack of water and poor personal hygiene create conditions favorable for their spread. The intestinal infections in this group also depend on lack of proper human waste disposal.
Water-based diseases	A necessary part of the life cycle of the infecting agent takes place in an aquatic animal. Some are also affected by waste disposal. Infections spread other than by contact with or ingestion of water have been excluded.
Diseases with water-related insect vectors	Infections are spread by insects that breed in water or bite near it. Adequate piped supplies may remove people from the biting areas or enable them to dispense with water storage jars where the insects breed. Unaffected by waste disposal.
Diseases related to fecal disposal and very little affected by water more directly	These are one extreme of a spectrum of diseases, mostly water washed, together with a group of water-based type infections likely to be acquired only by eating uncooked fish or other large aquatic organisms.

It can be assumed on the basis of current medical knowledge (summarized in Table 2.1) that if all water supply and sanitation facilities in a rural area were improved to the point where pathogenic bacteria or disease-carrying vectors did not exist, or the vectors were not contaminated, the health of the local population would be better than that of a population living in a similar but unimproved area. Conceptually, this statement is true although, in practice, with limited resources for water supply and sanitation improvement, there are at least four major problems to be considered by a potential rural water supply and sanitation investor. First, there are multiple sources of diseases. Second, a variety of physical and cultural factors must be taken into consideration in attempting to control diseases. Third, a water and sanitation improvement scheme which eliminated all water-associated health problems would, in most rural areas of developing countries, be very costly, if not impossible, in relation to available resources and the opportunity costs of those resources. Fourth, as the project engineer or economist attempted to make tradeoffs between costs and benefits, he would find it difficult (and sometimes arbitrary) to attach a meaningful value or measurable benefit to different levels of "better" health.

Multiple Disease Sources and Disease Control Factors

In rural South America, Asia, or Africa one potential source of a variety of diseases would probably be eliminated by improving and protecting a spring, digging a protected well and installing a hand pump, assisting a village with a pit privy program, or drilling a borehole and setting up a small pumping and storage facility, a distribution system with several standposts, and a few house connections. But in most rural areas where disease is a problem any number of the following situations may exist: (a) many members of the local population occasionally visit nearby areas with unimproved water; (b) much of the population still prefers to bathe or wash clothes in local waterholes or streams; (c) local cattle and insects are carriers of a variety of diseases; (d) much of the local fruit and vegetables is improperly washed; (e) local customs do not dictate the need for localized or sanitary excreta disposal; or (f) the drinking water dispensed at the spring or standposts is stored in containers that are sometimes open to flies and are frequently dipped into, thereby exposing the water to a variety of parasites, bacteria, and viruses.

In situations such as these, it is clear that while improved drinking water is probably a necessary condition for the improvement of people's health, it is not a sufficient condition. Because health is affected by numerous environmental, social, and cultural factors, it would be speculative to predict what the elimination of potential infections at the "official" water source would mean to the overall health of a community. In some cases an improved water supply might not significantly alter the health of the community; in other climates or types of terrain, however, or with house connections and other sanitary and health education measures taken in conjunction with the improvement of the supply of drinking water, a significant improvement in local health might be achieved. From a general sanitation point of view, permanent improvements in health are unlikely, if not impossible, unless a safe and convenient water supply either precedes or accompanies other sanitary measures. Improved excreta disposal, food and market sanitation, personal hygiene, and village cleanliness, undertaken to prevent and control filthborne diseases, are dependent on the availability of a good water supply.

The interrelations between water supply, other environmental sanitation measures, and health pose a difficult problem to the investor in rural or village water supply and sanitation. He must attempt to design a least-cost system of water supply and sanitation-related components which will, with an acceptable probability, bring the health of the specific community up to some predetermined level.

A necessary input in planning a water supply and sanitation program at least partially designed to improve health in rural areas is a knowledge of the extent of the improvements in health associated with past improvements in water supply and sanitation. The following section attempts to introduce and summarize some of the most important empirical work in this area.

The Empirical Evidence

From a survey of the existing literature that examined the relation between health and water supply and sanitation we have abstracted twenty-eight studies. While this is not a complete census of such studies, we feel that those presented are representative and contain many of the more important contributions. For purposes of our review, the studies are grouped according to the following five categories (not necessarily mutually exclusive): those dealing primarily with diarrheal diseases; those dealing with several diseases including skin and diarrheal diseases; those dealing with cholera; those dealing with schistosomiasis or bilharziasis; and those on childhood mortality.

The twenty-eight studies, summarized in Appendix A, are of two main types, cross-section and time series. Cross-section studies examine existing conditions at a specific time. Although it is not possible to show absolute correlation between a better water supply and lower disease rates, it can be shown that differences in water quantity or quality are associated with differences in disease rates. A cross-section study unfortunately cannot assign exact causes to the observed differences in disease levels. Unknown or uncontrollable factors of a cultural, social, economic, or environmental nature may have been at work, or perhaps the differences observed existed before differences in the water supply or sanitation conditions became significant. For example, an observed correlation between better water and health could, in fact, be the result of an already healthier population taking steps to improve its water supply.

It must always be assumed in cross-section studies that the investigators are aware of, and can account for, all differences which exist within or among the target population(s) at the time of the study. Tentative causation from the observed relationships may be imputed only if the investigators are confident of this assumption. It is only too easy to overlook, however, some of the many other relevant factors that could have been associated with observed differences in health or disease rates.[3]

The second type of study examines changes through time. In these studies the emphasis is on changes in health and disease rates and not on differences in them as is the case with cross-section studies. The major assumption in time series studies is that all changes taking place in all relevant variables are known and accounted for in the interpretation of the influences on health or disease rates of changes in water supply or sanitation levels. Generally, these studies are undertaken by improving water supply or sanitation facilities in one or more areas and monitoring health changes. This may be done with or without monitoring a control area: that is, an unimproved area which is otherwise similar to the one in which sanitation has been improved. Studies with a control area are preferred because investigators are better able to identify and account for hidden factors that change through time and may affect health. Using a control area identical to the change area, it can be assumed that, other than the explicit change in the water supply system or sanitation facilities in the change area, any hidden or subtle changes which occur in one area will also occur in the other area. The relevant study comparisons, therefore, are the differences in health in the two areas at some point in time after the water supply in the change area has been improved, rather than simply the changes in health which occurred sometime after improvements were made in the water supply or sanitation facilities.[4]

Because of a variety of conceptual and empirical factors the

---

3. Of the studies described in Appendix A, numbers 1, 2, 4, 5, 7–9, 11–16, 22, 23, 27, and 28 are essentially cross-sectional.

4. In Appendix A studies 3, 18, and 25 are studies which were made on a through-time basis without a control area, while 6, 10, 17, 19–21, 24, and 26 were made on a through-time basis with some type of control area.

twenty-eight studies which we have reviewed examining the association between water supply, sanitation, and health do not provide an exact statement of what will happen to specific health levels if certain specific water supply and sanitation changes are made in known locales. Empirically, all of the studies experienced one or more of the following problems:

1. It is almost always impossible to identify and account for all of the related factors (social, economic, environmental, and cultural) which are different or changing either among comparative populations or through time.

2. In particular it is difficult to deal with the systematic bias; for example, both cross-sectionally and through time better water supplies are usually associated with better housing, nutrition, education, sanitation, etc., each of which, quite independently, is expected to have a beneficial effect on health.

3. Sampling errors have undoubtedly been brought about by:
    a. incomplete reporting on disease and sickness;
    b. incomplete and inaccurate records;
    c. lack of cooperation, suspicion, or apathy on the part of the sample population;
    d. reliance on a mother's opinion or memory;
    e. inexperienced or untrained interviewers;
    f. language difficulties; and
    g. an attempt on the part of the sample population to tell the interviewer what the interviewer presumably wants to hear.

4. Different seasons of the year are associated with differences in disease rates.

5. Weather unpredictability influences control area or general water availability and the frequency of illness.

6. Even though sanitary facilities are installed, it is sometimes difficult to control the extent to which they will be used or properly maintained.

7. Breast feeding is an important factor difficult to control or measure in infant diarrheal and other disease rates.

8. In studying the health of older children, the sanitary condition of their schools, their jobs, and their most frequent play areas should be considered, as well as that of their homes.

9. Target populations are not fixed. Populations take periodic short trips and permanently migrate.

Although the many difficulties cited give us little confidence of being able to predict with acceptable accuracy the impact of investments in improved water and sanitation facilities, the studies we have examined have been informative. Thus the diarrheal disease studies provide some empirical evidence that the closer a family is to protected water, the lower will be the incidence of diarrhea. Other things being equal, those families with water inside the house tend to have the lowest infection rates, those with water very close outside the house have the next lowest, and those with the water source farther away have the highest. The ease with which reasonably good water can be obtained by users seems to be the key factor.

The observed relationship between the quantity of water and diarrhea prevalence shows that infecting agents can reach the mouth in many ways, including through unwashed food and unclean hands. It also partially reflects the fact that infants less than two years old, who generally have high diarrhea prevalence rates, probably are infected frequently, not by drinking unsafe water but by mothers who do not practice good personal hygiene. Gordon, for example, contends that "water for hygiene uses in adequate amounts and ready accessibility has more significance for this age group (less than two years old) than provision of a potable supply."[5] Related factors contributing to the incidence of diarrheal diseases are the availability of some form of sanitary excreta disposal and the extent to which a population is afforded health education. Furthermore, in a given culture, the need for health education seems to be inversely related to the population's socioeconomic state.

There is also a considerable body of opinion which holds that while water supply and sanitation are certainly important in controlling diarrhea, the most important factor as far as children are concerned is their nutritional state.[6] This is based on the argument that the usual route of transmission is by hand to mouth and not by some single controllable source such as domestic water, and therefore the nutritional state of the child host is more important in the etiology of the disease than is the method of transmission. It is still difficult, however, to evaluate these contentions since a thorough examination of possible tradeoffs between water supply and nutrition

---

5. J. E. Gordon, "Acute Diarrheal Disease," *American Journal of the Medical Sciences* 248 (September 1964):360.

6. Nevin S. Scrimshaw, "Synergism of Malnutrition and Infection: Evidence from Field Studies in Guatemala," *Journal of the American Medical Association* 212 (June 1970):1685–92.

has not been completed. In one study in which nutrition and diarrhea were examined, for example, it was stated that water supply had little role in the etiology of diarrheal disease even though the environmental sanitation program, which was to be implemented and monitored in a "treatment" village, was inadequately implemented and the water supply was in fact little improved.[7]

To the extent that diarrheal disease can be reduced or eliminated among young children (by improved water supply and sanitation, better nutrition, or other means), there will be an increased absorption of the nutrients consumed by the children. As a result, less food wastage will occur.[8] As in the case of the water supply-health relationship, studies are also currently being carried out attempting to measure more accurately the magnitude of this gastrointestinal disease, malabsorption, and its relation to food wastage.

As one would expect, the studies pertaining to skin diseases show that empirically skin disease prevalence is inversely related to the quantity of water available for use. The closer the protected water source is to the family, the greater the probability that family members will use larger quantities of it and that they will have a lower incidence of skin disease.

Cholera is a "waterborne" disease and the quantity of water available has nothing to do with infection rates. The three cholera studies examined show that protected water supplies in a specific area are associated with significantly lower cholera infection rates in that area. While people can travel out of the protected area, contract cholera, and bring it back into the area, if there is a protected water supply, the spread of cholera will be better contained. Improved and protected excreta disposal is shown to be another important factor in the control of cholera.

With regard to the overall prevention of cholera, an interesting study on the costs of alternative ways to prevent cholera was carried out on data collected in the Philippines. Given evidence that available anticholera vaccines are of low and short-lived effectiveness, the costs and effects of immunization were examined relative to the costs and

---

7. John W. Wall and J. Phillip Keeve, "Water Supply, Diarrheal Disease, and Nutrition: A Survey of the Literature and Recommendations for Research," draft working paper (Washington, D.C.: World Bank, September 1974).

8. Nevin S. Scrimshaw, Carl E. Taylor, and John E. Gordon, *Interactions of Nutrition and Infection*, WHO Monograph Series no 57 (Geneva: World Health Organization, 1968).

effects of providing simple privies in rural communities. The conclusion was that "sanitation (excreta disposal) proves both to be more effective and less expensive than vaccination, especially in long-term programs for control and elimination of cholera from endemic areas." [9]

Typhoid fever is another "waterborne" disease. Although no studies were reviewed that focused on an examination of the specific relationship between improved water and typhoid fever incidence, a simulation exercise was completed [10] comparing the costs and effects of typhoid vaccination with the costs and effects of improved sanitation. It was concluded that the antityphoid vaccine that gives high and long-lasting immunity is actually less effective and more costly in the long run than is the construction of privies.

Schistosomiasis or bilharziasis is a "water-based" disease, or a disease where a necessary part of the lifecycle of the infecting agent takes place in aquatic animals (see Appendix A). It results from infection by several species of worm which, as larvae, develop inside certain types of snails. Approximately a month after entering the snail, the larvae are shed back into the water and at this point can penetrate a person's skin on contact. One of the studies reviewed, dealing specifically with schistosomiasis, showed that children living closer to a river had higher infection rates and that children living in houses that did not have indoor water taps also had higher schistosomiasis infection rates. The other three studies showed that water supply or sanitary facilities designed to make it unnecessary for people to go near snail-infected waters generally resulted in lower human infection rates.

The Rockefeller Foundation is continuing its sponsorship of the schistosomiasis control study on St. Lucia.[11] One of the focuses of the

9. B. Cvjetanović, Sanitation versus Vaccination in Cholera Control: Cost-Effect and Cost-Benefit Aspects, in "Strategy of Cholera Control" (BD/Cholera/71.1) (Geneva: World Health Organization, 1971) pp. 17–24.

10. B. Cvjetanović, B. Grab, and K. Uemura, "Epidemiological Model of Typhoid Fever and Its Use in the Planning and Evaluation of Antityphoid Immunization and Sanitation Programmes," *Bulletin of the World Health Organization* 45, no. 1 (1971):53–75.

11. P. Jordan et al., "Control of Schistosoma Mansoni Transmission by Provision of Domestic Water Supplies in St. Lucia; a Preliminary Report" (New York: The Rockefeller Foundation, 1974); Gladwin O. Unrau, "Individual Household Water Supplies in Rural St. Lucia as a Control Measure against Schistosoma Mansoni" (New York: The Rockefeller Foundation, 1974); John M. Weir, "The Unconquered Plague," *The Rockefeller Foundation Quarterly* 2(1969):4–23.

study is to examine the costs and effects of alternative methods for combating schistosomiasis. As noted in the discussion of this study (Appendix A, abstract 26), one of the methods being examined is to encourage people to stay away from snail-infested creek water by providing alternative water facilities, such as piped water to each house, community laundry and shower facilities, and swimming–wading pools for children. Tentative results of the study indicate that "recurrent costs of the household water supplies project in the Riche Fond Valley are lower than annual costs of a mollusciciding operation in a nearby valley, and after a few more years overall costs of the water supplies will probably be no greater than those of mollusciciding." [12] With regard to treatment by chemotherapy, it was stated that "chemotherapy, whether used en masse or for the treatment of infected persons only, will probably reduce the risk of severe disease in many persons by reducing, if not eliminating, their worm load. Nevertheless, this method requires continued vigilance for infected immigrants, and the long-term effect of treatment on transmission has yet to be demonstrated." [13]

A portion of the St. Lucia study which examined the severity of the disease and the daily output of workers on a banana estate and in a light-industry plant failed to find any significant association between the two.[14] A follow-up study of the effects of the disease on productivity is, however, now under way.

Finally, the two studies reviewed which focus specifically on childhood mortality concluded, in general, that in Central and South America there is an inverse relationship between the availability of piped water and childhood mortality. Of course, many other unmeasured factors could have influenced the rather aggregate relationships which were presented.

To summarize, the twenty-eight studies provide evidence to reinforce the intuitive belief that the incidence of certain water-washed, waterborne, water-based, and water-sanitation associated diseases are related to the quantity or quality of water and sanitary facilities available to users. They give us little help, however, in determining exactly how much improvement in health can be expected from a

12. J. Jordan and others, "Control of Schistosmoa Mansoni," p. 36.
13. Ibid.
14. Burton A. Weisbrod and others, *Disease and Economic Development: The Impact of Parasitic Diseases in St. Lucia* (Madison: University of Wisconsin Press, 1973).

specific water supply and sanitation-related improvement in any particular area. Another question so far unresolved is how to translate improvements in health or disease rates into units of measurement comparable to the costs and benefits which might be generated by alternative investment opportunities. This question is discussed in the section of this chapter, "Placing a Value on Better Health."

The Water-Use Link

Critical to the results of any water supply or sanitation investment is the fact that the above studies have had very little to say about, and certainly have not been able to completely control, the actual ways in which the target populations make use of their water supply or sanitation facilities.

The following represents simplistically the crucial nature of the water-use link: [15]

$$\left\{\begin{array}{l}\text{Design, installation, and}\\ \text{operation and mainte-}\\ \text{nance of the water supply}\\ \text{or sanitation facilities}\end{array}\right\} \longrightarrow \left\{\begin{array}{l}\text{Actual water-use}\\ \text{patterns of the}\\ \text{population}\end{array}\right\} \longrightarrow \left\{\begin{array}{l}\text{Changes}\\ \text{in}\\ \text{health}\end{array}\right\}$$

Water is used for many purposes including drinking and washing, and there are wide variations in the amounts of water people want to, or are able to use. For example, The WHO Survey [16] showed the following average daily consumption figures in liters per capita per day (lcd) for rural areas of developing countries:

WHO region	Liters per capita per day	
	Minimum	Maximum
Africa	15	35
Southeast Asia	30	70
Western Pacific	30	95
Eastern Mediterranean	40	85
Algeria, Morocco, Turkey	20	65
Latin America and Caribbean	70	190
World average for developing countries	35	90

15. The authors wish to thank Dennis Warner and David Bradley for helpful discussions relating to this topic.
16. World Health Organization, "Community Water Supply and Sewage Disposal in Developing Countries (End of 1970)," *World Health Statistics Report* 26, no. 11 (1973).

Individual country data showed a minimum use of about 5 lcd for 7 countries; 20 lcd or less for 24 countries; and 40 lcd or less for 45 countries. Consumption which falls to as low as 5 lcd is probably about the minimum necessary to sustain life. From the review of the health studies it was concluded that, in general, at the lower end of the scale, as increased quantities of water are consumed, expected health benefits become greater.

Specific instances, of course, may contradict this generalization. Some of the ways in which a piped village water supply might be used without achievement of maximum expected health benefits are the following:

1. The piped water is used for washing, irrigating the small garden, and watering the goat or cow. Water for drinking, however, is still obtained from the traditional source because the villagers (or the village children) like the taste of the contaminated water better or do not like the taste of the well water which happens to have a high mineral content.

2. The piped water is used for drinking, but the personal sanitation habits of the village are such that piped water is rarely used for personal hygiene or clothes washing.

3. The piped water is used for drinking, but the villagers do not wash much of the food that they handle and then consume.

4. The piped water is carried from the standpost to the house and stored in open cans or jars before it is consumed. A variety of flies and other insects, as well as livestock and household pets, have access to the jars. In addition, when the water is being transported, unclean hands contaminate the rim of the jar, and the cans or jars are rarely washed out.

Water-use habits, wrapped up as they are in tradition, culture, and a simple lack of knowledge about consequences, to a great extent determine the magnitude of any health-related benefits a population may derive from a given water supply investment.

When a water supply system is introduced into a village or area, the villagers' water-use habits can be modified, first, by the passage of time and, second, by a water-use education and demonstration program. With regard to the first, it is reasonable to assume that the water-use habits of a population will gradually change once the water supply has been made more accessible and more dependable. While improvements in health may not be immediately noticeable, over a period of several years there may be distinct benefits.

A successful water-use or health education program could increase both the actual and the perceived benefits to be derived from an improved water supply and sanitation program. In turn, as perceived benefits increase, the population should be willing to pay higher water tariffs, reducing the need for subsidies and generally assuring the better operation and maintenance of their systems.

On the other hand, education programs are expensive and, depending on their design and acceptability, may or may not have a significant impact on the public. Like any other form of public sector investment, therefore, before an education program is initiated, its expected costs and benefits should be examined. Though a health education program could be the most cost-effective means of reducing water-associated diseases, there is little evidence to substantiate that this is so. Some evidence is available, however, on the significance of the time factor in conjunction with a health education program. On St. Lucia, for instance, about three years after several water supply systems were introduced to a rural population of about 2,000, water consumption rates increased from 15 liters per capita daily to 40 to 50 lcd.[17] The latter amount included the supply of water to public laundry and shower units, and taps at each house. The increased rates are significant because wastage was limited; all taps including those at the laundry and shower units were equipped with fordilla valves.[18]

In the context described, it is important to note that the amount of investment necessary to serve a given population depends partly on the extent to which water is not wasted but is used effectively for drinking, personal hygiene, food preparation, and household hygiene. If a given population makes effective use of its water supply, it can presumably achieve a given level of health benefits with a lower quality or different type of water supply service (fewer house connections and smaller system capacity, or only public standposts and a few bath houses). And, to the extent that a lower quality of service requires less investment in any one village, the same magnitude of program investment may be spread among a greater number of villages.

Any discussion of the association between better sanitation habits

---

17. Unrau, "Individual Household Water Supplies," p. 22.
18. It should be noted that generalizing on the basis of the St. Lucia case may not be entirely valid. In St. Lucia the rural population supplied with water has had Speed Unrau, a dedicated and capable engineer, keeping the system in excellent repair and providing continuous instruction and guidance on proper water-use and sanitation habits.

and health should note that cases have been reported where government attempts to encourage better water-use and sanitation habits have inadvertently brought about a decline in the health of the population. In one case it is reported that new water supplies plus governmental attempts to improve the sanitary habits of schoolchildren actually fostered the spread of trachoma. The government, having encouraged schoolchildren to wash their hands after defecating, failed to provide paper towels or instructions on the drying of hands. Consequently, the schoolchildren all dried their hands on the same handkerchief, thus promoting the spread of trachoma.[19] The authors are also familiar with an instance in Korea where a government handwashing campaign inadvertently facilitated the spread of diarrheal disease. In this case, immediately after defecating, children went to a well, picked up the bucket and rope, and then by lowering the bucket and rope into the well, contaminated the water.

Finally, an instance has been reported in which the introduction and use of primitive shell-type privies presumably caused an increase in the prevalence of diarrhea in several localities in Sudan. In arid areas, when people defecate on the sand, the excreta dries and is sterilized in a short time. The provision and use of primitive privies, on the other hand, to which dogs and other animals had access, prevented the rapid drying of the excreta and actually facilitated the spread of diarrhea among the local population.

Placing a Value on Better Health

In deciding upon the allocation of financial resources to a water supply or excreta disposal project, or choosing which project of several alternatives is the best for investment, the investor should ideally have some means of translating the expected improvement in health into units that can be used to compare the benefits of alternative expenditures. In practice, some means is required of assigning a monetary value to alternative mixes and magnitudes of better health. Unfortunately, there are many conceptual as well as empirical problems associated with attempting to place a value on better health.

---

19. Carter L. Marshall, "Some Exercises in Social Ecology: Health, Disease and Modernization in the Ryukyu Islands," in *The Careless Technology,* ed. M. Taghi Farvar and J. P. Milton (New York: Natural History Press, 1972), pp. 5–18.

These problems, however, do not belie the fact that if an investor is to make rational decisions he must have confidence in the theoretical foundation of his method of value or benefit measurement, or at least be aware of the limitations of his method of measurement so that he can exercise the right to make subjective judgments when necessary. A summary [20] follows of some of the conceptual considerations and suggestions for alternative approaches to the economic evaluation of better health.

Conceptual and Empirical Problems

A conservative way of measuring the value of better health to an individual or to a group is in terms of how much they are willing to pay for an improvement in health. Measured thus, a direct revenue comparison can be made with the investment and operating costs of a project designed to achieve that improvement. It may then be possible to estimate whether the economic benefits thus revealed indicate that the investment is worthwhile.

A specific investment project, however, will usually make some people associated with it better off, some worse, and the remainder indifferent or unaffected. One way of estimating the effect of the introduction of a water supply project in a village hitherto unserved might be to ask the villagers: "What is the maximum sum you would pay rather than go without the project?" Or, to those who do not want it, put the question, "What is the minimum sum you would accept to put up with the project?" Then the extent to which total welfare, as measured by willingness to pay, would be increased (decreased) by the project would be determined by the extent to which the sum of the payments made by those who would feel better off exceeds (or is less than) the sum demanded by those who would feel worse off.[21]

---

20. The discussion relies heavily on Edward J. Mishan, *Cost-Benefit Analysis: An Introduction* (New York: Praeger, 1971); A. R. Prest and R. Turvey, "Cost-Benefit Analysis," *Economic Journal* 75 (December 1965):683–735; Dorothy Rice, *Estimating the Cost of Illness,* Health Economics Series no. 6 (Washington, D.C.: U.S., Dept. of Health, Education, and Welfare, May 1966); and Herbert E. Klarman, "Present Status of Cost-Benefit Analysis in the Health Field," *American Journal of Public Health* 57, no. 11 (1967): 1948–53.

21. In a country where there was to be a reallocation of resources for the water supply project, urban dwellers (who would be giving up resources) would have to be quizzed as well as the rural dwellers in the specific project area.

This approach to project evaluation, however, presents several practical problems: First, there is evidence to suggest that the demand for health care (good water) increases as education and income increase even though the need for health care generally declines with increasing income and education.[22] Consequently, a better educated or higher income individual, while he may need a given project less, may be more able and willing to pay for it. Depending on the income distribution of the population, a few high income individuals might be able to control the final project result for the entire population.

Second, the "summation of individual welfare" approach is based on the premise that individuals are most qualified to judge what is best for themselves. It can also be argued that the poor, less educated segments of the population are not really able to determine what is the best water supply and sanitation system for themselves in the long run. Where a local water supply system is both a consumption and investment good, it can be argued that the uneducated poor generally perceive only the immediate consumption-convenience value of the system and therefore tend to undervalue the total system. Educating the poor to the total (consumption and investment) value of the system might be expensive and time consuming and, as a result, would raise the total cost of the system even before a project commitment had been made. Moreover, as we have suggested earlier, lack of knowledge of the health benefits of improved water supply and sanitation is not confined to the uneducated rural poor alone.

Third, questionnaire or personal interview methods of collecting answers to the above questions are probably largely unreliable. Essentially, people are asked to play the game of giving an answer to a somewhat hypothetical question. Income or education biases could easily develop, such that one or more groups would have a greater propensity or ability to exaggerate their answers.

In view of these problems, it is not surprising that the "summation of individual welfare" approach is seldom if ever attempted. While it is an approach consistent with the underlying premise of theoretical welfare economics, which holds that individuals should be able to judge what is best for themselves in the public sector of an economy just as they do in the private sector, this approach also illustrates a

---

22. Michael Grossman, "On the Concept of Health Capital and the Demand for Health," *Journal of Political Economy* 80 (March–April 1972):223–55; United Nations Research Institute for Social Development, "Cost-Benefit Analysis of Social Projects," Report no. 7 (a meeting of experts at Rennes, France, September–October 1965), (Geneva, 1966).

basic obstacle to the application of the theory: that is, that income distribution is implicitly taken as given. Yet a basic problem of many rural areas is that the communities are so poor that, almost by definition, the revealed willingness of consumers to pay will not demonstrate the economic justification for water supply projects.

There are, however, a number of other possible approaches to the problem of assigning economic values to improved health. While having only a minor association with the conceptually more appealing "total welfare" approach described above, they do assist in spotlighting factors decisionmakers generally feel need to be taken into account in making economic choices. All but one of the approaches examined below handle the problem of "differences in units of measurement" by converting into monetary units the health or disease rate changes brought about by an improved water supply system.

A brief description follows of five ways of attempting to value changes in an individual's health or life span.

1. Calculate the "economic worth" of his more healthful and lengthened life. To do so generally entails calculating the loss to the economy from his probabilistic sickness or death, by discounting—to use the simplest means—the future stream of changes in the individual's future gross earnings. A defect of this method is that it measures a person's income-generating power without considering the value of his life to him or to his family or friends. In practice such a measure assumes that one of the primary goals of the water supply investor, or national policymaker, is to maximize the country's national output (income).

2. Estimate a person's "economic worth" by calculating the present value of the output he will generate minus the amount that he will consume. This involves discounting the value of the economic losses which accrue only to others as a result of the person's sickness or death. The simplest method is to discount the difference between the person's future earnings if healthy and his future earnings if sick, or dead, minus the difference in the amounts he would have consumed. The assumption that what matters to society is its economic gain or loss following the death or sickness of one or more of its members underlies this "net-output" approach. No consideration is given to the gains, losses, or welfare of the individuals affected by the sickness or death. At an extreme, a program designed to eliminate elderly, unproductive people would generate positive benefits under this net-output valuation method.

3. Calculate a value of human life or health from that implicit in

previous governmental health improvement programs, and from the expenditures on, and the effect of, existing programs. The defect of this approach is that politicians or government leaders make investment decisions partly through a process of political compromise of conflicting goals, and almost certainly in the absence of even the crudest of approximations of the true benefits—and sometimes the costs—likely to occur. The implicit value, consequently, of life or health calculated from different programs would be somewhat arbitrary, would vary greatly, and, in developing countries, would probably depend on which programs were consulted, and where and when they were reviewed.

4. Calculate an estimate of the value of human life and health from an aggregate of the death and disability insurance premiums people willingly pay, together with the probability of their becoming disabled or dying. This approach, however, reflects concern only for the beneficiaries and not for the policyholder. Insurance primarily reflects a need and ability to provide for family and dependents and does not reflect the value of an individual's life or health to himself or to his family and friends.

5. There is one approach suggested which does not rely solely on measuring the economic effect of health changes on society, or on the individual: it is that the problem of the actual value of life and health need not be dealt with explicitly if a general index can be constructed reflecting changes in the standard of living or the "social-economic-environmental quality of life" in an area. A general index is, in concept, a step toward the "total welfare" approach of valuing changes in health brought about by changes in local water supplies. Rough approximations of such an index might be the level of living index suggested by the U.N. Research Institute [23] or some form of additive weights, as proposed by Bartone.[24] Indexes of this nature, unfortunately, are generally better suited for macro evaluation tasks, and in most cases would have to be specially modified with somewhat arbitrary changes in weights for each country, as well as for each culture and region within it, thus creating problems of comparability. In addition, numerous data problems would be encountered in any attempt to use such a general index on a micro-project, or program

---

23. United Nations Research Institute, "Cost-Benefit Analysis."
24. Carl R. Bartone, "Cost-Effectiveness Model for Establishing Investment Priorities for Water and Sewage Projects in the Guayas River Basin" (Lima: Pan American Health Organization, 1972).

basis, in developing countries. A more promising and more specific approach to indexing is discussed in this chapter's section, "Indexing and Cost Effectiveness."

Which Way to Proceed

For the economist and engineer who must go into the field, make decisions, and get things done, there is no one clear-cut method or procedure of avoiding all of the conceptual and practical problems associated with valuing changes in human health and life span.

The fact that problems exist, however, has not stopped empirical attempts at valuation of health improvement. Rather than struggle with the complex and perhaps costly total welfare approach to project valuation, investigators generally have relied on some of the less conceptually sound, but more manageable and still useful, alternative approaches. In the attempt to attach some form of comparable value measure to probabilistic changes in disease rates and expected lifetime earnings, the most common methods used are discounting changes in expected lifetime earnings [25] and discounting changes in expected lifetime earnings less changes in expected lifetime consumption.[26] Neither of these approaches values life, health, or satisfaction. They are simply attempts to quantify the economic output associated with life or health under the imperfect assumption that the economic output of humans reflects the value of life and health.

The issue of whether or not to subtract changes in consumption from changes in output depends essentially on whether the decision-maker decides to place a value on the personal consumption of the individual whose life span or health is altered. Those who do not subtract changes in consumption from changes in the individual's total output (earnings) argue that consumption is an end in itself and should be viewed as a final product. If it can be assumed that an individual's enjoyment increases with his level of consumption,

---

25. Method one discussed above was used by Rice, *Estimating the Cost of Illness;* Klarman, "Present Status of Cost-Benefit Analysis"; and Rashi Fein, *Economics of Mental Illness* (New York: Basic Books, 1958).

26. Method two discussed above was used by Edwin F. Pyatt and Peter P. Rogers, "On Estimating Benefit-Cost Ratios for Water Supply Investments," *American Journal of Public Health* 52 (October 1962):1729–42; Burton A. Weisbrod, *Economics of Public Health: Measuring the Economic Impact of Diseases* (Philadelphia: University of Pennsylvania Press, 1962); Louis I. Dublin, *The Money Value of a Man,* rev. ed. (New York: Ronald Press, 1946).

then any increase in satisfaction (through increased consumption) which is a result of a lengthened or more healthy life should not be subtracted.

With specific reference to (rural) water supply systems and sanitation programs, the factors which should be considered in benefit evaluations of better health are also the subject of some discussion. A set of guidelines, however, can be developed. Although it is imperfect, the most workable way, in general, to place a minimum value on the probabilistic improvements in the health of a population (assuming these improvements can be predicted) seems to be through discounted changes in potential or expected earnings. Discussion of this subject is somewhat involved; the factors to be considered will be outlined in Chapter 3.

Indexing and Cost Effectiveness

Another approach which, under certain circumstances, can be of use in examining the justification for, or composition of, investment in village water supply or sanitation programs involves viewing the projected results of the investment from a cost-effective rather than a cost-benefit point of view. The difference between the two methods is that benefits in a cost-effective exercise are not converted into monetary units.

In a simplified case, benefits would be left as changes in, say, disease rates, and the ratios of some summary measure of the reductions in disease rates to the costs incurred to secure those reductions would be compared for each investment alternative. This procedure would assist in the selection of the most cost-effective placement of investment funds, assuming the objectives of investment to be justified in the first place.

The problem, of course, is that a cost-effective comparison avoids the question of the relation between costs and benefits. If it is decided for social, political, humanitarian, or other reasons that a certain investment is to be allocated to a rural water supply or sanitation program, a cost effectiveness exercise can be designed to determine the way in which that allocation will have the greatest impact. The first steps in such an exercise are to identify the major water supply and sanitation investment alternatives and to cost these alternatives. Differences in items such as quality of service, quantity of service, type of service, areas to be served, training programs, educational activities, and administrative and maintenance organizations should be included. Next it would be required to identify (a) the existing diseases which could be affected by the defined water supply program alternatives; (b) the existing levels of those diseases in the areas or villages to be served; and (c) predictions of disease rate changes which might result from each of the investment alternatives (given assumptions about water-use habits).[27]

In view of the information likely to be at hand, attaining reliable estimates for items (b) and (c) will probably be difficult. Unless considerable time and money are available for data collection and research, very rough approximations will have to suffice.[28]

A fruitful alternative, however, to the complete enumeration and quantification of disease rates might be to derive a summary indicator or set of indicators of the "health state" of a community, region, or country, as the case may be. This could be attempted in one of two ways.

First, it might be possible to identify a few key diseases which would correlate well with the prevalence of the majority of water-associated diseases affecting the population, with the prevalence of these key diseases measurable by a relatively untrained layman. Thus, instead of making an attempt to identify the prevalence of the total possible spectrum of diseases, only the prevalence of two or three proxy or representative diseases would be examined. These, then, could be used to approximate the "health state" of the target population. The exact proxy diseases chosen would probably vary from region to region in a country, and from country to country around the world. As a point of beginning, the observer would probably want to look for evidence of disease prevalence in a very limited number of clinical categories such as diarrhea and other gastrointestinal disorders, eye diseases, skin diseases, and fevers.[29] In many areas of the developing world only the first and last of these would be relevant, and therefore the health-state observer could simply concentrate on measuring diarrheal morbidity (from household surveys or treatment clinic records), and on watching for indications of cholera and typhoid.

27. Disease rate changes could be either positive, negative, or some mix or both.
28. The problems of predicting disease reduction are discussed further in the first section of Chapter 5.
29. These categories were suggested to us by David Bradley.

A second alternative to the enumeration and measurement of the many water-related diseases affecting a community would involve defining the health state of the community not in terms of disease prevalence but in terms of the consequences of the collective diseases. It may be argued that if the ultimate goal of rural water supply and sanitation programs is to improve the well-being of diseased people, then from the point of view of the disease sufferer, it is the consequence of the disease rather than the disease itself which matters.

For example, it matters whether the patient is ambulatory, or in pain, or suffers minor discomfort. The sufferer will presumably be indifferent to a similar level of pain no matter what disease causes it, just as he will be indifferent as to what particular disease causes him to die. One method of comparability therefore is to classify diseases according to their effects on the patient, and then to sum those effects between which the patient is indifferent.

This concept is not new. White, Bradley, and White [30] mention making diseases comparable by attaching a value of "chronicity" and "severity" to each. Rosser and Watts [31] suggest a combination level of "dysfunction" and "distress" in order to show the severity of pain in any given functional category. A somewhat more precise application, however, has been proposed by Fanshel and Bush [32] in their health status index (HSI) approach which has a very simple basic idea. For a healthy patient, a prediction can be made of the probability of his spending time in a particular "health state" for any future year of his life. If, however, the patient contracts a certain disease, then the probability of his spending time in that particular health state may change.

For example, assume that a twenty-year-old man might be expected to spend 350 days of his twenty-fifth year in a state of "physical well-being." After contracting disease X, however, the "well" days may fall to 300. The number of days he is expected to spend in a state of dissatisfaction or discomfort will also increase. The difference be-

---

30. Gilbert F. White, David J. Bradley, and Anne U. White, *Drawers of Water*, p. 211.

31. R. Rosser and V. Watts, "The Measure of Hospital Output" (paper presented to the Operational Research Society Conference, September 1971, Lancaster, U.K.).

32. S. Fanshel and J. W. Bush, "A Health-Status Index and Its Application to Health-Services Outcomes," *Operations Research* 18 (1970):1021–66.

tween the time he can be expected to spend in each health state, with and without disease, therefore represents the "cost" of the disease. Conversely, the "benefit" of preventing the disease is the increment in prognosis. The "cost" of the treatment can then be summed over the rest of his lifetime.

The health-state approach has been used to evaluate the benefits of a tuberculosis prevention program in New York. For that purpose the following were listed:

(1) Well-being
(2) Dissatisfaction
(3) Discomfort
(4) Disability (minor)
(5) Disability (major)
(6) Disablement
(7) Confinement
(8) Confinement, bedridden
(9) Isolation
(10) Coma
(11) Death

These eleven health states were drawn up on the basis of functional disability, that is, each health state represents the extent to which the patient can perform his normal daily activities.

Of course, the definition and number of health states would depend on local conditions. For the case of developing countries and water-related diseases, a less detailed classification, say four or five states, may be appropriate. Appendix B illustrates the health-state approach in a village water supply context.

If cost-effectiveness tests and health-state approaches are to be successful, the physical effects not only of improved water supply and sanitation but also of other preventive or curative expenditures need to be understood. The problem still remains, however, of converting the HSI or disease-rate proxies, or whatever output measure is derived, into the same monetary units as those in which the costs are expressed. If this is not done, there is no means of evaluating investment justification in the first place, or of indicating the proper magnitude of the investment to be undertaken. On the other hand, if for social or political or humanitarian reasons a certain amount of investment is undertaken in the rural water supply and sanitation sector, a cost-effectiveness exercise might be helpful in screening alternative designs for the program.

3 | Economic Effects of Investments in Rural Water Supply and Sanitation

POTABLE WATER SUPPLY SYSTEMS in rural areas of developing countries may affect local, regional, and national economic output and growth.[1] The potential economic effects of rural water supply systems will be examined under the following headings which are, of course, not mutually exclusive: macroeconomic effects; direct economic effects on development and output; economic effects of improved health; effects of increased time for productive work; effects on income of increases in population; effects related to averted costs to the economy; and rural to urban drift and population relocation or stabilization.

Macroeconomic Implications

The macroeconomic effects of a rural water supply program on the national economy of a developing country are clearly not worth considering if the program is trivial in size in relation to total national economic output. Individual village pilot projects or other small-scale, local projects which are not part of a large national or

---

1. For a lengthy listing of almost every possible way in which water supply might affect populations in rural areas of the United States, see Dennis Warner and Jarir S. Dajani, *Water and Sewer Development in Rural America* (Lexington, Mass.: D. C. Heath and Co., 1975).

regional program would not affect the national economy significantly. But for rural water supply programs of a relatively large size, the macroeconomic effects may be viewed as being associated with economic growth, a redistribution of income, and possible balance of payments problems. Thus, if the aim is to reach the UNDD targets referred to in Chapter 1, Table 1.12 shows that macroeconomic implications are particularly important for Ethiopia but relatively insignificant for Iran.

Economic Growth

A country will experience an increase in overall economic activity as a result of the water supply program when funds are obtained from sources outside the country,[2] first, if these funds (see Tables 3.1 and 3.2) would not have flowed into the country except for the rural water supply program,[3] and, second, if the country is not already fully employing all of its resources. At a minimum, the increase in a country's economic activity or output will be equal to that proportion of the increase in direct program expenditures financed by outside sources, plus the increase in indirect expenditures made by those newly employed in the program and those directly or indirectly supplying services, equipment, and material to the program.

Similarly, if the country finances a portion of the rural water program through increased taxes or user fees, that is, from domestic sources, and if this additional government revenue is composed partly of money which the population would otherwise have saved, then the fact that the government immediately puts the money back into the economy, thereby increasing aggregate demand, results in a net increase in overall economic activity or output.

Finally, a water supply system is both a consumption and an investment good. It is a consumption good in that people begin using it immediately upon its completion. It is an investment good in that it is part of the local infrastructure and can indirectly generate

---

2. Tables 3.1 and 3.2 show the magnitude of international assistance for urban and rural water supply and sewerage projects in WHO regions, between 1966 and 1970.

3. In view of the changing priorities of bilateral and international aid agencies, this is likely to be an increasingly relevant condition. Note also that in these circumstances, the cost of foreign funds used in a village water supply project is the actual lending rate rather than the economic benefits that would have been obtained by use of those funds in alternative projects in the country.

Table 3.1. External Assistance Received for Community Water Supply Projects, 1966–1970
(Millions of U.S. dollars)

World Health Organization region	Water supply				
	Loans	Grants	Material and supplies	Other	Total
Africa	106.3	39.8	4.4	5.2	155.7
Central and South America	337.1	4.0	3.5	2.2	346.8
Eastern Mediterranean	102.3	2.8	4.0	0.4	109.5
Algeria, Morocco, Turkey	n.a.	n.a.	n.a.	n.a.	n.a.
Southeast Asia	5.5	8.3	2.4	0.8	17.0
Western Pacific	36.8	42.0	2.5	0.3	81.6
Total	588.0	96.9	16.8	8.9	710.6

n.a. Not available.
Source: World Health Organization, "Community Water Supply and Sewage Disposal in Developing Countries (End of 1970)," *Statistics Report* 26, no. 11 (1973): 747.

additional, future economic activity by attracting and assisting local commerce and village industry; and improved health of local human resources in turn can increase production. To the extent that village water supply systems are investment goods partly financed out of revenue from new taxes and user charges which would have been spent on consumption, then the result is a net shift from short-run

Table 3.2. External Assistance Received for Community Sewage Disposal Projects, 1966–1970
(Millions of U.S. dollars)

World Health Organization region	Loans	Grants	Material and supplies	Other	Total
Africa	7.9	1.0	—[a]	2.6	11.5
Central and South America	116.4	—[a]	0.2	0.3	116.9
Eastern Mediterranean	—[a]	—[a]	—[a]	—[a]	—[a]
Algeria, Morocco, Turkey	2.6	—[a]	—[a]	—[a]	2.6
Southeast Asia	3.5	0.1	0.5	—[a]	4.1
Western Pacific	6.0	1.3	—[a]	—[a]	7.3
Total	136.4	2.4	0.7	2.9	142.4

a. Nil or magnitude negligible.
Source: Same as Table 3.1.

consumption to investment. This shift could have a net positive effect on long-run economic growth in the regional or national economy.

Redistribution of Income

If the national government is bearing at least part of the cost of the water supply program (partial national government subsidy), and if it raises its revenues by taxing economic output or income, then a rural water supply program will generally result in a redistribution of income within the country from urban to rural and from higher to lower income population. This follows from the fact that per capita economic output and income are almost always higher in urban areas than in rural areas. A water supply program, therefore, entailing a flow of resources into nonurban areas and financed at least partly by countrywide taxes on output or income, would spatially redistribute resources. Income would be redistributed from higher income urban areas to nonurban areas and generally from higher income population to lower income population.

In addition, as noted above, disposable income would also be redistributed through time because, through taxation and user fees for water supply investment, income is generally shifted from current consumption (assuming low rates of saving in rural areas of developing countries) to consumption in the future at what will hopefully be at a higher per capita level.

Impact on Balance of Payments

Because most developing countries are continually hard pressed for foreign currency, a national rural water supply program requiring a country to import materials and a significant amount of equipment could be continually postponed in favor of national programs that could be carried out without an outflow of foreign exchange or national programs to generate exports which, in turn, would bring foreign exchange into the country. Within the water supply sector, however, rural water supply programs generally have a slight advantage over urban programs with regard to the foreign exchange component in that for rural systems (see Table 5.6). The percentage cost [4] of imported material to total construction costs is on average only 35 percent against 41 percent for urban water supply systems.

---

4. Based on statistics of the World Health Organization, *World Health Statistics Report* 26, no. 11 (1973):750.

The rural water supply–foreign exchange problem is more important in smaller or less advanced countries which lack a sufficient industrial base to manufacture a significant portion of the equipment needed. In fact, the WHO survey shows that for countries in the African and Western Pacific regions, 50 percent of total rural system costs are for imported materials while in the Americas and in Southeast Asia the figures are only 29 percent and 27 percent, respectively (see Table 5.6). Most developing countries are able to manufacture plastic pipe, but many of them still must import plastic pellets for the pipe extruders or at least some of the ingredients for the plastic. On the other hand, all but the more advanced (or larger) developing countries must import pumps, drilling rigs, and service vehicles for a rural water supply program. Although it may be cheaper in monetary terms to import and erect steel reservoir tanks, some countries, to avoid giving up foreign exchange, may opt to build tanks out of domestically manufactured cement at a higher money cost.

Labor is an abundant and low priced resource in most developing countries. Capital equipment, on the other hand, is relatively scarce and in many cases must be imported. Consequently, the balance of payments problems of a rural water supply program can be reduced by designing the program so that its construction, operation and maintenance, and expansion phases are as labor intensive as is technologically possible, given existing cost constraints. In many countries with viable rural water supply programs, particularly in Latin America, local village populations generally agree to contribute, during construction, as much manual labor as is needed, including digging and refilling trenches for the entire water distribution system. This limits the number of tractors or the amount of ditch-digging equipment that must be imported by the national program agency. In addition, it provides a way for villages to reduce the proportion of the cost of the system which they must bear.

Another means frequently used to reduce financial costs is for village populations to collect and furnish the sand and stones necessary for the construction of reservoirs and any other concrete or masonry structures.

A disadvantage of the use of labor-intensive construction techniques is in less efficiency; completion times for projects are generally longer, and somewhat greater amounts of supervision are usually required. Whereas this circumstance would not necessarily affect balance of payments problems, it should be considered when assessing both the real and financial costs of the project.

The extent of the impact of a village water supply program on a country's balance of payments will clearly vary from country to country depending on the natural and technical resources of each. The potential impact can be evaluated in advance and can, given a country's needs and resources, be influenced by designing the program and all individual projects to take advantage of local labor, materials, supplies, topography, and technology whenever possible. To do so effectively it is necessary to overcome a big hurdle by ensuring the recognition and use of shadow values for labor and foreign exchange. This is usually appreciated only at the central government level, and must somehow be conveyed to those responsible for project design, construction, and system operation. (Shadow-pricing is discussed more fully in Chapter 5.)

Direct Effects on Development and Output

There are several direct short- and long-run effects on the economic output of a community or region that can result from the introduction of potable water supply systems designed primarily to provide water for human consumption.

Short-Run Effects

When a system is designed in such a way that there can be excess capacity during some portion of the day (at nonpeak load times), it can sometimes be beneficial to allow limited irrigation of small garden plots near each dwelling or tap. A policy allowing (or encouraging) the watering of small gardens tends to produce the most benefits in areas which have acceptable soil but a dry climate, or in areas with at least one very dry season where the lack of water is the inhibiting factor to garden output. In these areas, times for watering might be allocated on a spatial basis to different groups of the population, and the type of plants allowed to be grown in the irrigated gardens could be restricted to those that consume relatively little water per unit of output. (A similar type of plant-water absorption restriction is enforced in some areas of the Dominican Republic.)

Gardens can also be irrigated with wastewater. An example of successful wastewater application is found in Lahore, Pakistan, where a significant amount of food for human and animal consumption is produced by this method of irrigation.

In other cases, direct economic benefits to local populations might derive from encouraging fish farming in a reservoir constructed for the local potable water supply, or in a drainage pool which collects water after it has been used by the village. A reservoir fish-farming operation is probably most feasible where a relatively large, open-air reservoir must be constructed and where the water must be filtered or otherwise treated prior to human consumption. Under these conditions, and depending on local costs of feeding the fish, a community could gain an extra food source and increase its water system revenue through a fish-farming operation requiring little additional capital investment in the water supply system.

Yet another possibility, in relatively arid areas or in areas with at least one very dry season, is for local animal husbandry to gain significantly through the provision of low-cost facilities for livestock watering at nonpeak load times. In Kenya it was found that one of the major benefits of the Zaina potable water supply scheme for human consumption was the increase, over a four-year period, in the number of cattle, pigs, sheep, goats, and poultry in the areas where there was access to watering troughs the year round. With cattle, both the number and the milk output per cow increased. All of the livestock increases were greater than occurred in a similar nearby area that did not receive a potable water supply system.[5] In Jordan, too, the loss of livestock during the dry season was significantly reduced by the installation of a village water supply and by the initiation of a livestock health program.[6] But there are cases where water supply systems designed primarily for human and livestock consumption have had little impact on livestock production or on general economic activity.[7]

If an excess system capacity at nonpeak load times is planned, usually little increase in investment is required to allow the watering of livestock. This practice may create an added small source of water system revenue. In several of the drier areas of the Dominican Republic, for example, the national rural water supply program

---

5. K. W. H. Fenwick, "The Short Term Effects of a Pilot Environmental Health Project in Rural Africa: the Zaina Scheme Reassessed after Four Years" (Nyeri, Central Province, Kenya: Ministry of Health, 1966).

6. Ralph L. Mendenhall, " 'Jash' Self-Help Program in Jordan," tenth annual report (New York: Near East Foundation, 1969).

7. I. D. Carruthers, *Rural Water Investment in Kenya: Impact and Economics of Community Water Supply* (London: University of London, Wye College, 1972), pp. 40–43.

(INAPA) allows water taps to be provided for the watering of livestock from a fixed trough at the same monthly charge as would be made for a house connection. The restriction made is that no more than approximately 600 liters per day be consumed at that tap (the estimated amount consumed at most house taps).

Finally, in areas where climate and local technology allow the growing and storage of fodder during a wetter growing season, it is possible that water troughs for animals might make beef cattle, hog, or poultry feeder operations feasible at an initial water-investment cost not significantly greater than the cost of the village potable water system for human consumption. If feasible, any of the small garden irrigation, fish-farming, or livestock-watering efforts described could conceivably generate additional direct economic benefits to a rural community in a relatively short time, by increasing community income and output.

One possible negative, short-run economic effect of a village water supply system might be a financially poorer population in terms of disposable income, or funds which low-income people have to spend. With the possible exceptions relating to gardens, livestock, and fish, it is difficult to argue that potable water for human consumption will directly increase the income of a population in the short run. This is particularly true of rural areas where water is not at present purchased from vendors, where there is general underemployment so that any improvement in health will not increase earnings, and where regional health services are free or at least heavily subsidized by the central government. In cases such as these, in the short run, the necessity of paying from 1 to 5 percent of yearly income as a water tariff in exchange for potable water, which does not immediately increase earnings or output, actually reduces the disposable income of each family and, in monetary terms, makes them poorer.

Long-Run Effects

A frequent economic argument made for rural, potable water supply systems over the long run is that such a system is an integral part of a community's infrastructure, without which it will not attract industry or, more likely, generate an expanding commercial and village-industry sector.

There are two observations to make about this contention. First, it is probably true in the sense that a potable water system is necessary for most forms of intensive local economic development.

As local commerce grows and village industry develops, the lack of a potable water supply system could retard the rate of local economic growth. Although, however, a potable water supply system is at some point usually necessary for long-run economic development, it is certainly not always sufficient to generate development. If there are several villages in a given region of a country, and if they all obtain water supply systems at approximately the same time, there is no reason to assume that all, or even most of them, will increase their rate of economic growth as a result. Given existing migration, marketing, and growth patterns, some of the villages may grow and develop. But the odds are that many will not.

It has been noted that two of the most important reasons for migration are a lack of educational opportunities for children and a lack of employment and income-generation opportunities for the total family. Because a village water system can at best generate only limited direct employment and income opportunities and has no effect on the amount of formal education available, it is generally unrealistic to expect a water supply system, by itself, to produce significant changes in long-run economic growth, development, and migration patterns in most rural villages.

Empirical evidence on the relationship through time between economic development and village water supply systems for human consumption in developing countries is difficult to find and even more difficult to evaluate for the reasons that (a) most rural water supply programs have been in existence for less than ten years and (b) many villages that received water in the early stages of the older programs have also received a number of other infrastructure and development investments through the years. As a result, it is very difficult to attribute an increase in local economic activity to any one particular government-induced investment in infrastructure, health, or village industry.

The second observation on the long-run economic effects of a water supply system is that firms or industries of a significant size are not generally attracted to small villages solely because a water system exists. Large companies, or even small water-using firms, will generally be able to develop their own water source in rural areas. They choose a specific location for a variety of economic reasons, most of them unrelated to whether or not the local village has a potable water supply system—indeed the proportion of business expenditures for water supply is normally infinitesimal. In northwestern Argentina, for example, there is a small village near Santiago del Estero where a tomato-processing factory was opened and began production shortly after the village inaugurated its new potable water system. The factory was immediately hooked into the system, and, in fact, required a water meter—which, in that area, is allocated only to "heavy" users (there were six other metered users in the town). On the surface this seems a perfect example of a water supply system attracting economic activity. Further investigation, however, revealed that another, older tomato-processing plant had been in the area some time and had developed its own water source. Furthermore, the new tomato-processing plant had been located in the area not because of the existence of a new potable water supply system but because of increasing economic opportunities for tomato production and processing. The existence of a potable water supply system which could be used at relatively low cost was, in this case, a small plus for the plant in that it eliminated the need to develop a private water source. But an already existing system was not a primary consideration in determining whether the plant would be located in the area. Rather, it was located there to take advantage of the growing opportunity to create profits and provide employment by processing tomatoes.

A related long-run economic consideration in financing village potable water systems is that if the water supply system should stimulate economic development, that activity would induce additional public revenue which might in turn be used to help expand, upgrade, or pay off any loans incurred in building the system. Public revenue derived from income and sales taxes would automatically increase with increasing economic activity.

Property tax revenue, which constitutes a large portion of local revenue in many developing countries, would also increase if property values were to increase. Such increases could occur in the following ways: first, new commerce and village industry might develop new property or might expand existing establishments; second, as the desirability of potable water becomes more widely recognized, property with on-premises water service or convenient access to potable water becomes relatively more attractive to population from areas without water, which in turn helps to increase the price (value) of the property; and, third, women who no longer have to spend a major portion of their day carrying water have more time to spend making improvements in, and attending to, their living facilities. As for empirical evidence, it has been reported that in some areas of the Dominican Republic in which potable water supply systems have been functioning only a short time, some villages have officially revalued homes by as much as 25 percent,[8] an increase attributed to improved water supply. The difficulties in making such judgments, however, are immense.[9]

Nevertheless, if a potable village water supply system does stimulate long-run economic activity in an area, the taxable stock of private investment, both commercial and residential, should increase along with the taxable flow of income and sales. This would allow consideration of alternative approaches to financing the system such as using the additional public sector revenue to help pay off water system debt, or further expanding and improving the system without resorting to higher future water rates. On the other hand, higher user charges may become feasible as local ability to pay increases; a gradual increase in rates, possibly on a deferred basis, might be desirable.

Improved Health and Labor Productivity

Although a direct link between economic output and improved health might seem obvious, it is empirically, especially on a program level, difficult to demonstrate. One attempt to find the effects of schistosomiasis and four other parasitic diseases on labor productivity on St. Lucia failed to demonstrate an association between the severity of the disease and the daily output of workers on a banana estate and at a light industry plant. This study, however, plagued not only by the normal problems of field studies, also prompted the valid question of whether or not schistosomiasis and the other diseases are sufficiently severe on St. Lucia to affect productivity.[10]

Empirical work does exist establishing a link between health factors and economic output on an aggregative international level. One study which compared health and economic output across twenty-two

---

8. Beatriz deGreiff, "First Stage of Planar Project" (Washington, D.C.: George Washington University, Dept. of Economics, Spring 1971).

9. Roy W. Bahl, Stephen P. Coelen, and Jeremy J. Warford, "Land Value Increments as a Measure of the Net Benefits of Urban Water Supply Projects in Developing Countries: Theory and Measurement" (paper presented at the Taxation Resources and Economic Development Conference, Madison, Wisconsin, 1972).

10. Burton A. Weisbrod et al., *Disease and Economic Development: The Impact of Parasitic Diseases in St. Lucia* (Madison: University of Wisconsin Press, 1973).

African, Asian, and Latin American countries found that the influence of health factors on economic output appears to be quantitatively large relative to the influence of other factors, including agricultural inputs such as labor and commercial fertilizer. In fact, this study went so far as to conclude that health inputs are associated with variations in economic output beyond those usually attributed to labor and capital.[11] These findings, of course, could be subject to considerable errors in data aggregation and interpretation.

The following sections focus on the effects of increased labor inputs (made possible by better rural health) and of a healthier and expanding population on a per capita income and economic output. If an improved water supply system has the effect of reducing mortality and morbidity in a local population, then a greater quantity of labor from that population will be available to use as an input in increasing local output, earnings, and income.

Reduction in Mortality Rates

When mortality rates in a locality decline as a result of better drinking water or improved sanitation facilities, the final calculated value of the economic impact depends on whether or not a person's consumption is viewed as a cost to society or as an objective of society. When a person dies prematurely, society loses the amount of output which he would have produced over an extended lifetime. What is generally debatable (as noted in a previous section on valuing health) is whether or not this loss to society should be calculated on a net basis (output he would have produced minus the amount he would have consumed) or on a gross basis (output he would have produced). If one is interested only in what the effect is on others, then the net basis would be an acceptable way to calculate society's economic loss. Alternatively, however, one could consider consumption to be an objective of society and therefore argue that the portion of a person's output which he would have consumed would have increased the total welfare of society and therefore should not be subtracted from total output. In this case the gross output calculation would be preferable. In either case, of course, the economic value of the loss due to the death would be calculated in terms of

---

11. Wilfred Malenbaum, "Health and Productivity in Poor Areas," in *Empirical Studies in Health Economics,* ed. Herbert Klarman (Baltimore: Johns Hopkins University Press, 1970).

its present value, which means that the flow of income (and consumption) would have to be discounted back to the value it could command at the present time.

The age at which a person dies does not affect the method of calculation. If an infant dies, the earnings flow to be discounted would include the following ten to fifteen years of zero earnings plus the expected earnings of an average individual of that sex over the remaining years of an average life span. If it were decided to subtract projected consumption from earnings, it would be discounted from the year of death (birth) throughout an average lifespan. The procedure is exactly the same for individuals who die at any other age.

It has been pointed out from time to time that from an economic resource point of view society loses more if a twelve-year-old dies than if an infant dies because, while neither has started contributing earnings to society, more of society's resources (consumption) have been invested in the twelve-year-old. From a program or project evaluation point of view, however, any costs incurred up to the time when the water project is initiated are sunk costs—costs which have been incurred but which cannot be recovered. The impact of a water supply project relates only to earnings and consumption in the future.

It is true that when discounting future earnings streams, if the same amount of earnings is attributed to both a twelve-year-old and a one-year-old, the twelve-year-old will have a greater present value because the twelve-year-old's earnings are realized years earlier. If it is assumed, though, that there will be some economic growth resulting in increases in the productivity of labor, the one-year-old during his working years may be more productive, in real terms, than the twelve-year-old.

Observation has shown, in numerous instances, that the greatest number of deaths from water-related diseases in developing countries occurs among children less than two or three years of age.[12] Consequently, a benefit valuation exercise that attempted to attach a "standardized" discounted earnings stream to probable changes in water-related deaths, regardless of age distribution, would probably

---

12. United States, Agency for International Development, and the Ethiopian Ministry of Public Health, "A Study of the Health Impact of a Protected Community Water Supply—Methodology and Baseline Findings" (Washington, D.C., December 1965); Ruth Rice Puffer, Carlos V. Serrano, and Ann Dillon, *Inter-American Investigation of Mortality in Childhood*, provisional report (Washington, D.C.: Pan American Health Organization, September 1971).

overvalue the short-run economic benefits of a reduction in death rates through improved water supply.

Reduction in Morbidity

The economic value of a reduction in morbidity, as a result of an improved water supply system, is also partly related to the age distribution of the population. A reduction in morbidity among children who are not economically productive would have little short-run economic value unless significant amounts of mothers' time were freed to be used productively. The long-run value, however, could be much greater. A population of children that suddenly has lower morbidity rates might, for example, be better able to utilize existing public sector investment in education.

A water supply-induced reduction in morbidity rates among those currently in the labor force could increase labor productivity and thus local earnings and output. The local economy might benefit by (a) reduced worker absentee rates (less lost earnings), (b) improved worker vigor and productivity on the job (higher productivity resulting in increased earnings), and (c) less earnings loss by members of families caring for others who are ill.

In a full employment economy, a reduction in morbidity affecting the labor force would induce increases in economic output. But in rural areas of developing countries there is generally substantial underemployment: for example, it has been estimated that in some parts of Mexico the population engages in productive economic activity only four months a year while in rural areas of the Dominican Republic the population can find work only 30 to 65 percent of their average workday. Since such situations are quite common, studies that attempt to value the economic cost of one or more water-related diseases by multiplying the developing country's minimum legal wage by an estimate of disease-caused sick days without considering existing employment opportunities probably considerably overestimate the "economic cost" of the disease.[13]

Merely a healthier population, able, on the average, to work more frequently and vigorously, does not mean that economic output will

---

13. See, for example, M. Farooq, "A Possible Approach to the Evaluation of the Economic Burden Imposed on a Community by Schistosomiasis," *Annals of Tropical Medicine and Parasitology* 57 (September 1963):323–31; "Medical and Economic Importance of Schistosomiasis," *Journal of Tropical Medicine and Hygiene* 67 (May 1964):105–12.

change. If the limited employment and work opportunities, as the population perceives them, remain unchanged, then the same will be true of economic output and earnings.

On the other hand, some increases in output might occur in areas where the planting and harvesting seasons are limited to several somewhat short periods and where labor is scarce during those periods. Under such conditions, lower absentee rates and increased population vigor during these periods could allow more intensive planting, cultivating, and harvesting efforts to pay off in increased output and earnings.

Attempting to place an exact economic value on these benefits would create some difficulty in estimating (a) the existence and duration of labor-scarce periods during the year, (b) the expected increase in energy resulting from a given reduction in morbidity rates, and (c) the effects of (b) as seen in increases in labor input and economic output. In addition, any attempt to simplify the problems of estimating the economic benefits of water supplies in rural areas by making use of aggregate per capita output and productivity figures for the total country would probably lead to an overestimate of the value of health benefits. Per capita output, or per capita contribution to GNP, is usually higher in areas where there are greater quantities of capital for labor to use, namely, in the large urban areas, in most countries. Consequently, unadjusted countrywide labor productivity figures would generally be too large to use in rural areas, and if used they would cause an overstatement of the estimated economic benefits.

Any dramatic improvements in health, to reemphasize a point, which have occurred as a result of improved water supplies, have been among children. The health-related potential for increased productivity among adults, consequently, even if employment were available, may not in many cases be very great. For example, in the Zaina scheme reviewed earlier,[14] it was found that adults were sick for less than one-half day per month and that the improved water system apparently caused no change in this rate. Even if the improved water had eliminated all diseases, the increase in the labor force would have been insignificant: no more than a half man-day a month.

14. Fenwick, "Short Term Effects."

Reduction in Spread of Disease

People who frequently come into contact with the residents of villages served by potable water systems might also show improvement in health and labor inputs. This could come about for two reasons. First, it has been well documented that potable water supply systems help retard the spread of epidemic diseases such as cholera and typhoid.[15] As a result, a given subset of a region's population which is served with potable water would have less likelihood of catching such diseases and of passing them on to others.[16] Conceivably, those having lower morbidity and mortality rates because the disease was not passed on to them by the population with access to potable water, could generate increased economic output. Second, a population unweakened by diarrhea and other water-associated diseases generally has a lower propensity to contract other more common sicknesses and to pass these sicknesses on to others. The population served by the potable water supply system and those with whom they come in contact therefore should have lower morbidity and mortality rates and should be able to generate a higher level of labor inputs which, in turn, might be translated into increased economic output.

Increased Time for Productive Work

A potable water supply system makes obtaining the water needed for drinking, washing, and preparing food more convenient for the local population. Those who must fetch and carry water for family use will have more time, therefore, to devote to other things. The provision of water for the family in the rural areas of most developing countries is the primary responsibility of women and children. Depending on season, location, and terrain, water carriers in many parts of the world could be expected to spend more than one hour each

---

15. World Health Organization, "Strategy of Cholera Control," abbreviated proceedings of the WHO Seminar on the Organization of Cholera Control, Manila, 6–9 October 1970 (BD/Cholera/71.1) (Geneva, 1971).

16. J. C. Azurín and M. Alvero, "Field Evaluation of Environmental Sanitation Measures against Cholera," *Bulletin of the World Health Organization* 51 (1974):19–26.

day carrying water or, in some cases, up to four hours.[17] Furthermore, again depending on location, terrain, and season, the distance between dwellings and a usable source of water is generally (at least in East Africa) less than a mile,[18] although examples have been cited where many of the women walk more than one mile, or even two miles.[19]

After the introduction of a potable water supply system, women would be able to spend that time formerly used in carrying water in more directly productive activities to increase economic output and earnings. Again, the opportunity to increase earnings and output may be relegated to those seasons, if any, in which planting, cultivation, and harvesting make labor a resource temporarily in short supply. During those limited periods of time, the additional woman-hours of labor, and perhaps the additional availability of water-carrying animals, may make it possible for the village to engage in a more intensive or extensive cultivation of land and thereby to utilize better existing land and agriculture-related capital.

Aside from seasonal factors, whether or not women would spend more time at measurably productive activities would depend on the opportunities for such work and on the personal and cultural factors affecting the inclination of the former water carriers to engage in such work. In a study of nine Tanzanian villages where agricultural work occupied the largest share of time of a majority of married women, when asked what they would do if they had more time available, less than half said they would spend it on agricultural work.[20]

In another study carried out in the small village of Kpomkpo in southeast Ghana,[21] women were asked how they would allocate their time if a new water supply system saved them about twelve hours per week. Their responses were:

---

17. Gilbert F. White, David J. Bradley, and Anne U. White, *Drawers of Water: Domestic Water Use in East Africa* (Chicago: University of Chicago Press, 1972).

18. White et al., *Drawers of Water*, p. 107.

19. Dennis Warner, *Rural Water Supply and Development: A Comparison of Nine Villages in Tanzania*, Economic Research Bureau Paper no. 69.17 (Dar es Salaam: University College, 1969), p. 14; World Bank, "Appraisal of a Rural Development Fund Project, Upper Volta," Agricultural Projects Dept. Report PA-127A (Washington, D.C., 16 May 1972), p. 21.

20. Warner, "Rural Water Supply."

21. G. E. Dalton and R. N. Parker, *Agriculture in South East Ghana*, vol. 2, Special Studies (Reading, U.K.: University of Reading, 1973).

Activity	Hours	Percent
Directly productive work	6.8	57
Household jobs	4.2	35
Leisure	0.9	8
Total	11.9	100

The interesting thing about this situation is that the women did in fact have the opportunity to engage in productive work, that is, in cassava and charcoal production. As a result, an estimate of the value of the time which would not have to be used fetching water was made by multiplying the average returns to labor from cassava and charcoal production (by month) times 0.57 times the time saved fetching water. In this exercise it was assumed that the returns to women were approximately equal to the returns to men, and that the returns to labor were constant, that is, marginal returns were equal to average returns.

To the extent that women spend a portion of their newly acquired free time on domestic chores such as washing clothes or tidying up their dwellings, there generally would be no directly measurable short-run economic benefit, except perhaps, as mentioned earlier, possible increases in property values.

Relieving children from water-carrying chores might, on the other hand, allow them to attend school more regularly and to take better advantage of existing investment in educational facilities, a situation that would probably have measurable economic impact only in the long run, if ever.

Effects of Increases in Population on per Capita Income

Given existing birth rates, investment in potable water supply or waste disposal, by improving health, can cause an increase in the rate of population growth. Whether or not this is economically desirable depends on what is happening at the same time to income or output in the country. It is obvious that economic output must grow at a rate faster than population in order to attain a goal of increasing per capita income. As noted above, however, only limited examples have been found where a potable water supply, which is primarily for human consumption, can be directly productive and result in a direct increase in economic output and income. Even with regard to better health and the extent to which potable water and better waste disposal improves labor inputs, there has been research at an aggregate level which contends that on average only a small proportion of economic growth is accounted for by increases in labor inputs.[22]

A water supply system, as mentioned earlier, is part of the local infrastructure and, as such, may indirectly increase production and output over the long run. There is insufficient evidence, however, to support an assumption that the direct and indirect increases in economic output caused by the potable water supply system would keep up with possible increases in population.

But there are two considerations which could modify the situation. First, it might be possible to stimulate the local economy with other directly productive investments which complement water supply and sanitation investment and which increase the rate of economic output to a point where it exceeds population growth. This possibility will be discussed in some detail in the sections on growth points and on multiple investment strategies in Chapter 4.

Second, more directly relevant to the population side of the problem is that the decline in infant and child mortality might also cause a decline in the birth rate.[23] This follows from the three primary reasons why people have children:[24] children between the ages of eight and eighteen, and particularly those of rural subsistence farmers, contribute work, and therefore income, to the family; children are a form of retirement annuity which rural parents purchase early in life and draw on later in life when they are no longer productive enough to sustain themselves; and there is the simple desire of people in many developing countries to continue their family line and to have sons to preside over their burial and inherit their belongings.

Given these reasons for raising children, conditions in which there is a substantial risk of infant and child mortality, as there is now in many rural areas with nonpotable water, would be expected

---

22. Simon S. Kuznets, *Modern Economic Growth: Rate, Structure, and Spread* (New Haven: Yale University Press, 1966).

23. John C. Snyder, "Population and Disease Control," *American Journal of Tropical Medicine and Hygiene* 21 (1972):386–91; David M. Heer and Dean O. Smith, "Mortality Level, Desired Family Size and Population Increase," *Demography* 5 (1968):104–21.

24. Warren C. Robinson and David E. Horlacher, "Population Growth and Economic Welfare," *Reports on Population/Family Planning* 6 (New York: The Population Council, February 1971).

to result in higher birth rates than if there were a much lower risk of infant and child death. If, through time, lower infant mortality rates bring about lessened birthrates, the problem of more rapid growth of water supply–induced population than corresponding increases in economic output may be less severe.

Unfortunately, very little empirical evidence exists to show what has happened to birth rates in rural areas of developing countries when death rates have been drastically lowered. One study, in which the consequences of malaria control in Sri Lanka were examined, did find that as mortality rates fell, the population was increasing rapidly. But on a cross-section basis it was also found that those areas with the lowest mortality rates had the lowest birth rates as well as the highest population density, literacy, and marriage age of women.[25] These conflicting results, of course, make it very difficult to support any cause and effect relationship.

Finally, considerable existing literature on the value of a prevented birth could be useful in estimating the real costs of a rural water supply system if it were concluded that, in a particular case, the water supply system would, over a foreseeable period, result in a more rapid increase in population than in income.[26] Essentially, the value of a prevented birth would be a person's discounted expected lifetime earnings subtracted from his discounted expected lifetime consumption. Presumably, it would be a cost to society if consumption were to exceed earnings, and a benefit to society if earnings exceeded consumption by a greater amount than that for the average person (so per capita net income increases). Of course, this calculation sidesteps the argument that consumption, as such, should be a goal of society and therefore does not represent a cost.

---

25. Harald Frederiksen, "Consequences of Mortality Trends in Ceylon" and "Malaria Control and Population Pressure in Ceylon," in *Readings on Population,* ed. David M. Heer (Englewood Cliffs, N.J.: Prentice-Hall, 1968).

26. Bruce Herrick and Ricardo Morán, "Declining Birth Rates in Chile: Their Effects on Output, Education, Health, and Housing," *Tempo,* April 1972 (Santa Barbara, Calif.: General Electric Company); Julian Simon, "The Value of Avoided Births to Underdeveloped Countries," *Population Studies* 23 (March 1969):61–68, and "The Per-Capita-Income Criterion and Natality Policies in Poor Countries," *Demography* 7 (August 1970):369–78; Harvey Leibenstein, "Pitfalls in Benefit-Cost Analysis of Birth Prevention," *Population Studies* 23 (July 1969):161–70; Stephen Enke, "The Gains to India from Population Control: Some Money Measures and Incentive Schemes," *Review of Economics and Statistics* 42 (May 1960):175–81.

Averted Costs

A rural water supply or waste disposal program could have the effect, in concept, of reducing some of the costs which the local or national economy of the developing country is currently experiencing such as possible one-time reductions in present expenditures, reductions in periodic revenue losses, and reductions in costs associated with personal consumption.

Possible Reduction in Current Expenditures

If a rural water supply or waste disposal program brings about lower water-related disease rates and thus a healthier population it might be possible for the country at least to reduce the rate of growth of some of the expenditures currently made for health and medical services. Specifically, fewer funds might be necessary for vaccination programs (typhoid, cholera, and so on), hospital and health center facilities and equipment, physicians and staff, drugs and medicines, and transportation for health purposes.

Whether or not a particular country would be able to reduce expenditures on health services as a result of a rural water supply or waste disposal program would depend on the extent of the improvement in the health of the population, on the supply of health care and the adequacy of health expenditures before the water supply program was initiated, and on the level of demand for public health care and services in the country. Little empirical information is available about what has happened to health expenditures in such a situation. Because most developing countries do not currently have an abundance of health care services and medical facilities, it is doubtful if many would choose to reduce current levels of expenditures on health.

What is more likely is that, in the short run, the quality of health services will increase because the same staff and facilities will be available to serve a population now healthier, thanks to improved water supply or waste disposal. In the long run, however, there might be some slowing in the rate of growth of public health expenditures which could be counted as reduced expenditures made possible by the rural water supply program.

Whether this were to happen or not, countries would now be able to exercise a new option as a result of the rural water and waste disposal program. They would have the option, at a specific time or over a period, of allowing the quality of health care in the country to improve, or of maintaining the same quality of care and reducing health-related public expenditures.

Reduction in Periodic Revenue Losses

A reduction in the frequency and magnitude of water-related epidemics could result in a smoother growth of the national economy. In particular, if a country relies to a significant extent on tourism and trade to generate income, and if epidemics necessitate travel restrictions, hurt tourism through unfavorable publicity, or result in embargoes on trade, then the country loses revenue and income. In situations such as this, a rural water supply program which contributes to a countrywide reduction in water-related epidemics would benefit the country by helping to smooth economic growth and reducing periodic losses in revenue. Estimates of the probable economic impact would have to be derived by estimating past frequency and magnitude of epidemic-related losses and by comparing these with probable changes brought about by a rural water supply and sanitation program.

Reduction in Costs Associated with Personal Consumption

One additional set of reduced costs which might be imputed to a rural water supply program relate to the fact that the majority of people served by the new system will now spend less effort procuring water for their personal consumption. The reduced effort is measurable in the cost of calories not now needed to carry water. If it is assumed, first, that carrying water requires more calories than the substitute activity, and second, that the person would reduce food intake (cost of personal consumption) proportionate to the reduced caloric needs, estimates of the value of the food not consumed could be made. Presumably, food not consumed would not be purchased, thereby reducing consumption costs (increasing disposable income) of the family. Alternatively, food not consumed could be sold, again increasing the disposable income of the family.

Estimates have been made, for several areas in East Africa, of the expenditure of caloric energy for procuring water over a variety of terrains, as well as daily caloric intake and caloric expenditure when one is not procuring water.[27] Another estimate, made in (Upper

---

27. White and others, *Drawers of Water*.

Volta), stated that 1 ton of sorghum was needed to meet the energy expended by 60 women fetching water, each walking 16 kilometers for 150 days of the dry season.[28] It must be kept in mind, however, that translating estimates of this sort into monetized benefits involves specific assumptions about corresponding changes in food intake and about what a person does with the extra time now available because of a new convenient potable water supply system.

Rural to Urban Drift and Population Location

In addition to the goals of improved health and an improved allocation of resources to increase economic output, a variety of other goals, or expected benefits, closely related to both health and economic development are frequently advocated. Prominent among them are the stemming of rural to urban drift, and population relocation and stabilization.

Population Drift

Most developing countries have been experiencing a migration of population from rural to urban areas. It is often true that this rapid flow of population puts a great strain on the social and economic overhead capital of the big urban areas, and it is argued that if the population inflow were slowed the big cities would be better able to absorb and generate employment for new immigrants and to cope with internal development problems. Rural water supply programs have been suggested as a means of slowing rural to urban migration because they can ease at least one of the basic problems of rural dwellers.[29]

A rural water supply and sanitation program would certainly help alleviate one of the "push" factors of migration. However, it is also

---

28. World Bank, "Appraisal of a Rural Development Fund Project, Upper Volta."

29. Other rural problems include lack of job opportunities, inferior social, economic, and health care amenities, and relatively poorer quality educational opportunities. For a summary of some of the developing country migration literature, see Mildred B. Levy and Walter Wadycki, "Lifetime versus One-Year Migration in Venezuela," *Journal of Regional Science* 12 (December 1972): 407–15; and Lorene Y. L. Yap, "Internal Migration in Less Developed Countries: A Survey of the Literature," Staff Working Paper no. 215 (Washington, D.C.: World Bank, September 1975).

probable that isolated improvements in rural water supplies will not, in most countries, slow migration appreciably. People migrate for a variety of reasons, and the relative short- or long-run lure of jobs, higher incomes, and educational opportunities in urban areas would generally be unchanged by the provision of improved rural water supply and waste disposal.

Of course, through time, if rural water supply systems, which are improvements in the local infrastructure, produce an increase in economic activity in rural areas, migration may be slowed. On the other hand, if improved rural water systems were to result only in a more healthy and vigorous rural population, more migrants might journey to the cities looking for alternative employment and education opportunities.

In summary, the contention that improving village water supplies in rural areas might significantly slow migration to the cities is an interesting theoretical possibility; however, at this time there is very little empirical evidence to support it, and there is some limited evidence to deny it.

A related contention deserving a brief review is that there is some statistical evidence from both developing and developed countries suggesting that migrants generally do not go directly from the dispersed population rural areas to the big cities.[30] Instead, in many cases there is a tendency to move first to the nearest regional population center (intermediate-size city or larger village) and, after an indeterminate stay, to move on to the capital city or to one of the country's other large urban areas.

In view of this kind of movement, the argument is sometimes made that if one of the objectives of a national development policy is to slow the migration into the very large urban centers, then resources should be channeled into the intermediate size regional population centers in an attempt to stimulate their economic viability and to

---

30. Arthur Redford, *Labour Migration in England, 1800–1850* (New York: A. M. Kelley, 1968); Appalachian Regional Commission, *Applachia* (Washington, D.C., May 1969), pp. 14–15; Barry J. Riddell and Milton E. Harvey, "The Urban System in the Migration Process: An Evaluation of Step-Wise Migration in Sierra Leone," *Economic Geography* 48 (July 1972): 270–83; Ira S. Lowry, *Migration and Metropolitan Growth: Two Analytical Models* (San Francisco: Chandler Publishing Co., 1966); Constantina Safilios-Rothschild, "Children and Adolescents in Slums and Shanty-Towns in Developing Countries" (New York: United Nations Economic and Social Council, March 1971).

make them attractive enough to hold the population flowing through them. Following this reasoning, and given a scarcity of national resources in the water supply and wastes sector, a country attempting to slow migration into the capital city would attempt to improve or install water supply systems in intermediate or secondary size cities and towns and not necessarily use up investment in the improvement or protection of the more rural systems (see the discussion on growth points in Chapter 4). Empirical studies having shown that migrants are primarily responsive to employment, income, and education opportunities, investment in water supply should be followed or supplemented by employment and education opportunities to increase the probability of a significant decline in out-migration.[31]

An alternative argument has been made that the very policies aimed at encouraging the growth of regional, intermediate-size cities or towns could eventually increase the flow of population to the largest or capital city. The more visible and prosperous regional centers might attract an increased number of migrants from the rural areas who in turn, after an indeterminate stay, would pass on to the biggest or capital city.[32]

Underlying the population migration argument for rural water supply and sanitation investment is the contention that the very large urban areas are already too large to be compatible with an efficient allocation of national resources, and that additional water supply and other social and economic investment in the big cities could result in an even greater misallocation of national resources. This argument is essentially that as cities grow they experience economies of scale up to a certain size. After reaching that optimum size, average costs of providing public services begin to rise, and as the cities grow even larger, significant diseconomies of scale are experienced. Although the optimum size for a city would depend on many factors, several studies based on a minimum public service cost approach suggest that the lowest average public service cost occurs with a population of between 30,000 and 250,000, with larger average costs in cities with populations of over 250,000 or in very small cities with population of less than approximately 5,000.[33]

---

31. Levy and Wadycki, "Lifetime versus One-Year Migration," pp. 407–15.
32. Riddell and Harvey, "The Urban System in the Migration Process," pp. 270–83.
33. Associazione per lo sviluppo dell'industria nel Mezzogiorno, "Ricerca sui coste d'insediamento" (Rome, 1967); William Alonso, "The Economics of

Other evidence suggests, however, that the cost of infrastructure for "an increase in industrial activity" declines or at least remains relatively constant with increases in city size.[34] Furthermore, a cursory examination of the relation of urban costs and total urban product with city size in West Germany, Japan, the USSR, and the United States suggests that the biggest cities are not too big from the viewpoint of economic efficiency, that is, as cities get larger average costs do increase, but not as rapidly as average output.[35] Herrara[36] has contended that if one of the objectives of Latin American countries is to create secondary growth centers, the leading cities should have a minimum population of 5 million to 6 million. In lagging countries or regions, moreover, boosting the size of the larger cities may be a sound strategy; the higher a city rises in the national or international urban hierarchy the greater is the tendency for it to benefit from growth diffusion.

One of the most recent and complete examinations of the urban size question has been carried out by Richardson.[37] He emphasizes that relative city size, city density, and hierarchical size distribution considerations are probably more relevant and productive topics of inquiry than an elusive search for any one absolute urban size optimum.

In summary, the economic theories which relate to city size are either too general to be of much use for policy guidelines (optimum size occurs where marginal social costs equal marginal social benefits or, depending on the assumptions, where net agglomeration economies are at a maximum) or very narrow in scope with extremely limiting assumptions. Furthermore, the interrelated nature of the subject, the difficulties of definition, measurement, and hypothesis testing, and the conflicting and general form of the goals give few

---

Urban Size," Center for Planning and Research Development Working Paper no. 138 (Berkeley: University of California, 1970); B. Khorev, "What Kind of City Is Needed?" *Literaturnaya gazeta* 14 (1969), reported in *Current Digest of the Soviet Press* 21 (23 April 1969).

34. R. Morse, "Costs of Urban Infrastructure as Related to City Size in Developing Countries: India Case Study" (Stanford, Calif.: Stanford Research Institute, 1968).

35. Alonso, "The Economics of Urban Size."

36. Felipe Herrara, "Nationalism and Urbanization in Latin America," *Ekistics* 32 (1971):369–73.

37. Harry W. Richardson, *The Economics of Urban Size* (Lexington, Mass.: D.C. Heath and Co., 1973).

results of use to policymakers. Accordingly, the consensus of advice would seem to be to stop wasting time on irrelevant optimum size considerations and to spend more time searching for the best allocation of resources to solve current problems, which are at least tangible. With regard to rural water supply systems, therefore, it would seem that arguments for investment should probably be based on something other than contentions that big cities are too big.

Population Relocation and Stabilization

Investments in village water supply and sanitation systems have sometimes been geared to specific relocation objectives or, particularly in the case of nomadic people, to stabilizing the population in order to improve efficiency in the construction and operation of infrastructural investments. A variety of reasons might be offered for a country's decision to move population spatially over a short period of time. In some cases, groups of people have been relocated from tropical river-basin areas where there existed a variety of diseases which could not be controlled. The population might be moved to an area on higher ground several miles back from the river. A sites and services area which included a potable water supply system and material for new dwellings might be the incentive for the move, on the assumption that, with these advantages, the population would be healthier and possibly more productive.

Other cases of relocating populations en masse occur where a new irrigation or hydroelectric project causes the inundation of a populated valley. In cases such as these, dwellings and a potable water supply system are usually among the relocation facilities provided.

Those countries that have constantly shifting populations and where population stabilization may be a desired objective experience a variation of the relocation problem. In Zambia, for example, the nomadic tradition is in part the result of wasteful agricultural practices. The burning of vegetation, which rapidly exhausts the soil, frequently means that the agricultural communities are provided with a certain basic infrastructure used only for a few years before the tribe abandons it and moves on. In this case, complementary investments —say in agricultural education, including the use of fertilizers—might in the long run permit cost savings to be achieved.

Relocation might also be encouraged when it provides an opportunity for the government to give people water and other public facilities at a lower unit cost (because of economies of scale) and to create the beginnings of a growth center which, as it develops, could become viable. This is one objective of the Ujàmaa villages program in Tanzania. Moreover, even in developed countries there is evidence that in certain instances it would be preferable from a strictly economic standpoint to relocate and provide essential services to a dispersed farming population than to provide it with public water supply and other services in its existing location.[38] But although the economies achievable in the public water supply field by population concentration may be considerable, social problems are likely to be encountered in attempting to use the relocation solution.

Finally, for reasons of political indoctrination or to generate long-run national political and economic power, populations have also been encouraged to move, on short notice, into newly created settlement areas which have potable water supply systems. An uninformed, dispersed, or nomadic population does not provide a central government with a very stable or reliable power base whereas a more concentrated and stable rural population is more easily informed of the government's merits.

Stabilization, or acceptance of relocation, normally implies much more than just physical investments in infrastructure. Water supply can be the catalyst for the local organization required for community development. A cohesive, problem-oriented organization of community leaders does not exist in the rural areas of many developing countries. There is often no formal group whose goal is to improve the community and to help it to grow and prosper. A community potable water supply project is one way to organize such a group and to demonstrate that it can carry on and can continue to function for community betterment long after the water supply project is completed.

It is frequently contended that if a rural water supply program is to succeed there must be involvement by leaders at the community level. Residents of the village must be induced to develop pride in the system, to feel that it belongs to them, or at least to feel that they have some ownership responsibility for it. This is usually accomplished by requiring the community to contribute some portion of the initial construction cost and pay, through time, at least the operation and maintenance costs of the system. Community contribution to construction can be in terms of money or labor, although in the case of

---

38. Jeremy J. Warford, *The South Atcham Scheme,* report submitted to the Ministry of Housing and Local Government (London: Her Majesty's Stationery Office, 1969).

piped water supply systems it is generally difficult to contribute much more than 10 percent of system cost through free labor.

The result of this need for community participation and contribution is that some form of local organization is usually created to help organize and administer the local effort. The organization may take various forms, although it is frequently a type of committee made up of local leaders. The committee (with the guidance and help of a community water program promoter provided by the national or regional water program office) is very active during the planning and construction phases of a project. After the project is completed, the committee meets occasionally to review system operations, finances, and possible system expansion.

A committee of this type, it is asserted, made up of local leaders, is a necessary part of the local infrastructure of a rural area requiring considerable self-help to make development progress. Evidence to this effect may be found in a number of countries in Latin America. Northern Argentina provided a particular instance observed by the authors. There, local committees were organized and involved in the rural areas when electricity was introduced several years ago. Now, similar committees, usually made up of the same people, are attempting to organize their villages and to petition the government for assistance in procuring village water supply systems. These cooperative electricity committees have survived and are now (with the help of a trained community water promoter) channeling their efforts in a new direction.

The introduction of a community water supply system, requiring the payment of a monthly fee by its users, is a means, it is sometimes suggested, by which the habit of periodic payments may be introduced into a population. Many rural populations do not understand or participate in periodic tax or revenue payments to the government. Water supply systems, therefore, in areas where the population pays for a recognized, tangible service, could be a means of introducing habits of payment for public services necessary to community development.

Summary

The preceding brief discussion of some of the economic effects of a rural water supply and sanitation program in developing countries covered its general growth and redistributive effects on the national economy; possible short- and long-run direct effects (gardening, animal husbandry, property values, commerce and village industry, and so on); its effects on labor inputs and earnings (death, morbidity, external health effects, additional time for productive work); the problems of population size and income; the possibility of averting some costs which the economy is currently bearing; and influences on population location and stability.

It is clear that any one particular country is unlikely to experience all, or even most, of these effects as a result of a rural water supply and sanitation program. But depending on national characteristics, each might experience a somewhat different mix of costs and benefits from the program.

Evident too is the fact that predicting the impact of a village water supply and sanitation program—whether in terms of health, income redistribution, productivity or population location—poses an immense problem. As we have observed earlier, these difficulties are not of such concern in the case of most urban systems, where beneficiaries are willing to pay for water and sanitation facilities and thereby provide an indication of the merits of those investments. That it is extremely difficult to extend this approach to project evaluation to rural areas is at the heart of the rural water supply problem. Even if ultimately, however, we cannot predict with adequate confidence the economic consequences of investments in this area, there are a number of courses of action that may be taken and information that may be acquired to improve this state of affairs, as we shall describe in the following chapters.

Part Three | *Program Planning*

4 | The Determination of Investment Priorities

IN A COUNTRY or region within a country considering the implementation of a rural water supply program, one of the important questions to be examined early in the planning stage is which areas, or villages, should receive priority. That question is now discussed under the headings of costs, economies of scale, and service quality; growth-point strategies; income redistribution and "worst-first" strategies; financial viability and community enthusiasm. Although these considerations are always cited and no doubt frequently used as criteria by which countries choose the towns or villages to receive water first, in practice political considerations or response to the most vociferous demands for service are also major determinants.

Costs, Economies of Scale, and Quality of Service

It is generally assumed that there are economies of large scale production in the provision of water supplies. If the objective of the rural water supply program is simply to maximize the number of people served (the implication of which is that the benefits of supplying an individual are the same wherever he lives), then water supply systems should be constructed in the largest towns and villages first. Eligible towns and villages (those with acceptable water sources, and so on) could simply be ranked by population size and provided with water supplies in turn as resources became available.

Evidence of Water Supply Economies of Scale: U.S. Data

There is empirical evidence from the United States that points to the existence of cost economies of scale in water supply. Although the absolute cost figures and the proportions of labor and capital may not be strictly applicable to the developing country situation, in general the technical relationships are. Furthermore, the developed country picture is not complicated by the extreme variations in service quality of developing countries. Thus, for statistical purposes, developed country data do not have to be adjusted to allow for variations in hours of supply, the degree of access to service, or water quality.

A study of over 300 water utilities in the state of Illinois yielded the following results: [1]

Population served	Median recurrent cost per thousand gallons produced (U.S. dollars)
1–1,000	0.843
1,001–5,000	0.589
5,001–10,000	0.409
10,001–25,000	0.445
Over 25,000	0.347

It can be seen that total expenditure per thousand gallons produced, excluding expenditure for capital additions, tended to decline from 84 cents per thousand gallons in utilities serving a population of 1,000 or less, to 35 cents per thousand gallons in utilities serving a population of over 25,000. These figures show that there are probably economies of scale with regard to recurring costs but do not give a complete picture since capital expenditure information is lacking.

Other analyses are available which make use of nationwide data on water utilities in the United States. An analysis of data collected by the American Water Works Association (AWWA) showed that in 1955 operation and maintenance costs of publicly owned water utilities varied as follows: [2]

---

1. Hamdy H. Afifi and V. Lewis Bassie, *Water Pricing Theory and Practice in Illinois* (Urbana, Ill.: University of Illinois, Bureau of Economic and Business Research, 1969).

2. Harris F. Seidel and E. Robert Baumann, "A Statistical Analysis of Water Works Data for 1955," *Journal of the American Water Works Association* 49, no. 12 (1957):1531–66.

Production of the utility (millions of gallons a day)	Operation and maintenance costs per capita (U.S. dollars)	Operation and maintenance costs per million gallons (U.S. dollars)
Under 2	5.55	163
2–4	5.63	122
4–6	5.77	114
6–10	5.82	109
10–20	4.90	98
20–50	5.35	92
Over 50	4.95	83

Declining costs are evident as utility size increases, particularly when measured in terms of gallons of output. In this case, however, the per capita costs are somewhat distorted in that they are based only on retail population (even though some of the utilities served large additional areas on a wholesale basis).

A similar result was found in an examination of AWWA data for 1960. In that year the average operation and maintenance costs for publicly owned utilities by volume group were as follows: [3]

Production of the utility (millions of gallons a day)	Cost per capita (U.S. dollars)	Cost per million gallons (U.S. dollars)
Less than 0.1	7.70	422
0.1–0.5	7.30	284
0.5–1.0	7.62	213
1–2	7.84	180
2–4	7.27	159
4–6	6.85	144
6–10	6.32	125
10–20	6.89	121
20–50	6.14	104
Over 50	6.04	106

As in the case of the 1955 data, these costs included all normal operating expenses and excluded items such as debt service, capital expense, and taxes, if any. Unlike the 1955 example, total retail and wholesale population served was used to calculate the per capita figures.

3. Harris F. Seidel and John L. Cleasby, "A Statistical Analysis of Water Works Data for 1960," *Journal of the American Water Works Association* 58, no. 12 (1966):1507–27.

A regression analysis of a sample of AWWA 1960 data was also carried out as a more exact test for the existence of scale economies (or diseconomies) in supplying water. Water utilities in the United States were the subject of the examination, partly because of the availability of the AWWA data and partly because of the need to assume a constant quality of service among the utilities. As noted earlier, a major advantage of using a sample of water utilities from the United States is that it minimizes quality-related distortions in the relation between costs and quantity of output. The results of the analysis, which are detailed in Appendix C, supply additional evidence of the presence of economies of scale in water supply.

Evidence of Water Supply Economies of Scale from Developing Countries

Empirical evidence also supports the existence of economies of scale in supplying water to smaller communities in developing countries, although in these cases it is more difficult to assume a constant quality of service across the observations. Lauria, for example, found probable economies of scale when he estimated cost regressions in studies of community water supply in Guatemala and Honduras.[4] Carruthers, examining the rural water supply program in Kenya, estimated that, for a project, the increase in average cost for a fivefold increase in water supply is about 2.5.[5] The rural water supply program in the Dominican Republic also has experienced declining per capita costs in construction, administration, and operation and maintenance of systems.[6]

Economies of scale are further illustrated by the more detailed figures in Table 4.1, based on estimates prepared in November 1973 for a rural development project in Tanzania, adjusted where neces-

---

4. Donald T. Lauria, *Planning Water Supplies in Developing Countries,* final report submitted to the U.S., Agency for International Development, Office of Health (Chapel Hill, N.C.: University of North Carolina, Dept. of Environmental Sciences and Engineering, School of Public Health, 1972).

5. I. D. Carruthers, *Rural Water Investment in Kenya: Impact on Economics of Community Water Supply* (London: University of London, Wye College, 1972), p. 104.

6. Tito H. Cairo, *Acueductos Rurales en República Dominicana,* annexes 8, 14 (República Dominicana: Instituto Nacional de Aguas Potables y Alcantarillados, August 1974).

Table 4.1. Specifications and Cost Estimates for Four Village Water Supply Systems in Tanzania

Item	I	II	III	IV
Basic assumptions				
Village population	1,750	2,500	3,500	5,000
Per capita consumption (liters per day)	30	30	30	30
Average daily consumption (cubic meters)	52.5	75	105	150
Raw water main length (meters)	2,000	2,000	2,000	2,000
Elevation difference, source—village (meters)	100	100	100	100
Distribution mains length (meters)	4,000	5,500	8,500	11,300
Public hydrants	12	18	26	36
Persons per hydrant	146	139	135	139
Costs (U.S. dollars)				
Preparatory works	950	950	950	950
Intake	150	220	300	430
Pumphouse	1,280	1,280	1,280	1,280
Pumps	4,160	4,160	5,120	5,370
Rising main	3,310	3,720	4,670	4,700
Storage tank	1,680	2,130	2,910	3,240
Distribution systems	8,760	11,970	18,540	24,820
Hydrants	380	570	820	1,140
Construction plant costs	950	950	950	950
Transportation	2,190	2,920	4,380	5,840
Subtotal [a]	23,810	28,870	39,920	48,720
Overhead and contingencies (30 percent)	7,140	8,660	11,980	14,620
Total	30,950	37,530	51,900	63,340
Total per capita	17.70	15.00	14.80	12.70

a. Figures rounded.
Source: Project data assembled by Richard Middleton.

sary according to unit cost curves derived from other projects.[7] The typical Tanzanian system was infiltration at a river, with diesel-driven centrifugal pumps drawing from a well, lined with concrete rings, delivering water to an elevated storage tank made from concrete blocks, with distribution through public hydrants.

Additional evidence on economies of scale is apparent from the following figures taken from a project appraisal report prepared by

---

7. The authors are indebted to Richard Middleton for the preparation of this example and for summarizing the following Inter-American Development Bank example.

the Inter-American Development Bank in 1974. The project supplies a rural population totalling 87,000, distributed over 90 rural localities with populations ranging from 100 to 2,000. Where possible, the systems were to be fed by gravity, by diverting streams or springs, with treatment limited to chlorination. At the request of the villages, the supply is through house connections, not public hydrants. Per capita consumption is estimated at 50 to 100 liters a day, depending on the community. Typical costs (in dollars per capita) are calculated to vary as follows:

Present population	Present population	Design population, 1995
100–200	137	86
201–400	93	58
401–600	79	49
601–1,000	58	36
1,001–2,000	43	27
Weighted average	59	37

A more detailed example, based on data assembled from a number of actual projects, illustrates more completely how cost differences related to system size can originate among villages in a developing country.[8] It is essentially a comparison of two villages, one with a population of 10,000 (A) and one with a population of 1,000 (B). In the two villages it is assumed that the levels of service, per capita water consumption, and source of water are the same. It is also assumed that 50 percent of the service is provided through house connections and 50 percent through public hydrants; that there is adequate groundwater at a depth of 100 feet; that dependability is conditional on the use of one well and one pump; and that distribution costs are US$8 per capita.

A. *1,000 cubic meters per day production*	Cost (*U.S. dollars*)
30-centimeter well complete with screen, pump	5,500
Transmission, 20 centimeter	8,000
Storage	20,000
Distribution	80,000
Total	113,500
Per capita	11.35

8. The authors are indebted to Harold Shipman for the construction of the substantive parts of this example.

B. *100 cubic meters per day production*

15-centimeter well complete with screen, pump	2,800
Transmission, 10 centimeter	3,600
Storage	6,000
Distribution	8,000
Total	20,400
Per capita	20.40

It can be seen that cost differences are particularly evident in the source works, transmission, and storage elements. In fact, there might also be some scale economies for the distribution facilities, but for purposes of this example, it is assumed that per capita distribution costs are the same for each village.

The effect of dependability of supply and its cost may be noted in the above example where only one well is provided for each village. Should the well pump fail, the village would be out of water until it was repaired. If this were deemed to be a major problem, two wells could be provided and in that case the following figures might be typical:

Village A:	One 12-inch well	$5,500
	Two 8-inch wells	$7,600
Village B:	One 6-inch well	$2,800
	Two 6-inch wells	$5,600

For Village A the cost of greater dependability would be $2,100, or $0.21 per capita. For Village B it would be $2,800, or $2.80 per capita.

There are, of course, many other factors besides scale-related economies which influence costs across villages. Table 4.2 represents an attempt to summarize the implications of some of these factors. As can be seen, two of the more important ones are transmission costs and source works. Both of these are partly associated with the quality of water service provided to a village population. It can be seen that a lower level of water use brought about by the fact that a greater proportion of the population is supplied through public hydrants results in a lower per capita cost.

Costs also vary according to the severity of any constraints imposed by local sources of water. For example, if Village A is unable to find additional water from wells nearby, it may have to go to a river, hence the water must be treated. If the river flow is irregular, a small dam may be required to store water for the dry periods. What began as a well source costing, with limited transmission and no

Table 4.2. Hypothetical Capital Cost Implications of Service Levels and Treatment

Village population	Service level[a]	Assumed daily per capita water use (liters)	Daily village water use (cubic meters)	Water source	Treatment	Typical costs (U.S. dollars per cubic meter)[b]				
						Source works	Treatment	Storage and distribution	Total	Cost per capita
1,000	PH	40	40	Well	None	70	—	195	265	10
1,000	PH, HC[c]	100	100	Well	None	28	—	176	204	20
1,000	PH	40	40	Clear surface water	Chlorination	10	10	195	215	9
1,000	PH, HC[c]	100	100	Clear surface water	Chlorination	10	8	176	194	19
1,000	PH	40	40	Contaminated or turbid surface water	Filtration and chlorination	10	200	195	405	16
1,000	PH, HC[c]	100	100	As above	As above	10	150	176	336	34
10,000	PH	40	400	As above	As above	5	40	158	203	8
10,000	PH, HC[c]	100	1,000	As above	As above	4	18	108	130	13

a. HC = House connections; PH = Public hydrants provided at one for each 100 population.
b. Costs are at 1973 levels and for illustration only.
c. Each 50 percent of total.

treatment, around $11 per capita may increase to $30 or $50 per capita depending on how far the river is, what pumping is required, and how complex the dam construction may be.

Many urban areas in developing countries are now facing the fact that the accessible water sources are fully committed and new sources farther away must be employed. In some instances, then, the incremental costs of new urban water supply investment may be equal to, or exceed, per capita costs for smaller village systems. Where such is the case, the country could maximize the number of people served for a given expenditure by investing in water supplies in rural areas. This solution could have favorable income distribution implications, although the effects on the long-run growth of economic output in the country would have to be closely examined.

When discussing the costs of supplying water to villages, some consideration must be given to public bathing and laundry facilities. Depending on climate and health problems, facilities for bathing and clothes washing might be needed in villages where few homes have water connections. Such units are usually constructed in locations convenient to the village and adjacent to, or in conjunction with, public standposts. The same structure may incorporate both bathing and laundering facilities. Costs depend, among other things, on the number of people to be served, whether the facility includes some toilet facilities, and whether both laundry and bathing arrangements are provided. The cost range could extend from $500 to $3,000. If a satisfactory means of disposing of the waste and sewage in the immediate vicinity is not available, additional costs will, of course, be incurred.

Finally, the costs of the promotion, construction, and operation and maintenance phases of a rural water supply program may be reduced if the projects are clustered on a spatial basis. Unless there are specific strategy-based reasons (such as a desire to achieve a demonstration effect) for scattering village water supply projects throughout a region or country, it should be less costly to supply most of the high priority villages in one geographic area before moving on to other areas. If this is done, pipe, construction equipment, or drilling rigs will not usually have to be transported great distances between projects, and the supervisory maintenance and administrative body, if there is one, can organize initially by areas, in an attempt to minimize transportation and communication problems.

Clustering of projects could be generally consistent with a growth-point or growth-area strategy of village selection. All projects in a limited growth-point area could be completed before the construction equipment is moved elsewhere. The procedure would require, of course, coordinated advance promotion work geared to having all of the villages ready to receive the systems and to contribute their share of the cost at approximately the same time. Clustering is also highly relevant to the problems of operation and maintenance that plague village water supply programs, and that can in part be ascribed to the relatively high cost of servicing spatially separated water supply systems. It will, however, be appreciated that there are political and staffing obstacles to this solution, such as the need for a government to avoid giving the impression of regional bias.

Scale Economies Related to Waste Disposal Facilities

The existence of scale economies in the provision of sewage disposal is less well documented than in the case of water supply. One reason for this is that there are many more possible variations in the quality and type of sewage collection, treatment, and disposal than exist in the provision of water. Consequently, to isolate by statistical means the impact of system size on unit costs is relatively difficult.

With regard to the treatment of sewage, an examination of the operating and maintenance costs of a number of small and medium-size secondary treatment plants in Massachusetts in 1953 yielded the following results: [9]

Sewage flow (millions of gallons a day)	Estimated annual cost per capita (U.S. dollars)
0.14	2.00
0.15	3.20
0.40	1.50
0.48	1.40
0.50	0.60
0.58	0.90
0.60	2.60
0.60	1.40

9. Walter Isard and Robert E. Coughlin, *Municipal Costs and Revenues Resulting from Community Growth* (Wellesley, Mass.: Chandler-Davis Publishing Co., 1957), p. 79.

1.20	1.30
1.26	1.10
1.49	0.60
1.70	0.70
1.70	0.60
3.50	0.50
4.00	0.60
32.00	0.40

In general, per capita costs declined as plant size increased, although there were obviously other factors besides size which affected costs. Perhaps the most comprehensive examination of the costs of sewage disposal, however, was carried out by Downing.[10] See Table 4.3 for his estimate of the costs incurred for different types of treatment facilities. Overall, he concluded that the geographic area which a sewage utility should serve "is determined by the existing size of the utility, the density of the fringe area, and the distance between the fringe and the treatment plant. For a city of 100,000 people, the service area would cover all areas within a distance of 10 miles from the treatment plant and serve a density as low as 4 people per acre." With regard to the number and location of treatment plants he found that "the savings in treatment costs for regional plants (scale economies) is rapidly offset by the increase in transportation costs. This relationship indicates that only one plant should be built for a contiguous metropolitan area. It also indicates that, unless a small city is very close to a large city, the small city should build a separate treatment facility."[11]

Downing's conclusion has more recently been supported by Dajani and Gemmell[12] who, using a nonlinear programming algorithm, found that, after a certain size of wastewater collection system is reached, diseconomies of scale set in. They then conclude that "this implies that a number of smaller and simpler networks may be constructed at a greater economy than a large, enveloping system."

The situation in rural areas of developing countries, of course,

---

10. Paul B. Downing, *The Economics of Urban Sewage Disposal* (New York: Praeger, 1969).

11. Ibid., p. 121.

12. Jarir S. Dajani and Robert S. Gemmell, "Economic Guidelines for Public Utilities Planning," *Journal of the Urban Planning and Development Division, Proceedings of the American Society of Civil Engineers* 99, UP 2, no. 9977 (1973):171–82.

Table 4.3. Estimated Cost of Sewage Disposal

Type of plant	Capacity (number of people)	Annual average total cost (U.S. dollars[a] per capita)	Capacity (millions of gallons a day)	Annual average total cost (U.S. dollars[a] per million gallons a day)
Primary	1,000	7.16	0.1	75,870
	10,000	3.59	1.0	29,565
	100,000	1.97	10.0	13,461
Trickling filter	1,000	10.55	0.1	102,830
	10,000	4.12	1.0	36,615
	100,000	2.00	10.0	15,972
Activated sludge	100	19.23	—	—
	1,000	8.79	0.1	97,100
	10,000	4.66	1.0	45,589
	100,000	2.68	10.0	24,836

a. 1957–1959 dollars.
Source: Paul B. Downing, *The Economics of Urban Sewage Disposal* (New York: Praeger, 1969), p. 35.

is much different from that in the cities in the United States which provided Downing's and Dajani and Gemmell's frame of reference. Sanitation facilities required for most villages are generally determined by their size, the density of housing, soil and drainage conditions, and level of development. The design, means of financing, and the approaches to project development are all affected by these factors.

Most water piped or carried to the house ends up as waste, and in rudimentary systems, the waste is primarily from the kitchen area. Because of the limited volume, this waste can be discharged by a small-diameter pipe to a leaching pit next to the house. Costs range from $5 to $50 depending on the pipe, curbing material, and labor.

Vault and borehole latrines are the least-cost solution to disposal of body waste in uncongested areas. When properly located, constructed, and maintained, latrines meet all public health requirements. Financial costs may range from $10 a unit, where labor and the shelter are provided by the household, to around $200 if vault, slab, and a reasonably good structure are supplied. The shelter structure is of little importance from the public health standpoint if the slab and vault are properly constructed. Depending on the size of the vault and the care given it, frequency of cleaning may vary from one to ten years.

For large villages where density of housing is high, where the space surrounding houses is insufficient to permit construction of latrines or individual sewage disposal units, and where soils are impervious or groundwater level high, a community sewer system with low-cost oxidation pond treatment might be considered. Such systems are expensive, however, and function only if a sufficient number of houses have inside toilets, to ensure a flow in the sewers adequate to scour the piping and prevent clogging. Because only a few houses have indoor water flush toilets, and these are frequently widely dispersed, few villages find it technically feasible to construct sewer systems. Householders who wish to install inside toilets thus need individual sewage disposal facilities. For sand and gravel soils, and where water wells are located away from the area, simple leaching pits curbed with rock, brick, or concrete can be constructed at costs ranging from a few dollars up to $200, depending on labor and materials used.

Where soils are less pervious, and where larger volumes of sewage must be disposed, septic tanks, discharging either to leaching pits or tile fields, are employed. Costs can range from $100 to $1,000 depending on the size and material used in the tank and on the type of soil absorption system required. The higher figures apply where a tile field of substantial length is required, and where no free contribution of labor or materials is involved. Disposal of septic tank effluents to road ditches, while a common practice, is not satisfactory because of ensuing public health and environmental problems. Connection is sometimes possible to drain lines constructed for other purposes. This practice is not generally recommended, but it may be done for a limited number of houses, to dispose of septic tank effluent until there are enough connections to warrant construction of a sewer system with low-cost oxidation pond treatment. Community toilets, while not uncommon, normally are not a suitable facility for village use except to serve market areas and places of assembly. They are difficult to maintain and generally do not meet household needs.[13]

---

13. The authors are again indebted to Harold Shipman for providing many of the cost estimates and much of the write-up on village sanitation.

Overall, the conclusion on effecting scale economies in the provision of sewage and sanitation services is that, for a given quality of service and with specific population density constraints, significant economies of scale can be realized. With regard to villages in developing countries, however, the possible variations in quality and quantity of service, together with the great variability in local conditions and need, preclude generalization.

Growth-Point Strategies

It is well known that economic growth and development do not take place at the same rate in all localities. At any time some areas are growing rapidly, some are stagnant, and others are declining.

Rural communities of most developing countries are generally not among those participating in rapid economic growth. Urban areas are the ones which are attracting people, capital, and firms. People move to urban areas because of the possibility of better jobs and higher earnings, better educational opportunities for children, and sometimes better public facilities and services. Capital flows to urban areas because of greater demand and higher rates of return. Business firms tend to locate in urban areas because there is a better trained labor force, a large and more accessible market of higher income buyers, better transportation facilities, locally manufactured inputs, and legal, technical, and governmental services.

It is clear why it is difficult for smaller towns and villages to compete with the larger urban areas for skilled labor, innovative entrepreneurs, and financial resources. It is sometimes argued that the creation of points or centers of rapid economic growth in rural areas is a viable and desirable means of coping with the problem of rural-to-urban population drift. These points of economic growth could be a limited number of selected towns or villages having reasonable transportation access to the surrounding areas and, preferably, having natural or marketing advantages that have brought about a generally higher level of economic activity. Once the potential growth points had been selected, government investment in educational facilities, roads, and sanitary facilities, including water supply, market places, and so on, would be necessary. The goal of such investment would be to create centers which would attract and hold economic activity and therefore hold population.

The contention is that, in general, if a specific amount of government investment is spatially concentrated, rather than distributed in small amounts throughout rural areas, it is likely (a) to maximize the flow of income to regional earners in the short run; (b) to attract the maximum possible flow of enterprise and capital from outside the area or region; (c) to provide the most job opportunities in the shortest time; (d) to generate a concentration of people so that adequate public services can be provided at a reasonable per capita cost; and (e) to provide a situation in which employment and income will spread, or trickle out, into the nongrowth areas of the region.

There is a voluminous literature on growth points, or growth poles, and the problems of selecting and stimulating them. This literature tends to support our view that village potable water supply investment, spread randomly among villages in rural areas of developing countries, will not directly or indirectly generate a significant quantity of economic activity. As we noted earlier, while a potable water supply is usually necessary for significant economic development, it is not sufficient by itself to induce development. If economic development is an objective, then the limited water supply investment should be directed into selected high potential areas or regions with a relatively concentrated population, and should be accompanied by complementary investment in other public services. This, of course, is a rationale for the emphasis normally given to urban, as opposed to rural, water supply projects.

Income Redistribution and "Worst-First" Strategies

The goal of redistributing real income from higher to lower income groups could also be a consideration when selecting which villages should have a high priority for receiving a water supply system. Where subsidization of village schemes is involved, investment in rural areas might result in a high-to-low-income redistribution, because rural populations are generally poorer than urban populations and because the major portion of national public sector revenues (on a per person basis) is usually generated from the higher income urban areas. This situation is probably true for most developing countries, even if a rural-growth-point strategy is pursued. Areas selected for rural-growth-point development, although they would not be the very poorest rural areas, would, nevertheless, generally be low-income areas relative to the largest urban centers of the country.

Methods currently used by countries for selecting areas which should have a high priority for water service are somewhat diverse, and are generally not well defined. An exception is the well-defined system of village selection used in Thailand,[14] a country in which a worst-first [15] strategy has been pursued. There, villages are ranked according to their need for water, and those villages with "very extreme need" or "extreme need" are given the highest priority. Ranks are assigned by a team comprised of two individuals who visit four to six villages a day. Both members of the team are equipped with a simple checklist of questions such as, how far each villager walks for water in the dry season, and how long must he, or members of his family, wait or queue up to obtain domestic water. Similar questions are asked concerning how far livestock must be driven for water in the dry season. At least nine villagers in scattered parts of each village must be interviewed.

The team members rate on a scoring sheet the degree of village need for domestic and livestock water during the dry season. Villages receiving a score of between 0 and 10 points fall into the very extreme-need category. These villages are usually more than 5 kilometers distant from sources of domestic water during the dry season, and the villagers must wait up to and exceeding twenty-four hours for water at the source of supply. Their livestock must be driven more than 8 kilometers for water in the dry season.

Villages receiving a score between 11 and 14 points fall into the extreme-need category. These villages are more than 3 kilometers distant from sources of domestic water in the dry season, and villagers must wait for up to several hours for water at the source of supply. Livestock in these villages must be driven more than 5 kilometers for water in the dry season.

Of the first 24,785 Thai villages surveyed, 450 fell into the very extreme-need category while 1,872 fell into the extreme-need class. In this case, villages farthest from water are also generally smaller and, in many cases, poorer than average. As a result, some of the poorer villages have a good chance of attaining a high priority for water service.

14. "Accelerated Rural Development Manual for Domestic Water Resources Development Planning" (Bangkok: Office of Accelerated Rural Development, 1971).

15. The term "worst first" means those villages which are deemed to be worst off in terms of whatever criteria are being used: income, disease rates, bad water, and so on.

The Determination of Investment Priorities

In most countries with a viable rural water supply program, however, there seems to be a built-in bias in the system of selection which, for several reasons, works against the very poorest villages and areas. First, in most Latin American and in several Asian countries, villages must contribute some portion of the cost of the construction of the system, a contribution to be made in terms of money, labor, or both. Many times, the required local contribution is more than can be feasibly given through labor and local materials, so that at least some monetary contribution is necessary. Villages too poor or too backward to raise the required local contribution are therefore usually unable to participate in the water supply program.

Second, in a number of countries the villagers, or system users, are requested to pay water charges at least sufficient to cover local operation and maintenance costs. Among the reasons offered by water program officials for water-use charges are that (a) they reduce the subsidy the national government usually must contribute to the program; (b) they help the local populations achieve feelings of pride, ownership, and responsibility toward the system; and (c) they help rural populations develop a habit of payment and a feeling of achieving something by cooperating with the government. The poorer villages, however, sometimes find it difficult to generate a sufficient flow of extra income to cover their share of system operation and maintenance costs. Consequently, as in the case of requiring a local contribution to construction costs, the result of charging water-user fees is that the poorer villages are in some cases pushed to the bottom of the priority list.

Third, in countries where the criteria for selecting villages for participation in the rural water supply program are loosely defined, those villages that agitate, petition, and frequently demand assistance are those that receive the systems first. And those villages first to recognize the value of a potable water system, and to be the most effective agitators for water supply systems, are generally populated by relatively better educated and higher income people. Here, again, it is not the poorest rural villages which receive the first systems.

Finally, the Inter-American Development Bank (IDB) and the Pan American Health Organization (PAHO) have discussed a formula for choosing which villages in a country or region should be supplied with water first. One version of a formula developed by the PAHO and used experimentally by the IDB is as follows:

$$I = 100 \cdot \frac{P}{C-A} \cdot r \cdot k,$$

where I is an index of project selection priority in which higher values of I indicate a higher priority for early water supply system installation; $\frac{P}{C-A}$ is the inverse of the cost per capita of the system, excluding the distribution network costs and excluding the local counterpart contribution, in which P is the design population (the expected population of the village in twenty years), C is the total cost (less household connections, if any), and A is the counterpart contribution supplied by the community; r is an index of the physical availability of water derived as a ratio between the existing water flow at the point of capture (presumably for surface water sources) and the requirements foreseen in the twentieth year of operation of the system; and k is an index of the concentration of houses in the community to be served, measured as that proportion of the total number located within 50 meters of the proposed main conduits.

This index (I) tends to assign a higher priority to villages which require the lowest per capita investment by the national water agency. The result would be consistent with a strategy of maximizing the number of villages served.

Per capita investment which must be contributed by sources outside the village could be low because the village contributes a relatively large proportion of the costs; the village is relatively large and experiences cost economies of scale; or the village is fortunate enough to have a water source nearby which can be tapped at a low cost. The first two reasons might be consistent with a high financial viability criterion or with a growth-point strategy. The third reason would be consistent with a strategy designed to serve the maximum number of villages.

As a result of the inclusion of the availability of water index (r), villages which tend to have water sources exceeding the projected village water requirements twenty years hence would also tend to be given a high priority by the priority index (I). In a technical sense this is probably a good idea, up to some physical limit which is considered an "adequate" water source. It does not seem fruitful, however, to assign a higher priority to a community with a water source which is 750 percent of expected community needs in twenty years than to one with a water source which is only 350 percent of expected needs in twenty years. There also seems to be a problem with regard to borehole water where, presumably for a small village, r could almost be infinity.

In addition to the results achieved by applying the priority index formula, the IDB suggests that some attention should also be paid to (a) the distance to the existing water source, (b) the degree of unemployment in the community (it is not stated whether a high or low rate should generate a greater priority), (c) the type of service and the percentage of houses to be connected, (d) land tenure, (e) existence of other infrastructure facilities, and (f) operating and maintenance costs.

In summary, while any water supply emphasis on rural areas tends to foster a redistribution of income, in most developing countries with rural water supply programs, the direct income redistribution in the short run is technically not as large as it could be because the higher income, better educated, larger rural villages tend to be the ones being served.

This result, however, is not necessarily bad. If some variant of a growth-point (or a high development potential) strategy is being followed, the villages which should be served first would be the higher income, better educated, larger towns and villages. A worst-first strategy, or a strategy of providing water to villages which generally are among the smaller, poorer, and least educated, is a high-cost and low probable-payoff venture. The poorest villages would have difficulty (a) in contributing financial resources for the construction of the system, (b) in maintaining adequate user fees to cover operation and maintenance, and (c) in generating and maintaining sufficient local expertise to assist in operating the system. In addition, if the villages are relatively small, as the poorest ones usually are, the per person construction and maintenance costs would be high relative to larger, higher income villages. It is difficult to determine, from experience, exactly how much more costly (on a per capita basis) a serve-the-poorest, worst-first strategy would be because water supply systems in the poorest villages of many countries have become inoperable after a short period of time through lack of maintenance or financing.

Furthermore, the poorest villages in a country or region are poor for a reason. These villages simply may not have a sufficient current or potential economic base to support the existing population at other than a subsistence level. As a result, a government policy which provides nonviable villages with amenities encouraging the current nonviable, subsistence-level existence of the population is not productive and may even serve to the long-run detriment of the population. As described previously, an alternative policy to help relocate the population closer to a growth center offering opportunities for increased earnings, employment, and education may be more productive in the long run. Canada is among the countries in which such a policy has been proposed. In 1969, the Quebec provincial government proposed that eleven backwoods villages be wiped off the map. The residents were to be given cash incentives to relocate in larger towns where schools, hospitals, and vocational training centers are available.[16]

Thus far, we have discussed worst-first policies in a purely rural context. If, however, for purposes of income redistribution, a true worst-first policy were to be adopted by a developing country, the rational water supply sector policy in many cases might be to concentrate on providing improved water for urban slum dwellers. A case can be made that in many instances the residents of slum and squatter areas in the big cities of developing countries are worse off than their rural counterparts. Urban slum dwellers usually have very few alternatives for procuring drinking water and, in expanding slums, the quality is questionable and the cost of water is generally high (particularly if purchased from vendors). In addition, in densely populated areas, wastewater seepage into water pipes (a possible occurrence where intermittent water service is the consequence of policies which have brought about water shortages) can cause the water supply distribution system to become a vehicle for the transmission of the very diseases the system was designed to prevent. It will frequently be the case, therefore, that the water supply and sanitation needs of urban slum dwellers should have priority if a worst-first policy is to be pursued on a national basis.

Financial Contribution and Community Enthusiasm

As noted above, a number of Asian and South American countries allow villages to participate in the rural water supply program only if the flow of income which the villages generate through time is sufficient to support a water supply project at least partially. In several countries, villages are expected to contribute between 10 and 30 percent of the construction cost and to pay a water-user fee which at the minimum covers operation and maintenance costs (see Chapter 7 for a more complete discussion of financing). This strategy

---

16. Edgar M. Hoover, *An Introduction to Regional Economics* (New York: Knopf, 1971), p. 279.

of providing villages with water supply systems only if the projects are on a financially acceptable footing generally increases the probability that the population will accept, use, and maintain the system.

A condition requiring a financial contribution covering some portion of capital and all operation and maintenance expenses is probably not consistent with a worst-first strategy. On the other hand, it could be consistent with a growth-point or growth-area strategy, and if the national government partially subsidizes the program, it could tend to redistribute real income in favor of the rural poor.

It is frequently noted in rural water supply literature that the probability of project failure is much greater in cases where the recipient village is not outwardly enthusiastic about the project. No matter how badly (in the opinion of an external appraiser) a village "needs" a better water supply system, if the population itself does not perceive the value of the system, the usage rate will be low, system maintenance and local administration will be inadequate, and vandalism could be a problem.

On the other hand, an enthusiastic community will be more likely to have its contributions completed and its payments submitted on time. It will usually attempt to see that the system is used and well maintained, and will report any problems it is having with the system. As a result, in several countries with viable rural water supply programs, only those villages which are actively enthusiastic about obtaining a water supply system are considered to be eligible. An example is found in Peru in the criteria for selecting target villages for participation in the rural water supply program. Villages there which have expressed interest, have requested the system, and have offered assistance in construction and operation are designated as high priority villages.[17]

Villages which, for health or economic development reasons, need improved water, but which do not perceive that need, might be stimulated or educated to their need by community water program promoters. Unless community or village enthusiasm is present, however, at the time the system is being constructed, there is a much greater probability that the system will not be widely used, or that it will fall into disrepair in a short time. An underutilized or nonfunctioning system reflects an overinvestment in the project area and a misallocation of investment on a national level.

17. Guido Acurio, "Agua Potable Rural, Perú," report to Rural Water of Peru, Lima, October 1969.

The link between community support for a water supply project and the quality of service provided is obviously close. In this regard, one particular country in Latin America ran into several difficulties. The country set out to provide water supply systems in approximately 400 rural villages. As the program got under way it became apparent that much of the rural population desired a better quality of water service than the project designs called for. In many villages the population complained that they wanted water taps at their houses and that they did not like the public fountain arrangement being constructed. In addition, they complained that the water reservoirs were too small and that as a result they kept running out of water. The result of these quality-of-service problems, and a lack of promotional work and demand analysis which should have been done in the villages before the project began, was that many villages allowed the systems to fall into disrepair by not assisting with necessary maintenance work, and by not supporting user-fee collection.

To alleviate the situation, the central program administration authorized additional construction to be undertaken in some villages in an attempt to raise standards and quality of service. Increasing the quality of service after the system was already completed, however, increased overall system cost above the cost of a better system in the first place. Because of these increased costs and because an unexpectedly high proportion of the villages experienced costly water source problems, water supply systems installed in villages which were served later in the program were underdesigned even further in an attempt to keep costs down so that the program could serve the total of 400 villages specified in the loan agreement with the international agency. This led to further problems of population acceptance and nonpayment and, as a result, the program slowly came to a halt.

Conclusions

The problem of determining investment priorities may in essence be reduced to one of ranking projects according to their costs and benefits. As we have observed, although cost estimates are relatively easy—although sometimes not made—the measurement of benefits is fraught with difficulty. It is frequently impossible to predict with acceptable accuracy what the physical consequences of an investment will be, let alone to place a monetary equivalent on them. Furthermore, even if we could do so, value judgments often have to be made: for example, should we supply people with water even if the economic costs of so doing are not matched by any measurable economic benefits, and, if so, who should be supplied first and what quality of service should be provided?

Ranking of projects, therefore, unfortunately has to rely ultimately and heavily upon that sometimes questionable tool, judgment. Choice of, or among, projects that cannot be described adequately in cost-benefit terms has to be made somehow, and the criteria presented in this chapter, including per capita costs on the one hand and such factors as community enthusiasm, development potential, and quality of existing supply on the other, should be seen as a checklist by which each project should be judged. These variables are not commensurate—indeed this is the heart of the matter—but if a systematic use of the checklist is made it should at least help to make explicit the subjective weights that are implied by any project ranking.

Although the methodology outlined above may not seem very satisfactory since we cannot measure project benefits properly, it will probably serve as an adequate screening device at least for projects designed to provide a minimum supply of water for basic health needs. Once this has been achieved, however, a far more rigorous test is available to us, namely the willingness of consumers to pay for improved supply. We argue that introduction of this requirement as a test of project acceptability should be implemented as strictly as possible, at least for all supplies in excess of the basic minimum. A fuller discussion of this approach follows in subsequent chapters.

5 | Special Problems of Program Planning

SEVERAL FACTORS COMMON to the planning of water supply systems have unique aspects when related to rural areas. Among those that require discussion are tradeoffs between health and project costs, quality of service, population acceptance, estimating the money value of village labor contributions, shadow pricing, level of technology, complementary programs, and the time frame for investment.

Tradeoffs between Health and Project Costs

When designing a water supply system, the engineer commits to the project resources which cannot then be used by the investor for other water supply projects, or for other purposes. Ideally, the engineer should have guidelines that give him some probabilistic statements about what the possible alternative levels and quality of service mean in terms of different magnitudes of improved health. In addition, he should be able to calculate how the value of the expected improvements in health compare to the costs of the alternative levels of service which could be designed into the system. The general question of the valuation of improved health was discussed in Chapter 2. Now we shall examine the more specific question of exactly how much improvement in health might be expected from an improvement in the water supply of a local area.

The twenty-eight studies summarized in Chapter 2 were reviewed in order to derive from existing literature some guidelines concerning the amount of health improvement that might be expected from different types of water and sanitation improvements. Generally, the study results are insufficient to give us a specific statement having acceptable predictive accuracy for all cultures, types of locations, and types of diseases. Many relevant variables have been identified, however, and the derivation of rather crude but nevertheless useful estimates by rule-of-thumb methods may in certain circumstances be possible.

A number of studies have made assumptions about the extent to which disease rates would decline if water supply improvements were undertaken in developing countries. Wagner and Wannoni,[1] in attempting to estimate savings in Venezuela which would result from the construction of safe water supplies in rural areas, chose what they considered to be a conservative figure of 75 percent expected disease reduction.

Pyatt and Rogers,[2] in a cost-benefit calculation of the potential effects of water supply systems in Puerto Rico, assumed that 60 percent of the recorded typhoid, diarrhea, and dysentery cases (excluding infant diseases) reflected actual water-related disease. The authors implicitly assumed, therefore, that improved water would reduce the reported prevalence of disease by approximately 60 percent.

If an environment were found which approximated the one investigated by J. Watt et al.,[3] and if sanitary improvements were introduced which eliminated *Shigella,* a major cause of diarrhea, then an estimate of a two-thirds reduction in diarrheal disease might be justified. For the situation he investigated in rural California, Watt estimated that diarrheal diseases would be reduced by approximately two-thirds if *Shigella* were eliminated.

White, Bradley, and White[4] have provided perhaps the most

---

1. Edmund G. Wagner and Luis Wannoni, "Anticipated Savings in Venezuela through the Construction of Safe Water Supplies in Rural Areas" (WHO/Env. San. 40 (paper presented to the Expert Committee on Environmental Sanitation, World Health Organization, Geneva, 1953).

2. Edwin F. Pyatt and Peter P. Rogers, "On Estimating Benefit-Cost Ratios for Water Supply Investments," *American Journal of Public Health* 52 (October 1962):1729–42.

3. James Watt et al., "Diarrheal Diseases in Fresno County, California," *American Journal of Public Health* 43, no. 6 (1953):728–41.

4. Gilbert F. White, David J. Bradley, and Anne U. White, *Drawers of*

extensive set of estimates of the proportions of different diseases in rural areas of East Africa which may be prevented by the introduction of improved water supplies. Overall they estimated that approximately 52 percent of water-related disease could be abolished if excellent water supplies were available. The following list shows a detailed breakdown of their estimates of expected rates of reduction:

Disease	Percent
Typhoid	80
Paratyphoid and other *Salmonella* diseases	40
Bacillary dysentery	50
Amebiasis	50
Dysentery, unspecified	50
Louseborne typhus	40
Urinary schistosomiasis	80
Intestinal schistosomiasis	40
Schistosomiasis, unspecified	60
Ascariasis	40
Guinea-worm infestation	100
Louseborne relapsing fever	40
Leptospirosis	80
Yaws	70
Trachoma	60
Trypanosomiasis (*T. gambiense*)	80
Trypanosomiasis, unspecified	10
Scabies	80
Inflammatory eye diseases	70
Otitis externa	40
Dental caries	10
Gastroenteritis (age 4 weeks to 2 years)	50
Gastroenteritis (over 2 years)	50
Skin and subcutaneous infections	50
Chronic skin (leg) ulcer	40
Diarrhea of the newborn	50
Tinea	50

The authors qualified the reliability of their estimates as follows: "These estimates can be little more than guesses, but a basis for them is set out in the discussions of disease given above and, although they are in error, a far greater error probably would be introduced by

---

Water: Domestic Water Use in East Africa (Chicago: University of Chicago Press, 1972), pp. 190–91.

assuming that these conditions would either disappear or remain unchanged by improving [water] supplies."

The above sets of estimates implicitly concede that there are many ways in which a person can become infected with water-associated disease other than by drinking the water available in his home village. Generally, given the current state of the art, in order to have any confidence in an estimate, the impact on health resulting from a given water supply improvement should probably be estimated individually for each project, taking into consideration the health, geographic, climatic, economic, and cultural mix of the project population at that time.

Of course, those factors that affect benefits also affect the costs of a project. Figure 5.1 illustrates two of the many possible relationships between health levels (those which can be influenced directly or indirectly by water supply) and the cost of a water supply project. Here, health is measured by a hypothetical index from zero, representing the level of health prior to water supply improvements, to 100, the level of health where there are no diseases related to the

Figure 5.1. Hypothetical Relations between Village Health and Costs of Water Supply Project

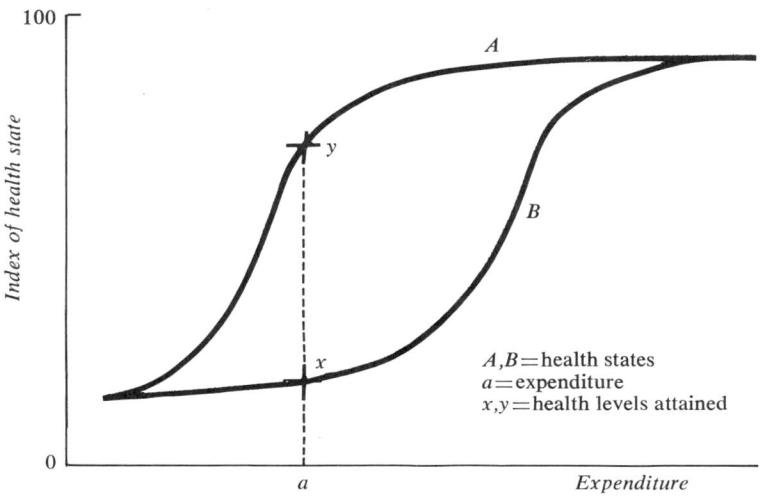

water supply. Cost reflects the total cost of the water supply project including engineering, construction, administration, maintenance, and any additional costs for training, sanitation, continuing technical assistance, and so on.

Curve A represents a hypothetical case in which health begins to improve rapidly after an initial relatively small, low-cost improvement in the local water supply system, such as protecting an existing supply, digging a series of wells and installing hand pumps, or extending water service into homes. Curve B represents a case where a much greater initial investment is required before there is a significant improvement in health.

It is important for the project engineer and the investor to have some feel for the type of situation they are facing. For example, suppose they assume that the particular case will be like A, requiring only a small investment for substantial results; they therefore decide to invest a dollars in order to bring health up to y. Suppose, however, the situation is actually like B, then a dollars will bring health only up to x and, in effect, a significant expenditure of resources will have resulted in an insignificant change in health.

One approach to this problem might be to reformulate it in the following manner: What amount of improvement in the major disease rates would it take to make a given investment worthwhile? In an attempt to answer that question all related health information and empirical study results, as well as an epidemiologist, could be consulted to judge whether the "target" rate of health improvement (that rate necessary to make the project worthwhile) could, with an acceptable degree of probability, be achieved.

While answering the above question, other estimates could be made of the possible health effects of additional investment (more people served or a higher quality of service, and so on) and of somewhat less investment. This exercise would, in effect, be an attempt to find the placement (on curve A, curve B, or some intermediate curve) of the initial projected point and the approximate slope of the line at that point.

Some attention should also be given to the program "mix" of physical facilities, water use and health education, system maintenance training, and so on, which go into a given investment amount. For example, it is possible that curve B could be shifted to the left (which would result in a greater health improvement for a given investment, or alternatively a smaller investment necessary to achieve a target health improvement). This shift might be brought about by changing the proportions of the investment such that a larger proportion would be spent on water use and health education for the local population and a smaller proportion on physical facilities. The end result of this change in emphasis could be a lower quality of water supply service but a greater and more healthful use of the water provided. This follows from an observation repeatedly found in rural water supply literature that the best water supply system in the world will not affect local health if the population is not willing or able to use it. (This point was discussed in greater detail in "The Water-Use Link" section of Chapter 2.)

When in Chapter 2 the relation between health and water supply and sanitation was examined, it became apparent that an adequate quantity of good water is a necessary condition for good health. It is not in itself a sufficient condition, however, since good drinking water and a population with a significant number of water-associated disease problems can exist in the same village. From the analysis and review of literature undertaken in Chapter 2, it appears that the water supply investor who is interested in "health" benefits must make use of inputs from at least four different analytical focuses: sanitary engineering, economics, sociology or anthropology, and epidemiology.

The engineer can provide technical designs and cost estimates for a given water supply system, or for a program with several different cost and quality–quantity-of-service alternatives. Furthermore, if he has good knowledge of that country he might, with some sociological input, also be in a good position to exercise judgment concerning the possible social and cultural water-use problems which may affect the efficiency and use of alternative designs of the system.

The epidemiologist can then provide a rough estimate of the extent to which health or disease rates might improve if each alternative project/program design were implemented. Although, in most instances, this task will be very difficult and subject to considerable error, subjective judgments made by experienced epidemiologists are, in the authors' opinion, the only feasible way to carry out project health-impact evaluations at a reasonable cost. B. Cvjetanović of the World Health Organization recently related to the authors one example of an informal survey carried out by two experienced epidemiologists. Several years ago Cvjetanović and a colleague spent a morning driving around Phoenix, Arizona, in an automobile. From the car they observed types of neighborhoods, the location of privies, refuse, standing water and water taps, and so on. Upon leaving each area they marked on a city map their estimate of the prevalence of diarrhea in that area. That afternoon they checked their "automobile estimates" with recorded city health statistics and found almost no significant deviation. The forecasting of water supply and sanitation-induced health-state changes in rural areas of developing countries presents a slightly different problem but the same form of expertise should nevertheless be valuable in dealing with it.

Given this input, the economist can assist in project development by estimating shadow values (where appropriate) and by then attempting to place a monetary value on the estimated health improvements. He can also make a comparison between these benefits and the alternative engineering costs and possibilities for water supply investment in that or other programs. In other words, after valuing the probable health improvements in each alternative, the economist can attempt to put together the engineering, social, and epidemiological inputs in such a way as to select a project which comes closest to meeting the overall objectives of the investor, within the constraints of the available resources.

System Design and Quality of Service

The focus of this section is on tradeoffs related to the more technical design aspects of quality-of-service problems. (Administrative considerations are covered in Chapter 6.)

The quality of the water service designed into a water supply system should depend primarily on the goals which the system is supposed to achieve. Most rural water supply projects have both health and economic objectives. As has been discussed previously, every project should be designed in such a way as to maximize the probability that the objectives will be achieved, subject to the constraint that there are other uses, and corresponding benefits, for each additional dollar spent on the project.

In the design stage, other things being equal, increasing the probability that the goals will be achieved generally involves an increase in the cost of the project. Whether or not the increase in cost is worth the increment in the probability of success must be assessed by examining the alternative uses to which the additional resources could be put. Overinvestment in a project could easily be as bad as underinvestment when the overinvestment is viewed in terms of its opportunity cost.

A helpful way to view the question of what level of service should be designed into a project is to consider the two basic water supply factors which most determine the amount of benefits to be expected: the quality of the water consumed and the quantity of water consumed. In the review of the twenty-eight health studies in Appendix A, both of these factors were found to be important in controlling water-associated diseases.

Quality of Water

Whether or not it is desirable to lower standards of water quality in order to achieve cost savings is debatable.[5] It is certainly true that a water system which would, from time to time, distribute highly contaminated water would not be acceptable. But it may be difficult to justify significant expenditures (in terms, say, of the number of new consumers who could otherwise be served) to eliminate marginal taste, color, or odor problems, unless of course these problems make the water absolutely unacceptable to the consuming population.

Clearly, a statement that "reasonably safe" water is better than no water, and that money spent on supplying absolutely safe, tasteless, colorless, and odorless water could be better used by supplying more people with only reasonably safe water, depends upon one's definition of the term, "reasonably safe." The problem, of course, is to decide whether or not it is desirable, in some cases, to relax World Health Organization water quality standards in defining what is reasonably safe water. In practice, as shown in Tables 5.1, 5.2, and 5.3, many countries have either relaxed or simply not been able to implement the water quality standards suggested by WHO.

In several of the studies reviewed in Appendix A the quantity of water consumed was found to be more important than the quality of the water in reducing disease incidence rates. It must also be assumed, however, that the quality of the water in those cases was, on average, of a "reasonable" quality.

For the sanitary engineer, the particularly difficult design decisions arise when several village water supply projects need chlorine or filtration only during the one- or two-month dry season, or during the wet season when there is high sedimentation and slope wash, when it

---

5. For an interesting discussion on this point, see Harold R. Shipman, "Policies Affecting the Financing of Urban Water Supply in Developing Countries," International Standing Committee on Problems of Water Supply in Developing Countries, Subject no. 2 (Washington, D.C.: World Bank, 1972).

Table 5.1. Responsibility for Surveillance of Drinking Water Quality
(Number of countries)

	Public health authority		Other agency only
World Health Organization region	Alone	With another agency	
Africa	12	8	3
Central and South America	13	7	1
Eastern Mediterranean	9	7	1
Algeria, Morocco, Turkey	3	—[a]	—[a]
Southeast Asia	5	1	1
Western Pacific	6	1	1
Total	48	24	7

a. Nil or magnitude negligible.
Source: Same as Table 1.1, pp. 762–63.

is considered possible that fecal residue or bacteria could get into the system. The difficult question is whether or not chlorine and filtration facilities should be built into the village systems, to be used only one or two months a year, or whether the funds should be used to help provide a year-round water supply system for an additional village. Adding to this cost-quality tradeoff problem is the fact that the best

Table 5.2. Extent and Frequency of Bacteriological Examinations of Drinking Water
(Number of countries)

World Health Organization region	Every supply regularly		Some supplies regularly		Every supply occasionally		Some supplies occasionally		No examination	
	U	R	U	R	U	R	U	R	U	R
Africa	8	2	11	3	8	2	8	13	—[a]	9
Central and South America	8	2	13	6	2	—[a]	10	16	—[a]	6
Eastern Mediterranean	6	3	8	4	5	2	9	13	2	3
Algeria, Morocco, Turkey	—[a]	—[a]	2	1	1	1	2	2	—[a]	—[a]
Southeast Asia	2	—[a]	4	2	1	—[a]	5	8	—[a]	1
Western Pacific	6	1	1	4	—[a]	2	3	5	—[a]	1
Total	30	8	39	20	17	7	37	57	2	20

Note: U = urban; R = rural.
a. Nil or magnitude negligible.
Source: Same as Table 1.1.

estimates of probable bacteria levels, or possible fecal contamination, under different circumstances and with different levels of treatment, are generally subject to considerable error.

The quality of water question has no general solution. Aside from adherence to the general principle that on average, at the source, groundwater is safer than surface water, the best means of handling the problem probably is to approach it afresh for each project, keeping in mind the dual goals of providing so-called reasonably safe water and keeping project costs as low as possible.

Quantity of Water

As previously noted, the quantity of water individuals consume has been found to be associated with the incidence and prevalence of several of the diseases common to rural residents in developing countries. Worldwide, as shown by the WHO survey data in Table 5.4, there are great variations in the amount of water consumed, with rural and urban standpost consumers always consuming less than those supplied with house connections. Of course, since rural dwellers do not have a significant number of water-using appliances, and generally do not have flush toilets, the major physical factors influencing the amount of water consumed by villagers are (a) the distance of the water tap from an individual's dwelling, (b) the degree of regularity with which water flows from the system, and (c) the rate or ease of water flow from the tap.

The relative convenience (or nearness) of a water tap influences the health of water users both because they tend to consume more if the tap is near and because, when water is carried to the dwelling and stored in a container until it is used, there is a much greater likelihood of contamination. One study in St. Lucia, in fact, found significant differences in the schistosomiasis infection rates between a group of villages served with individual house taps, public laundry and shower facilities, and public wading pools, and a group of villages served only with widely dispersed public standposts.[6]

In some areas in East Africa where water supplies are scanty at the end of the dry season, both tsetse flies and people tend to congregate around the residual muddy water holes. As a result the trans-

---

6. P. Jordan et al., "Control of Schistosoma Mansoni Transmission by Provision of Domestic Water Supplies in St. Lucia: A Preliminary Report" (New York: The Rockefeller Foundation, 1974).

Table 5.3. Adoption of Standards for Quality of Drinking Water
(Number of countries)

World Health Organization region	WHO standards adapted to suit country needs	WHO standards adopted in toto	National standards prepared before	Other standards	None contemplated	Contemplated in near future	In preparation
Africa	5	5	1	2	7	3	5
Central and South America	7	4	3	2	2	3	1
Eastern Mediterranean	7	3	—[a]	1	1	6	2
Algeria, Morocco, Turkey	1	—[a]	—[a]	—[a]	—[a]	—[a]	2
Southeast Asia	1	2	—[a]	2	—[a]	1	2
Western Pacific	2	—[a]	1	1	2	1	2
Total	23	14	5	8	12	14	14

a. Nil or magnitude negligible.
Source: Same as Table 1.1, pp. 762–63.

mission of African trypanosomiasis, or sleeping sickness, may become intense. In situations such as this it can be argued that the provision of piped water supplies in alternative locations is more important than improving the quality of existing supplies.[7] (A similar argument can be made for certain strains of onchocerciasis, river blindness.) The array of possibilities for tap location are, of course, endless: from one public fountain (standpost), or hand pump, in the center of the village to a series of public fountains along a main trunk line and several smaller lines, to taps at each individual dwelling.

The question of whether rural water supply systems should be constructed primarily with public fountains or with an individual tap at each house is one with no fixed answer. Basically, it is a decision which depends on the philosophy or goals of the country or ministry which is providing the financial subsidy, the demands, or perceived needs, of the rural residents, and the ability of the water consumers to pay for the more convenient house installation.

The philosophy of countries concerning the question of house taps versus public fountains can vary greatly even among those in similar regions of the world. For example, in Tanzania the rural water supply program focuses almost entirely on the provision of public standposts. The philosophy of the program is that as many people as possible should have access to improved water and that this can be facilitated by providing only low-cost public standpost installations. Water at the standposts is provided free, which means that the program generally has significant implications for income redistribution and requires continuing government subsidies.

In some regions of Ghana, on the other hand, the program has focused on providing only individual household connections. All dwellings which are served are expected to pay user fees, and if a user falls too far behind on his payments his water service is cut off. Any family which cannot afford to pay the user fee is not officially supplied with water, although some do buy water from those who have house taps. More recently some public standposts are being introduced.

In the relatively higher income Latin American countries most of the successful programs have encouraged the installation of house connections. Generally, village systems are designed with a capacity of 100 percent house connections even if all dwellings in the village

---

7. The authors wish to thank David Bradley for suggesting this point.

Table 5.4. Daily Water Consumption from Community Water Supplies
(Liters per capita)

World Health Organization region	Urban				Rural	
	House connections		Public standposts			
	Minimum	Maximum	Minimum	Maximum	Minimum	Maximum
Africa	65	290	20	45	15	35
Central and South America	160	380	25	50	70	190
Eastern Mediterranean	95	245	30	60	40	85
Algeria, Morocco, Turkey	65	210	25	40	20	65
Southeast Asia	75	165	25	50	30	70
Western Pacific	85	365	30	95	30	95
Average	90	280	25	55	35	90

Note: Average daily consumption rounded to nearest 5 liters.
Source: Same as Table 1.1, p. 771.

do not hook up initially. For example, when a system is built, only 20 to 50 percent of the houses might pay the additional fee for an individual house connection. The remaining residents of the village use public fountains. As time passes, however, an increasing number of households pay the connection fee and receive taps at their houses. In several countries, after a certain proportion of the houses have house connections (60 to 80 percent), all or most of the public fountains are disconnected. This is done in an attempt to provide a further stimulus for additional house connections. In a few localities, notably in northern Argentina, villages also provide one free water tap at which private water vendors can secure safe water which they in turn sell to the more dispersed population in the surrounding areas.

The additional cost of constructing a system with house taps rather than public fountains varies widely. Undoubtedly, more water per capita is consumed when all dwellings have house taps. This, of course, means that a larger design capacity of the system is required (perhaps in some cases as much as two to three times larger). The additional cost of physically extending water lines from a main line to individual dwellings depends on how extensive the main line distribution system would be if the house tap option were not planned. In view of the many possible system configurations and variations in population density and service costs, it is almost impossible to generalize about the relative cost of household versus standpost supplies.

But a specific calculation carried out by Unrau [8] for five rural settlements on St. Lucia, led him to conclude that "once the essential equipment and materials for an adequate public hydrant supply have been purchased and installed," the added capital costs for individual service lines and fordilla valves amounted to an average of 10 percent of the total expenditures, excluding engineering and supervision overhead expenses. "On computation of the costs of the service line (plastic), fittings and (fordilla) faucets, the additional expense averaged slightly over US$12 per house (1972 dollars), or approximately $2.40 per capita served." [9]

Also, an interesting case study of the extension of a water supply distribtuion system to individual dwellings in three barrios in Asunción, Paraguay, showed that per capita installation costs which in-

---

8. Gladwin O. Unrau, "Individual Household Water Supplies in Rural St. Lucia as a Control Measure Against Schistosoma Mansoni" (New York: The Rockefeller Foundation, 1974).

9. Ibid., p. 24.

cluded fordilla valves were in the neighborhood of $5 to $6 (at 1962 price levels). This low-cost system which made use of small-diameter pipes and so-called "pod" configurations compared very favorably with a conventional distribution system constructed in Asunción which in 1958 cost $42.60 per capita.[10] (With regard to the Paraguay example, it seems to us that the differences in the two figures are so great that there may be some problems of comparability.)

In most developing countries, of course, so-called house connections or house taps are not connections inside the house. A house connection is either a patio connection (a connection on the inside wall of an enclosed courtyard-type area) or a connection in the yard beside, or in back of, the house. A connection inside a house implies a drainage system, which does not exist in most rural villages.

The single house connection (in the yard) does permit considerable versatility in the use of the water. In several countries it is not uncommon to see a plastic garden hose connected to the water tap so that the residents can convey water to an enclosed area where they can take a shower, to a tank in which animals are watered, and to the area where they prepare food for personal consumption.

When a decision must be made about whether the residents of a certain village should be encouraged to have house connections rather than to use public fountains, the income and education level of the residents should be considered. Generally, the demand for improved water, and particularly water located at a dwelling, is a consequence (rather than a cause) of economic development. Therefore, higher income villages (and countries) are more inclined to demand house connections and, of course, are also more able to pay for them. In other villages (and countries), the money value of the house connection might in some cases exceed the value of the dwelling.

Whether or not villagers should be asked to pay the full cost of their house connections at the time of installation depends partly on their ability to pay, on the relative certainty of collecting the payments at a later date, and on the strength of the health-benefit goal which might dictate that a lower (below cost) hook-up fee should be charged in order to encourage house connections. With regard to the health-benefit goal, the issue that should be raised is whether an

10. E. K. G. Borjesson and Carlos M. Bobeda, "New Concept in Water Service for Developing Countries," *Journal of the American Water Works Association* 56, no. 7 (1964):853–62.

Table 5.5. Rural Water Supply House Connections in Peru, 1967–72
(Percent as of December 31)

Year of work completion	1969	1970	1971	1972	1973
1967	45	48	62	68	77
1968	39	44	48	53	55
1969	—	35	46	51	54
1970	—	—	39	47	49
1971	—	—	—	47	49
1972	—	—	—	—	39

Source: Assembled from project data supplied by the Inter-American Development Bank.

acceptable level of health improvement can be attained without—or with just a few—house connections.

In the higher income developing countries, an attempt should probably be made to construct village systems that can be upgraded by village residents at some future date. For example, if the initial subsidized system involves only the provision of a few standposts, the capacity of the source, storage, and treatment facilities should be such that the villagers can provide individual house connections for themselves whenever they are able to pay the full cost of the extensions to the distribution system. In this way, as income levels in the village improve, and as the demand for and appreciation of water increases, the villagers will be able to adapt the system to their new situation without lengthy central office delays, and without an expenditure of funds for the upgrading of the entire system. One report describing the Latin American experience has stated that it has usually taken from eight to ten years for villages to convert themselves from 100 percent public fountains to 80 percent house connections,[11] although in many villages, particularly in Peru, the transition time has been less. The increase in the percentage of house connections in Peru between 1967 and 1972 is shown in Table 5.5.

In the lower income or poorer developing countries such as India and Nepal, the construction of village systems that can be cheaply upgraded at some future date may not be the best way to use existing resources. In these countries the need for basic sanitation is very great, relative to existing resources, and as a result there may be little

---

11. David Donaldson, "Water for the Rural Community," *Gazette* 6, no. 1-2 (1974):2–9 (Washington, D.C.: Pan American Health Organization).

room for trading off the number of present villages served for possible future systems' upgrading.

The other two factors influencing the quantity of water consumed, that is, the degree of regularity with which water flows through the system and the rate or ease of the water flow from the tap, have been discussed previously. Possibilities for, and implications of, flow-limiters are discussed in Chapter 7. The fact that intermittent supplies introduce a considerable danger of contaminating the system through a seepage of wastewater has also been noted, although this problem is not usually as serious for rural systems as it is for those in urban areas.

Population Acceptance

If the majority of the population of a village does not actively support the installation of a water supply system, the probability that the health and development goals of the system will be attained is greatly reduced. As noted previously, if the demand for improved water is generally a derived demand, then the higher income, better educated villages will be among the first to request a water supply system. Because these villages have an initial enthusiasm for the water supply system, it remains to translate their enthusiasm into concrete action in the form of a local contribution (labor or money) to system construction cost and to operation and maintenance; to ascertain the level of service the village can afford, and will be pleased with and support; and to design and support the operation and maintenance phase of the program so that the village population does not become disenchanted through inefficiencies and inadequacies.

Villages selected as having particularly high priority but which do not themselves perceive the advantages of a piped water supply system must receive considerable attention in the form of water supply promotion and education. The objective would be to stimulate a sufficient enthusiasm for an improved water supply system so that the village would willingly make the local contributions required, and would enthusiastically support the operation and maintenance function. In the case of very low income and backward villages, it is possible that the large amount of promotion necessary to stimulate an acceptable level of enthusiasm, together with the lack of sufficient local ability to assist in, and support, system operation and maintenance, could increase the costs of the system to the extent that better uses for the funds could be found elsewhere.

In a more general sense, there are three factors which must be considered in gaining or maintaining a community's enthusiasm about a water supply system: promotion, community involvement, and efficient operation and maintenance. Promotion and operation and maintenance are discussed in Chapter 6. The remaining factor, community involvement, is generally advocated on the psychological grounds that a community involved in a project and contributing labor or financial resources to it will value the project more highly.

Community involvement and participation may be encouraged by a water program promoter, who helps organize a community water supply committee which, in turn, decides how the community will raise its portion of the cost of construction. The community contribution may be raised in a variety of ways, including asking each family for a cash payment, holding several village-benefit fiestas or bazaars, and organizing a free labor crew to dig trenches for water lines, to collect sand and gravel, and to provide a general-purpose supply of unskilled labor.

In at least one Latin American country, the job of encouraging villagers to donate their labor to a village water supply project was made easier by the World Food Program. In that country the World Food Program had an arrangement with the national rural water supply agency whereby, for each day that a villager donated four hours work to the water supply project, he received a free food ration which was supposed to feed a family of six for one day.

In addition to the psychological and obvious financial reasons for advocating community involvement, there may also be solid economic reasons for supporting such a policy. For example, community involvement, by providing local labor for construction, could lower the real cost of projects because of the general underemployment in rural areas of developing countries. If construction should take place other than at harvest or planting time, then the opportunity cost (or shadow price) of the labor involved could be close to zero. Of course, a community contribution of labor would require additional promoter or supervisory time, a factor tending to reduce, somewhat, the real cost advantage of the free labor. Moreover, while ministries of regional or rural development often pay lip service to the economic advantages of self-help schemes, water supply engineers frequently take a more pessimistic view, citing the problems of labor organization and efficiency. A World Bank study on the use of labor-intensive methods in highway construction tends to confirm this view.[12]

Estimating the Monetary Value of Village Labor

In practice, there is some uncertainty about how to place a monetary value on the "free" labor villages donate to the water supply project as part of their contribution to construction costs. Some of the problems of valuing the local labor contribution are illustrated by the following methods which have, at one time or another, been suggested in several Latin American countries.

Water supply authorities frequently estimate the money value of local labor by multiplying the number of man-days of work contributed by villagers times the national minimum legal wage. Although this is probably the value as perceived by the village itself, it represents a considerable overestimate of the real social value of the labor because few of the workers would have had an alternative opportunity to earn income or engage in production activities during the time they were working on the water supply project.

Another method is to value the donated labor as equal to the market value of the family food rations given to workers who contribute labor to the water supply project. As noted previously, in at least one Latin American country the World Food Program made arrangements with the rural water supply agency to provide free food rations, enough to feed a family of six for one day, for each four-hour workday of donated labor. In the country referred to, the market value of the food ration was approximately one and one-half times the legal minimum wage for one-half day of work. Equating the value of the donated labor with the value of the food allotment would therefore result in an even greater overestimate of the real value of the labor.

A more legitimate method of calculating the value of donated labor for purposes of determining the financial amount to be credited to the village's contribution to construction costs would be to compute the cheapest alternative way the job could be done. For example, if a job

12. World Bank, "Study of the Substitution of Labor and Equipment in Civil Construction: Phase II Final Report," Working Paper no. 172 (Washington, D.C., January 1974).

that the donated labor completed in three weeks could have been done in three days by a tractor with a back-hoe, the value of the donated labor is the amount it would have cost to get the job done with the tractor (the foreign exchange components of which should be appropriately shadow-priced).

Shadow Pricing

Closely related to the analysis of donated labor is the problem of shadow pricing, which frequently arises in investment decisions in developing countries. For any public investment project, some estimate of the real resource costs to society should be made, so that (a) the real costs can be compared with the expected benefits to determine whether the investment should be made; (b) the real costs of alternative methods by which the project can be completed can be compared so that project costs can be minimized; and (c) beneficiaries can be asked to pay for the real resource costs their consumption entails, or alternatively, any subsidy they receive can be estimated in real terms.

The real costs to society of the resources needed for a water supply project are, in principle, scarcity prices which are determined by supply and demand. In developed countries, real costs can be estimated with some degree of accuracy by using market prices. In developing countries, however the cost of foreign exchange is often underestimated, and the cost of protected goods and unskilled labor are overestimated, when market prices are used. Moreover, the rate at which the investing agency borrows frequently does not represent the true cost to the economy of the capital it employs. In cases such as this, when market prices do not reflect real resource costs, other estimates of real costs (shadow prices) are necessary.

Various techniques for computing shadow prices have been proposed. Among the more important is the Little and Mirrlees (LM) method,[13] which uses foreign currency as the numéraire by which costs and benefits of projects are evaluated, while not involving an explicit use of a shadow exchange rate. The best-known alternative

---

13. Ian M. D. Little and James A. Mirrlees, *Manual of Industrial Project Analysis,* vol. 2, *Social Cost-Benefit Analysis,* Development Centre Studies (Paris: Organization for Economic Cooperation and Development, 1969).

to the LM method is the UNIDO approach,[14] which uses domestic currency as the numéraire and employs a shadow exchange rate to derive estimates of social costs and benefits.

Important practical advantages are sometimes claimed for LM over other methods. Because the LM method measures costs and benefits in terms of world market prices for traded and tradable goods, it avoids making the explicit statement that a currency is overvalued. Another advantage is that it permits a more sophisticated measurement of costs and benefits by not using a blanket shadow exchange rate, but by valuing different commodities individually simply by making use of the appropriate world market prices.

In practice, however, this benefit is likely to be more apparent than real. It is very difficult to measure these factors in the precise manner implied by such a procedure, and some averaging is always necessary. The LM proposals suggest that, where measurement becomes impossible, a "standard conversion factor" should be used instead. The standard conversion factor is simply the reciprocal of the shadow exchange rate, so in these circumstances there is even less choice between LM and the other procedures.

In the case of projects for which benefits and costs can be estimated in commensurable terms, there is indeed little to choose between the LM, UNIDO, or a number of other shadow-pricing approaches that have been developed. The basic differences between the methods lies in the choice of numeraire, that is, the unit of account used to measure benefits and costs. Thus if a numéraire is used consistently, the same investment decision will be signalled, whatever the numeraire actually is. Unfortunately, there are a number of areas—water supply being a notable example—where project benefits cannot be measured directly, and where, as we shall explain in more detail in Chapter 7, the key to efficient investment decisionmaking depends on setting prices equal to true economic costs. The role of shadow pricing is then to provide an estimate of the absolute economic cost of incremental supplies of water, so the choice of numéraire becomes critical. In this regard the LM method fails, the UNIDO method being more suitable in that it provides such an estimate. In other words, while obscuring the extent to which a currency is overvalued (an advantage of the LM method from the viewpoint of coun-

14. United Nations Industrial Development Organization, *Guidelines for Project Evaluation* (ID/Ser. H/2) (New York: United Nations, 1972).

tries' sensitivity), LM also obscures the true economic cost of water consumption, thereby making it difficult to arrive at sensible domestic pricing policies.

There are a number of practical and conceptual problems that are of general application to the LM, UNIDO, and other methods, but are not of direct concern to us here. More specific practical problems do concern us. First, the use of shadow prices may result in the selection of a village water supply project which, although in terms of the economic resources used in its construction and operation is estimated to have the least cost, may not be the cheapest in purely financial terms. The additional financial resources then have to be raised by the water supply agency. The water consumers can argue—and on theoretical grounds would be justified in so doing—that the additional financial cost should not be passed on to them. The alternative, of course, is for the water supply ministry to be allocated a larger subsidy from national general revenues. Given the scarcity of public funds in most developing countries (which implies that they should be appropriately shadow valued), the problems associated with this alternative will be apparent.

Second, consultants would presumably have to employ an experienced economist to enable project design and selection to be made in accordance with shadow-pricing guidelines. As a result, the cost of feasibility and design studies might rise significantly—not simply by the cost of hiring the economist but because the employment of the latter could mean that very different schemes are evaluated, for example, labor- versus capital-intensive projects. This possible high cost and delay owing to carrying out precise shadow-value calculations implies that, unless there are very good apparent reasons for believing that large savings can be achieved by use of shadow values, an acceptable procedure would be to use blanket values, such as the shadow exchange rate as suggested by UNIDO.

Third, the complexity of the interaction between the appropriate project selection and design and the appropriate method of construction will be increased by use of shadow pricing. The problems of trying to frame tender documents to reflect the need for the use of shadow values by bidders will also be immense.

The difficulties of handling these problems do not, however, excuse the general absence of shadow pricing in rural water supply investment programs. The fact remains that rural areas of developing countries tend to be characterized by underemployment and by overvalued local currency. As a result, a failure to shadow-price these factors, together with the availability of development funds at interest rates below the opportunity cost of the capital, could tend to distort the choice between labor- and capital-intensive methods of construction and operation, and to distort the choices among alternative water supply investment projects. It is clear that the merits of labor-intensive methods which are widely proclaimed by those with responsibilities for village water supply, rest essentially upon the notion of shadow pricing, although they are rarely estimated or expressed in those terms.

Level of Technology

A further manifestation of the concept of shadow pricing can be found in the choice of the technology that is appropriate for village water supply services. One of the primary considerations in designing and building a rural water supply project is to keep the technology as simple as possible, so that local operators will be able to operate and maintain the system for long periods of time in the absence of an engineer. The potential, however, of low-level or intermediate level technology is debatable. The Intermediate Technology Development Group has done some work in this area,[15] as have engineers at the Asian Institute of Technology in Bangkok.[16] A document containing both a technical description of some existing rural water supply and sanitation facilities and a review of selected problems encountered in designing and maintaining unsophisticated systems, is distributed by the International Development Research Centre.[17] Also, a brief discussion of small-scale rainwater collection schemes is available in Rees.[18]

---

15. Intermediate Technology Development Group Ltd., "The Introduction of Rainwater Catchment Tanks and Micro-Irrigation to Botswana" (London, September 1969).

16. Richard J. Frankel, "Research on Rural Community Water Supply at the Asian Institute of Technology, Bangkok" (paper presented at the WHO Regional Seminar on Rural Water Supply, Khon Kaen, Thailand, 4–14 March 1970).

17. Ian Burton, Yves Maystre, and Emanuel Idelovitch, *Technology Assessment Research Priorities for Water Supply and Sanitation in Developing Countries* (Ottawa: International Development Research Centre, November 1973).

18. Judith Rees, "Domestic Water Supply," in *Infrastructure Problems of the Cities of Developing Countries* (New York: The Ford Foundation, 1971), pp. 13–97.

A vast number of ingenious devices for making use of intermediate technology have been proposed in recent include bicycle-operated pumps, small-scale rainwater c storage facilities, bamboo pipes or aqueducts, coconut f rice husk, or charcoal water filters, and the never-ending se ι ιne perfect handpump. The most significant recent innovation, however, in the village water supply field has been the introduction of plastic pipe. If plastic pipe represents an intermediate level of technology, then it is clearly one example of a successful adaptation. Polyvinyl chloride is used in rural water supply programs throughout the world. It has the advantage of being relatively cheap and simple to manufacture so that most developing countries can purchase an extruder and produce it locally, of having a very smooth internal surface, and of being relatively easy to assemble at the construction site by semiskilled labor. The minor disadvantages of some plastic pipe are sensitivity to light and weather and decreasing strength with increases in temperature.

Besides the platitude that technical installations and equipment should be kept as simple as possible, and that water treatment should when possible be limited to easily maintained infiltration galleries, settling basins, and slow sand filters, there are also the economic considerations that, when feasible, local materials and equipment should be used and capital costs and capital imports should be kept to a minimum. This is, of course, in keeping with lowering the economic costs of the water supply program, with stimulating economic activity within the country, and with making the program more attractive to the national government by requiring the expenditure of a minimum of foreign exchange. As the WHO survey data in Table 5.6 show, imported material generally constitutes a smaller percentage of construction expenditures in rural water supply systems than in urban systems. This circumstance is probably somewhat a result of lower standards of service and of so-called free labor contributions in rural areas. The relevance of shadow pricing, however, in making decisions on the appropriate level of technology is clear. Unfortunately, as with the use of labor-intensive methods, such decisions are usually based on intuition, or at best on purely financial implications, rather than analysis of economic costs.

Complementary Programs

There may be a number of investments, complementary to a rural water supply program, which either increase the probability that the

Table 5.6. Percentage Cost of Imported Material to Total Construction Cost in Community Water Supply and Sewage Disposal Projects

World Health Organization region	Community water supply		Urban sewage disposal					
			Public sewerage system			Household system		
	Urban	Rural	Conventional treatment	Oxidation ponds	Without treatment	Pit privy	With septic tank	Other
Africa	58	50	57	30	31	23	43	10
Central and South America	33	29	18	4	7	8	8	2
Eastern Mediterranean	46	41	45	43	10	1	5	10
Algeria, Morocco, Turkey	20	15	—[a]	—[a]	—[a]	—[a]	—[a]	—[a]
Southeast Asia	38	27	43	33	33	—[b]	4	—[b]
Western Pacific	50	50	44	13	26	3	12	—[b]
Total	41	35	41	27	21	7	14	4

a. Data not available.
b. Nil or magnitude negligible.
Source: Same as Table 1.1, p. 750.

ultimate objectives of the water supply program will be accomplished, or lower the costs of the water supply program. An example of the first type of complementary investment is a sanitary education and latrine program designed to increase the probability that the health objectives of the water supply installation are accomplished. Another example of this type of investment would be a directly productive capital investment necessary to provide an opportunity for a productive life to those whose health is improved as, for instance, a program to educate rural water users in the new opportunities for increasing village livestock production and garden output.

A comparable complementary investment always to be considered when a water supply project is being designed is an investment in drainage. A drainage system, or a means of draining water away from public standpost or cattle watering areas, is not necessary in all instances; the need is related to the slope of the ground, proximity of residential areas, and the absorptive capacity of the soil. Most rural water supply systems do not have drains near water outlets. In cases, however, where, because of heavy usage and level terrain, wastewater tends to collect, a significant health hazard can result. This health hazard would be greatest in areas where there is a potential for malaria, schistosomiasis, or other parasitic diseases. In such areas, drainage facilities must be provided if the full potential of health benefits is to be realized.

An example of the second type of complementary program would be a rural electrification program: it not only contributes to the development objectives but lowers the operating cost of the water supply system itself by allowing the use of an electric-powered pump, rather than one requiring the continued purchase of gasoline or diesel fuel.

In general, any form of growth-point strategy (discussed in Chapter 4) requires complementary investments. Suggestions for complementary development investments, in addition to those built into the water supply project, include sanitation and education programs, feeder roads, rural electrification, village industry, crop improvement, and marketing information programs. If the full psychological as well as physical impact of these complementary programs is to be realized, they should be undertaken at approximately the same time as the construction of the water supply system.

The Time Frame for Investment

If increases in population do not live up to the estimates which were used in designing a water supply system, overinvestment results. On the other hand, if a water supply system reaches capacity quickly, and if deficits in supply capacity are not acceptable, then the secondary expansion of the system can raise unit costs above what they would have been had a larger capacity system been constructed initially.

The amount of water supply excess capacity which should be constructed is essentially a function of economies of scale and of the discount rate.[19] Economies of scale signify that, other things being equal, average or unit construction costs decrease as scale increases (marginal cost is less than average cost). Therefore, since economies of scale exist in the construction of water supply systems, the unit cost of a project designed to reach full capacity in twenty years will be less than the unit cost in twenty years of a project which had an initial design capacity of five years and which was expanded in size three times over the period.

Empirical evidence supporting the existence of economies of scale has already been discussed at some length in Chapter 4. Given this evidence, and the assumption that when a system reaches capacity it will be expanded, it makes good sense to design systems with excess capacity (with larger potential economies of scale corresponding to longer design periods).

The best length for the design period depends on the discount rate, or the rate at which the cost of probable system expansion is discounted back to the present. Generally, the higher the discount rate the shorter will be the optimum design period because, of course, a higher opportunity cost of resources corresponds to a higher discount rate.

Very simplistic estimates of the optimum design period for rural water supply systems can be computed from calculations done by Lauria,[20] using a model developed by Manne,[21] and using estimates

---

19. Donald Lauria, *Planning Small Water Supplies in Developing Countries*, final report to the U.S., Agency for International Development, Office of Health (Chapel Hill: University of North Carolina, Dept. of Environmental Sciences and Engineering, School of Public Health, 1972), p. 13.

20. Ibid.

21. Alan S. Manne, ed., *Investments for Capacity Expansion: Size, Location, and Time Phasing* (Cambridge, Mass.: M.I.T. Press, 1967), p. 85.

of economies-of-scale elasticities made by Lauria and by Carruthers.[22] (Economies-of-scale elasticity estimates show the percentage increase in system construction cost brought about by a 1 percent increase in system capacity.) In general, if the discount rate is assumed to be 10 percent, then the optimum design period for a rural water supply system would be somewhere between a low figure of four or five years, derived by using Lauria's economies-of-scale elasticity estimates for Guatemala (0.77) and Honduras (0.85) and twelve or thirteen years using the elasticity estimate (0.50) resulting from Carruthers' calculations. If the discount rate is only 5 percent, the optimum design periods would be seven to ten years and slightly over twenty-five, respectively. This contrasts with the relatively common practice in Africa, Asia, and Latin America of designing rural water supply systems with a twenty-year capacity.

An additional factor complicating optimum design period calculations is the difficulty of making accurate projections of population changes. Rural-to-urban population migration in most developing countries has been increasing rapidly. Design capacities would have to be larger if it is assumed that rural water supply systems can slow out-migration. On the other hand, if out-migration is not slowed, then faulty assumptions could result in significant excess capacities.

Rural-to-rural migration also causes significant differences in population growth rates among villages. In most countries some villages will not grow and some will even suffer a significant net loss of population during the next fifteen years. Others may experience a much greater increase in population (because of improved health and migration pattern changes) than they have in the past.

One way to approach the difficulties of estimating population changes among villages in rural areas is to tie population forecasts to forecasts of potential changes in economic activity. The assumption would be that those rural areas which begin to experience an increase in economic activity will be the areas which attract and hold population. Consequently, those areas should be afforded a higher figure than the majority of rural villages for population growth rate in water system design capacity calculations. The point is that using a fixed average population growth rate for all villages could result in a much greater amount of overinvestment and underinvestment on a spatial

---

22. I. D. Carruthers, *Rural Water Investment in Kenya: Impact and Economics of Community Water Supply* (London: University of London, Wye College, 1972), p. 104.

basis than would be the case if different estimates for growth rates were used for different classes of villages.

Finally, when possible, the phasing of investment should be practiced. For example, suppose a water supply system is designed so that it must have two storage or reservoir tanks when it reaches capacity in fifteen years. Suppose further that the system will not need the second tank during the first seven years of its existence (the first tank will reach capacity in seven years). The rational investment policy would be to construct the system without the second tank and then construct the second tank in seven years.

An advantage of this course of action is, first, that there is an initial cost savings in terms of real investment; and, second, that if the population of the village grows at a slower rate than projected, investment in the second reservoir may be postponed for more than seven years. The problem with phasing investment is that it assumes resources will be available at the time when they are needed, so that the additional tank can then be constructed. This, of course, implies an efficiently managed and well-planned and financed program that has, in practice, usually been difficult to achieve.

6 Administration of Rural Water Supply Programs

THE ADMINISTRATION OF RURAL water supply programs may be viewed as composed of three interrelated stages: planning, construction, and operation and maintenance. Factors which should be considered by the central administrative body during the planning stage have been the topic of much of the preceding chapters. Most important in the planning stage is that existing alternatives, not only on the supply but also on the demand side, be explored, and the implications (costs and benefits) of each alternative be considered.

Construction Phase

Administration of the construction phase of the program should not present many new problems to engineers who have worked in developing countries, although a natural resistance to a financially more costly yet economically preferable solution (that is, using shadow pricing) may, in a few instances, have to be overcome. When communities have agreed to contribute labor but have not been adequately motivated to be ready at the exact time the labor is needed is the kind of practical difficulty that could arise. There is no doubt that, from a purely administrative point of view, community participation agreements lead to greater local management difficulties than if the program ministry or the contractor were able to undertake the project in the most technically efficient way. These increased management difficulties are costs which, together with longer construction times associated with labor-intensive methods, must be incorporated into the cost-benefit calculations.

A second problem in administering the construction phase of rural water supply programs is in asking private contractors for bids on the construction work; the biggest and most experienced contractors frequently do not bid. In some countries, the more experienced and financially stable contractors are interested only in relatively large jobs in the urban areas, leaving smaller, more financially marginal contractors to bid on water supply construction projects in the rural areas. This circumstance has led to difficulties in getting the contractor to work with the community, in having him follow through and complete the job, and in helping him to gain timely access to the imported materials necessary for him to complete the job.

In one Latin American country the construction contract was written in such a way that the financially marginal contractors received a very large portion of the total payment when they began the project. As a result, they exhibited a propensity to begin construction on as many village projects as they could in order to receive that payment. The outcome was that the program found it had a significant number of partially completed projects being rapidly overgrown by weeds. Furthermore, a number of village water committees and populations became discouraged with the delays and lost much of their enthusiasm for the projects.

Operation and Maintenance

Problems of initial planning and construction are usually slight when compared with problems of operating and maintaining rural water supply systems after they have been constructed; without doubt, these are the major administrative problems associated with providing water supplies in rural areas of developing countries. In almost all countries with viable water supply programs, it is not difficult to find villages where the water supply system is either not working as planned (either technically or financially) or not functioning at all.[1]

---

1. For an interesting introduction to a number of problems frequently encountered when observing the administration of the operation and maintenance phase of water supply programs in rural areas, see Robert S. Anderson, "People and Water in Rural Bangladesh (1972–1973)" (Vancouver, B.C.:

In fact, in two countries we visited, one in East Africa and one in Central America, systems were actually failing at a more rapid rate than they were being constructed.

In Thailand a survey [2] by students at the Asian Institute of Technology in 1971 showed that 69 of 79 rural water supply systems studied had some difficulties in operating their plants. Among the more frequent complaints catalogued were: (a) continuing difficulty in collecting money from consumers because of broken taps, the great distance to public fountains, and the people's low incomes; (b) operators' salaries too low to support families; (c) pumps or public fountains broken or batteries not charged; (d) inadequate tanks or water sources; (e) insufficient pipe to extend the distribution system; (f) a lack of knowledge about system operation and chemicals; and (g) a lack of assistance from the central water supply authority.

Another example of typical operation and administration problems was observed in a Latin American country where one of the authors and several country engineers were accosted by irate villagers because of a technical problem they were having with their water system pump. The pump was not delivering enough water to fill the reservoir and, as a result, the village had water only about two hours a day. Because of this defect, many of the villagers were refusing to pay their water-use fees and the system was in danger of being shut down for a lack of operating revenue. In addition, the village had borrowed money in order to finance their initial contribution to the system and, due to inadequate revenues, they were in arrears on the loan.

The village water committee had written the central and regional water program offices about their problem and had received no response. They had also taken the pump to a nearby town of approximately 100,000 population and had paid a mechanic to rebuild it. The mechanic now guaranteed that the pump was functioning properly but they were still getting only a trickle of water. The water committee members had done everything they could think of to solve the problem and had not succeeded. They were in-

---

University of British Columbia, Department of Anthropology and Sociology, July 1974).

2. Charnvit Athikomrungsarit, "Benefits and Costs of Providing Potable Water to Small Communities in Thailand" (Master's thesis no. 566, Asian Institute of Technology, Bangkok, 1971).

dustrious, responsible, and concerned, but unable to solve their problem because they could not get two or three hours of an engineer's time to check out the system and pinpoint the real trouble.

Although this case occurred in a country where the target rural population is relatively well educated, it is a case typical of many countries where there is poor technical support and inadequate replacement and expansion inventories for systems once they have been completed.

Part of the general lack of technical support is the result of a lack of planning and adequate administrative organization, and part is the result of the inability, in many countries, of local country or district engineers to leave administrative work in their offices to see at firsthand what needs to be done to improve operation and maintenance efforts. Another adverse influence is the greater political impact and glamour attached to construction expenditures over expenditures for continuing operation and maintenance. Finally, in many cases, national budgetary authorities simply do not recognize the extreme importance of operation and maintenance and hence do not institute tariff policies that generate adequate revenue from village consumers for operation and maintenance.

Centralization versus Decentralization

The question of whether a rural water supply program should be administered by a central agency, or whether it should have a considerable amount of local, or at least regional, autonomy, has no unique answer. The organization should be such as to (a) assure the technical and administrative reliability of the program, and (b) be as efficient as possible in financial and economic terms. The latter goal implies that there must be at least a reasonable level of local interest and cooperation. In general, whether or not these goals can be best accomplished through a centralized or decentralized administrative structure in a given country depends upon the stage of the program we are talking about, the size of the country, the level of education and skills existing among the rural population, and whether there are economies of scale in that country in administering rural water supply programs.

In most countries, during the initial planning phase of the program, efficient administration can probably best be accomplished at the national level, or at that level of government which has authority for regional development planning. This administration could be at the regional or state level in very large countries; in most smaller developing countries, initial planning of the program requires more of an overview than is usually found at the subnational level.

The construction and the operation and maintenance phases of the program can be carried out efficiently at the national or the state or local level. To take advantage of a knowledge of local conditions, resources, and problems, these phases of the program should be conducted, as a general rule, at the lowest possible level which has the necessary technical expertise.

If a village population is capable of carrying out part of the construction and a significant portion of the local operation and maintenance, it is best to design the administrative system so that this can be done. Costs might be lowered (at least real costs), and the probability of community acceptance and appreciation would be increased.

On the other hand, if the rural target population is relatively backward, with few technical skills and with little income and education, then a structure more centralized around regional or national level expertise might be the most efficient and, indeed, the only way to administer the program. In Latin America, a more localized authority with local promoters, pump operators, revenue collectors, and bookkeepers has worked well in several countries. In parts of Africa, however, where the income and education levels of the rural population are much lower, a greater degree of central administration has generally proved to be the best solution. In situations such as this, however, it is wise to have local advisory committees so that local populations feel that they are participating in the program and take some pride in the systems.

In countries where there are relatively few professional engineers, it is sometimes difficult to associate qualified people (who prefer to work and live in large cities) with rural systems. In cases such as this, ensuring an adequate operation and maintenance function may require a broad and fairly centralized administrative authority.

The size of the country also affects the decision concerning what the level of administrative control should be. A national control program in a small country could be the exact equivalent of a regional control program in a larger country in everything except name.

Table 6.1. Types of Agencies Responsible for Planning of Community Water Supply

World Health Organization region	National or regional water authority		Municipalities		Ministry of public health		Ministry of public works or power		Other ministries		Other agencies	
	U	R	U	R	U	R	U	R	U	R	U	R
Africa	6	5	1	1	—[a]	3	16	10	7	6	6	10
Central and South America	9	7	11	4	2	12	4	3	—[a]	—[a]	4	5
Eastern Mediterranean	4	6	5	2	1	3	4	4	6	7	4	4
Algeria, Morocco, Turkey	—[a]	—[a]	1	—[a]	—[a]	—[a]	1	—[a]	1	3	2	1
Southeast Asia	2	1	2	1	3	4	3	—[a]	1	1	3	2
Western Pacific	1	1	4	1	—[a]	1	5	5	1	1	2	2
Total	22	20	24	9	6	23	33	22	16	18	21	24

Note: U = urban; R = rural.
a. Nil or magnitude negligible.
Source: Same as Table 1.1, p. 760–61.

Agency Responsibility

In countries with rural water supply programs it is not unusual to find several national ministries or agencies with separate water supply programs serving rural areas. The ministry of health, ministry of hydraulic resources, ministry of agriculture, ministry of public works, and a national planning agency might all have water supply programs of a similar nature, focusing on slightly different aspects of rural problems, on different sizes of towns, or on different regions. The variety of agencies currently reported to be involved in various stages of water supply and sewerage programs in developing countries are reflected in Tables 6.1 to 6.6, containing WHO survey data. There are usually historical or political reasons for this multiplicity of rural water supply agencies. In some cases, this multiple-agency arrangement even seems to work reasonably well.

Conceptually, however, it can be argued that to achieve efficient management control, reduce repetition, and assure better allocation of resources, the national rural water supply program should be under the control of one agency. The specific agency to be in charge should depend on the goals of the program, and the expertise required for the job. Periodic evaluation of the appropriateness of an agency to handle the program—or particular elements of it—is therefore necessary as goals and the relevance of available expertise tend to change over time.

If the primary objective of the program is to stimulate economic development or to attempt to redistribute income, a national planning ministry or some other national agency with those goals would be well suited to operate the program. To facilitate national-level cooperation for the ministry in charge of the rural water supply program, the heads of related ministries (health, hydraulic resources, agriculture, and so on) might be made members of the program's board of directors. In this way, expertise and cooperation from several sources could be solicited, yet one agency alone would have the operating responsibility for the program.

Because the most commonly cited justification for investment in rural water supplies is health (see Chapter 2), either as an end in itself or as a means of stimulating productivity, it is sometimes argued that the ministry of health may be best suited to administer the program. This contention may be particularly true in lower income countries where the chances of rural economic development in the short run are not great.

Table 6.2. Types of Agencies Responsible for Construction of Community Water Supply

World Health Organization region	National or regional water authority		Municipalities		Ministry of public health		Ministry of public works or power		Other ministries		Other agencies	
	U	R	U	R	U	R	U	R	U	R	U	R
Africa	10	7	1	3	—ᵃ	2	15	10	3	4	6	11
Central and South America	8	7	12	5	1	10	4	3	—ᵃ	—ᵃ	4	6
Eastern Mediterranean	4	6	7	5	1	4	4	3	5	6	5	4
Algeria, Morocco, Turkey	—ᵃ	—ᵃ	1	—ᵃ	—ᵃ	—ᵃ	2	1	—ᵃ	2	2	1
Southeast Asia	2	1	2	1	2	4	4	—ᵃ	—ᵃ	1	2	1
Western Pacific	1	1	4	1	1	2	5	5	—ᵃ	—ᵃ	2	2
Total	25	22	27	15	5	22	34	22	8	13	21	25

Note: U = urban; R = rural.
a. Nil or magnitude negligible.
Source: Same as Table 1.1.

Table 6.3. Types of Agencies Responsible for Operation and Maintenance of Community Water Supply

World Health Organization region	National or regional water authority		Municipalities		Ministry of public health		Ministry of public works or power		Other ministries		Other agencies	
	U	R	U	R	U	R	U	R	U	R	U	R
Africa	13	8	3	6	—[a]	—[a]	14	9	3	5	2	8
Central and South America	10	7	15	10	2	11	3	3	—[a]	1	5	4
Eastern Mediterranean	3	5	12	9	—[a]	1	4	3	2	2	5	4
Algeria, Morocco, Turkey	1	1	1	2	—[a]	—[a]	1	—[a]	—[a]	1	—[a]	1
Southeast Asia	1	1	5	6	2	3	1	—[a]	1	1	2	1
Western Pacific	1	1	6	3	—[a]	—[a]	4	4	—[a]	—[a]	2	2
Total	29	23	42	36	4	15	27	19	6	10	16	20

Note: U = urban; R = rural.
a. Nil or magnitude negligible.
Source: Same as Table 1.1.

Table 6.4. Types of Agencies Responsible for Planning of Sewage Disposal Systems

World Health Organization region	National or regional water authority		Municipalities		Ministry of public health		Ministry of public works or power		Other ministries		Other agencies	
	U	R	U	R	U	R	U	R	U	R	U	R
Africa	—[a]	1	3	2	—[a]	3	8	6	4	5	7	3
Central and South America	11	9	11	4	4	14	5	3	—[a]	—[a]	3	—[a]
Eastern Mediterranean	1	—[a]	2	—[a]	—[a]	1	—[a]	1	5	4	1	—[a]
Algeria, Morocco, Turkey	—[a]	—[a]	—[a]	—[a]	—[a]	—[a]	—[a]	1	1	1	2	1
Southeast Asia	1	—[a]	—[a]	—[a]	2	6	3	—[a]	—[a]	—[a]	2	1
Western Pacific	—[a]	—[a]	2	1	1	5	6	4	—[a]	—[a]	1	—[a]
Total	13	10	18	7	7	29	22	14	10	10	16	5

Note: U = urban; R = rural.
a. Nil or magnitude negligible.
Source: Same as Table 1.1.

Table 6.5. Types of Agencies Responsible for Construction of Sewage Disposal Systems

World Health Organization region	National or regional water authority		Municipalities		Ministry of public health		Ministry of public works or power		Other ministries		Other agencies	
	U	R	U	R	U	R	U	R	U	R	U	R
Africa	1	1	3	—a	1	4	9	6	1	1	6	5
Central and South America	13	9	11	5	4	14	5	3	—a	—a	1	—a
Eastern Mediterranean	2	—a	5	1	—a	1	—a	—a	2	3	2	—a
Algeria, Morocco, Turkey	1	—a	—a	—a	—a	—a	—a	1	1	1	1	—a
Southeast Asia	1	2	2	—a	2	6	2	—a	—a	—a	1	1
Western Pacific	2	2	3	1	1	5	6	4	—a	—a	—	—a
Total	22	14	24	7	8	30	22	14	4	5	11	6

Note: U = urban; R = rural.
a. Nil or magnitude negligible.
Source: Same as Table 1.1.

Table 6.6. Types of Agencies Responsible for Operation and Maintenance of Sewage Disposal Systems

World Health Organization region	National or regional water authority		Municipalities		Ministry of public health		Ministry of public works or power		Other ministries		Other agencies	
	U	R	U	R	U	R	U	R	U	R	U	R
Africa	1	—a	5	4	—a	2	4	1	—a	—a	4	2
Central and South America	10	6	15	9	1	7	1	1	—a	—a	2	1
Eastern Mediterranean	2	—a	5	2	—a	1	—a	—a	1	1	1	—a
Algeria, Morocco, Turkey	—a	—a	—a	—a	—a	—a	—a	—a	—a	—a	1	1
Southeast Asia	2	1	7	2	—a	4	—a	—a	—a	—a	—a	1
Western Pacific	1	—a	4	—a	—a	3	6	3	—a	—a	—a	—a
Total	16	7	36	17	1	17	11	5	1	1	8	5

Note: U = urban; R = rural.
a. Nil or magnitude negligible.
Source: Same as Table 1.1.

The World Health Organization has generally been encouraging developing countries to establish health centers throughout rural areas. These rural health centers are, in some cases, the only central government administrative units in the region and could be used by the ministry of health as a local administrative base for a rural water supply program. The water supply program could make use of the existing health-center facilities in an attempt to hold costs down and to facilitate community acceptance of the water supply program by operating out of a facility already locally known and accepted.

One problem, however, frequently mentioned by engineers, with placing the rural water supply program in the ministry of health, is that the orientation of health ministries in many countries is toward dispensing pills, buying more hospital beds, and giving vaccinations. The contention is that ministries of health, staffed primarily by physicians, have insufficient interest in allocating their scarce resources to building and administering water supply systems in rural areas. Another important problem with ministries of health is that, in many countries, they have relatively little influence on the central finance ministries.

In whatever administrative unit the program is ultimately placed, for the relatively unsophisticated rural system it is usual practice that the ministry that builds it should also be charged with its ongoing operation and maintenance. This procedure reduces administrative changeover and coordination problems, and allows a less encumbered feedback from the operation and administration groups to the construction group on problems of quality of work and materials, and on problems of design. It could also simplify, somewhat, problems which might be encountered in recruiting qualified engineers and administrators to oversee the operation and maintenance phases of the program.

Training and Incentives

To assure a reasonable probability of success, a water supply program that is to be implemented in rural areas of developing countries must have a specialized personnel training function. Basically, three kinds of training programs have to be undertaken. First, there must be a program designed to train the lower level employees of the system. Depending on how the system is organized, this level

Table 6.7. Relation of Number of Professional Water Supply Staff Requiring Training during 1972–76 to Availability of Adequate In-Country Training Facilities

World Health Organization region	Managers		Finance personnel		Engineers		Chemists and biologists		Other		Total	
	a	na	a	na	a	na	a	na	a	na	a	na
Africa	8	45	43	55	17	245	19	51	137	57	224	453
Central and South America	406	87	255	47	562	139	130	39	220	51	1,573	363
Eastern Mediterranean	28	220	84	338	70	254	20	156	65	81	267	1,149
Algeria, Morocco, Turkey	—[a]	—[a]	—[a]	6	—[a]	24	—[a]	6	21	—[a]	21	36
Southeast Asia	30	57	1,569	31	33,040	316	41	2,525	680	22	35,360	2,951
Western Pacific	—[a]	285	4	393	178	567	7	144	3	151	192	1,540
Total	472	694	1,955	870	33,867	1,645	217	2,921	1,126	362	37,637	6,492

Note: a = available; na = not available.
a. Nil or magnitude negligible.
Source: Same as Table 1.1, pp. 774–75.

would usually include bill collectors, bookkeepers, and pump operators.

The training program for the pump operator whose duties include maintaining the technical operation of a local system is particularly important. The extent or depth of the training would depend on the amount of technical support he could call on from the regional program headquarters if something in the system began to malfunction. Even after the construction phase of the water supply program has been completed, there must be a periodically recurring training program to assure qualified replacements for operators who leave their jobs.

The second type of training or orientation program necessary would be one for community promoters. The promoters would have to be acquainted with the construction and operation procedures of the program, be equipped to organize the villagers, and should also know the advantages potable water could bring to rural villages. Promoters in most countries generally have a better formal education than the villagers with whom they will be dealing, for example, they are former schoolteachers, sanitarians, and so on.

Third, some form of education or orientation program for the residents of the villages being supplied with water would be desirable. If, for example, the full health impact of the water supply investment is to be realized, the villagers should be encouraged to utilize the system to its fullest potential, including practicing good water-related sanitation. Many of the empirical health studies reviewed in Appendix A implied the importance of educating the population in good sanitation and water-use habits (see the section, "The Water-Use Link," Chapter 2).

Of course, other, more traditional training efforts are required in all water supply and sanitation-related programs. WHO Survey data presented in Tables 6.7 and 6.8 give some idea of the types and expected training needs of existing programs in developing countries.

In many instances there is the problem of motivating the employees of the rural water supply program to concentrate on reaching the objectives of the program. Junior-level public employees are frequently paid so low a wage that they are forced to hold more than one job. A method by which water supply employees might be encouraged to focus on the purpose of their jobs would be to create a bonus incentive system tied to accomplishing specific program objectives.

Such a system is functioning fairly well in several states in Argen-

Table 6.8. Relation of Number of Subprofessional Water Supply Staff Requiring Training during 1972–76 to Availability of Adequate In-Country Training Facilities

World Health Organization region	Supervisors		Specialized artisans		Special clerks		Drillers		Other		Total	
	a	na	a	na	a	na	a	na	a	na	a	na
Africa	332	206	1,181	25	397	—[b]	71	111	574	117	2,555	459
Central and South America	382	191	1,928	7	427	250	148	38	1,053	156	3,938	642
Eastern Mediterranean	273	465	4,880	2,470	2,375	1,170	22	133	239	441	7,789	4,679
Algeria, Morocco, Turkey	—[a]		208	—[a]	96	—[a]	—[a]	—[a]	43	—[a]	347	—[a]
Southeast Asia	4,060	315	2,000,205	620	40,280	140	606	240	9,059	810	2,054,210	2,125
Western Pacific	18	2,000	90	4,004	25	3,550	3	402	255	558	391	10,514
Total	5,065	3,177	2,008,492	7,126	43,600	5,110	850	924	11,223	2,082	2,069,230	18,419

Note: a = available; na = not available.
a. Nil or magnitude negligible.
b. Source information unclear.
Source: Same as Table 1.1.

tina. There, national water program authorities, when setting up a rural water supply program administered through the various provincial or state governments, found, first, that the central planning and administrative staff at the state level would be composed mostly of existing personnel who would be serving the rural water supply program in addition to their regular duties; and, second, that state-level engineers and administrative staff were paid very low wages. As a result, the majority of them worked only part of a day so that they could hold other jobs in addition to their state employment.

To solve these problems and to stimulate functionaries at the state level to devote time and effort to achieving success for the rural water supply program, a system of financial bonuses was instituted whereby state engineers and administrators earn financial rewards by achieving specific objectives during given time periods. Details of the incentive plan have changed from time to time, but engineers have been known to double their base salaries by this means.

During the construction phase of the projects the bonuses are based mainly on finishing a certain portion of the project during a given period of time. If 100 percent of the goal is accomplished the engineer receives a 100 percent bonus in salary; if 60 percent is achieved during the allotted time he receives a 60 percent salary bonus, and so on.

During the operation and maintenance phase of the project the bonuses are designed to promote frequent visits by the engineer to villages to advise on maintenance, administration, and expansion, to check chlorine levels, and so on. The engineer must send reports by specific dates to the national program office outlining his visits to villages, the problems he encountered, and the solutions he worked out. The reports must be detailed and must follow a specific outline. If, during a given period, the engineer is able to accomplish 100 percent of his quota visits with 100 percent satisfaction, he then receives a 100 percent salary bonus.

There are several provinces in Argentina, however, where the bonus system has not worked. The reason for the failure of the system in these provinces is that the state engineers and staff who are working on the rural water supply system are in a department (or organization) closely tied to several other departments employing engineers and staff of equal qualifications. When the bonus system was proposed for the people who would be working on the rural water supply program, their colleagues, who were equally qualified but who would not be working on the rural water supply program, complained so vigorously about salary discrimination that the system was not implemented. The possibility of falsifying records might also be a drawback to a bonus incentive system, as well as the necessity for engineers to spend a considerable amount of their time filling out report forms.

Another factor that enters where rural water supply employees are paid a very low wage is the considerable pilferage of supplies by employees who, in turn, sell the supplies on the open market. One such situation has been described in Bangladesh.[3] While turning a blind eye to pilfering may be the only way in which the real wages of water employees reach a level sufficient to retain their labor, the inefficiencies of such a situation are obvious.

Related specifically to the rural aspects of a rural water supply program is the difficulty of recruiting and retaining qualified employees—for example, engineers—if they must spend a significant portion of their time living in relatively backward rural areas. Dependent on the specific case, this problem might have various solutions, including a salary premium for living in areas without many public services, a personnel rotation system to pull staff back to the city every other year, and so on.

Financial and Income Distribution Considerations

Existing arrangements for the financing of village water supply and sanitation programs depend upon economic conditions in the rural areas of the country, manifested primarily in ability or willingness to pay for water; the philosophy of the central government about who should pay for the facilities; and, quite often, the agreement with an international or bilateral lending agency. The most common financial arrangement in Latin America, encouraged by the Inter-American Development Bank, is that the village raise between 10 and 20 percent of the construction cost of a project, with the national and state government picking up approximately 20 to 30 percent, and the international agency loan covering the other 50 percent. The national government usually agrees to pay back the international agency loan from national-level tax revenues.

In Asia and Africa the situation varies widely. In Thailand and Zambia, for example, villages normally contribute nothing toward

---

3. Anderson, "People and Water."

the cost of construction of rural water systems. In other countries, including Sri Lanka and several states in India, local contributions of 25 to 50 percent of investment cost are required. It is unusual for a country to succeed in generating a significant amount of funds for payments on interest and loan principal from user fees paid by low-income rural water consumers.

Two major problems arise in trying to set water-use charges to cover at least operation and maintenance costs. First, in many countries it is difficult to ascertain what operating costs really are, or what they should be because existing systems in most cases are not being properly maintained. As a result, the costs of proper operation and maintenance of village systems are probably greater than generally realized or revealed in the accounts of rural water supply authorities.

The second problem is that pricing schemes are badly designed and only randomly enforced. In some countries the same water use rate is charged to all villages in the country. Elsewhere the water use rates are subject to few guidelines and there is an implicit acceptance that the village populations will pay as little as they can get by with. The haphazard pricing policies generally observed do not recognize any of the variations among villages in ability to pay, benefits received, or costs of supply.

Financing a significant expansion of existing systems, and an expansion through time of the number of villages served, usually requires additional funding from outside the water supply program. Several Latin American countries have attempted, under the guidance of the Inter-American Development Bank and the Pan American Health Organization, to handle program expansion demands by instituting a so-called revolving fund concept. This method essentially requires charging a user fee to cover not only operation and maintenance costs, but also to generate additional revenue for a central program fund. As money accumulates in this fund, it can be used for system expansions, or for building new systems.

Because the revolving fund concept is relatively new in Latin America it is probably premature to judge whether or not it is working. In practice, however, it is still difficult to find a country where a significant surplus of revenue above operation and maintenance costs is being generated by user fees.

For project expansion purposes it is also possible to allow individual villages to accumulate their own surplus revenue fund by charging a user fee greater than needed to cover operating and maintenance expenses. This practice in Peru, in some of the higher income rural villages, has made the population very proud of the fact that they are generating a water-supply expansion and contingency fund which is drawing interest for them in a bank.

One of the major problems in areas where rural water user fees are not generating sufficient revenue to cover operation and maintenance costs is that the availability of the revenue subsidy depends on decisions made by a central government far removed from the rural population. Consequently, in a year when competing needs for funds from national general revenue sources are great, the operation and maintenance subsidy for rural water supply systems can be cut back, forcing many systems to operate even more inefficiently and sporadically. There is usually no intent on the part of the national government to shut down rural systems, but that is sometimes the result of subsidy cutbacks occurring in the absence of a successful effort to increase the amount of revenues generated locally.

One method by which rural water supply systems may be removed from a dependence on general revenues allocated by the national government is to provide a financial link between the rural water supply program and the water supply systems of urban areas. A national or regional water authority might be created which includes both higher income urban areas and lower income rural villages. The water authority could adjust water prices so that it could establish itself on a financially sound footing. By charging higher prices in urban areas the authority could use the surplus revenue generated to subsidize water supply systems in the lower income rural areas.

This system, in fact, is being followed in Costa Rica. There, the national water and sewerage authority (SNAA) attempts to collect 70 percent of the costs of rural water supply systems from the tariffs paid by the rural consumers. Urban areas outside San José are supposed to pay water tariffs sufficient to cover their total costs of supply, while San José users are supposed to generate revenue sufficient to cover their total supply costs, plus the amount necessary to cover the required financial subsidy for the rural areas.

Urban-rural subsidy systems such as this have also been planned in a number of countries, including Ghana, Brazil, and India. In these countries, it is planned that national or state water authorities should determine water supply prices in urban and rural areas so that surplus revenues in the urban areas could be generated to subsidize the operation and maintenance of the rural systems.

There are five main factors to be considered in deciding on whether or not to establish a regional or national urban-rural pricing authority of this type. First, if one of the country's goals is redistribution of income, this system is a way of accomplishing that. Higher income urban-area residents are taxed through a water-use tax; the proceeds are then distributed to lower income residents of rural areas in the subsidizing of the ongoing costs of their water supply systems.

Second, if the demand for water is relatively inelastic in urban areas (as has been shown in a number of water-demand studies), then there should be little misallocation of resources as a result of the higher price in these areas. Even though urban prices could be higher than marginal costs of supplying urban areas, relatively inelastic demand implies consumption of approximately the same quantity of water at the higher price. In the rural areas, where the demand for water is probably somewhat more elastic, theoretically, people might, in the end, consume more water at the lower price. The relevant consideration here, however, is that, without the lower subsidy price, the system might not have been constructed, and therefore rural users might not be consuming improved water at all. Furthermore, because it is frequently not feasible to charge consumers in rural areas on the basis of use, rural demand elasticity is not always a relevant consideration.

Third, to the extent that urban systems are able to maintain financial viability, a constant source of revenue for subsidizing the operation and maintenance of village water supply systems would be assured. This revenue could be counted on through time and, hopefully, would not be subject each year to the revenue and expenditure problems of the central government. As pointed out earlier, dependence on the central government for operation and maintenance subsidies frequently leads to periodic system failures.

Fourth, in attempting to achieve income redistribution, the structure of tariffs in the urban area must be such that prices are not increased in the slum or ghetto areas. The middle- and high-income areas should bear the brunt of the higher urban water prices while the slum dweller, who uses a low volume of water, should still be able to purchase the amount he needs at a low price. In other words, do not raise the price of water to the urban poor in order to subsidize the rural poor, particularly where the latter generally have better alternative sources.

Fifth, the rural-urban pricing and revenue authority may not always be able to generate sufficient revenues from urban areas to subsidize adequately the operation and maintenance costs in rural areas. For example, in a country where a great majority of the population resides in serviceable rural areas, the potential amount of surplus revenue which could be generated from the relatively small, higher income urban population may be insufficient to cover the water supply subsidy needs of the rural population. This problem, of course, might be handled in a number of ways, including providing water under the regional pricing board scheme only to those villages that could be subsidized.

Income redistribution can also take place among rural areas within the framework of a so-called revolving fund. If revolving funds are used not only for their stated purpose of providing funds for expansion but also as a fund from which operating and maintenance subsidies can be drawn, then higher income rural villages, which generate a flow of user payments greater than is needed for their operation and maintenance, can subsidize operations in lower income villages. In fact, this is probably what is happening in several Latin American countries. Of course, a potential problem with this use of the revolving fund is the possibility that if prices are set by a national authority at a similar level in all villages, a low income village with a cheap water source and low operation and maintenance expenses might be subsidizing a higher income village which, for geographical or geological reasons, has relatively high operation and maintenance expenses.

One final consideration in the financing of rural water supply programs relates to so-called conditional grants. From time to time, developing countries have made economically bad investment decisions because of conditional grants from more developed countries. For example, it is not necessarily an economically sound decision to accept a $5 million gift from a developed country to begin a rural water supply program if the gift specifies that all, or a large proportion, of the funds must be spent in the donor country for capital equipment and materials. The capital equipment might have been purchased elsewhere at a cheaper price, and lower-cost local materials or a lower level of technology might have been substituted for items purchased in the developed country.

Furthermore, when the rural water supply program becomes tied to expensive capital equipment manufactured in the grant-bearing country, adverse effects may be felt for many years if there is need to purchase relatively costly replacement parts and compatible equipment. Through time, a considerable drain of resources may occur, and the real value of the original gift can actually become negative.

It is not that conditional grants or gifts for specific program purposes to developing countries are bad. It is simply that before a grant is accepted, it would be wise for the recipient agency in the developing country to have an economist and an engineer examine the short- and long-run costs and benefits of the grant. These costs and benefits should be compared with the real ones which would be generated if the country initiated the program with its own funds or with unconditional grants or loans from bilateral or international agencies.

In this section, financial arrangements and the concept of fairness —or income distribution—in water charging policy have been emphasized, a reflection of traditional practice. Price has another role, however, namely to influence consumption, and thereby to provide guidance to decisionmakers as to the merits of investment decisions. The relevance of this fact for water supply in general, and rural water supply in particular, is dealt with in Chapter 7.

7 Water Charges and Project Evaluation

A MAJOR THEME OF THIS BOOK is the extreme difficulty of predicting the effects of investments in rural water supply and sanitation. A satisfactory basis on which to allocate funds to the sector as a whole is therefore lacking, as well as a method of ranking projects within the sector. We have described at length the problems, not simply of quantifying in economic terms, but even of identifying the impact of such investments on public health, normally accepted as a primary objective. Improved water supplies can support the achievement of other objectives, such as stemming rural-to-urban drift, creating more time for productive activity, and so on, but at present intuition is the primary guide as to the merits of competing projects. Moreover, we are pessimistic of the hope of improving knowledge in this area by conventional benefit-cost analysis, which would seek to evaluate water and sanitation investments by direct observation of how such services are used, and to impute to them money values based largely on the judgment of the analyst concerned. Experience suggests that in the public utilities field in general, such attempts have tended to be futile: the only way in which the minimum economic worth of investments can be determined is by giving consumers themselves the chance to let authorities know how much they value the service concerned, by being charged a price that reflects the full economic cost of supply.

Some Basic Principles

We shall outline the role of economic pricing theory in the water supply field, and show that, while rigorous application of the theory may not always be feasible in rural areas, the principles remain highly relevant. Indeed, we contend that, combined with the financial and administrative arguments for recovering costs from consumers discussed in earlier chapters, recognition of the concept of consumers' willingness to pay as a guide to resource allocation is absolutely essential to the achievement of any noticeable improvement in the rural water supply situation in the developing world.

Economic Efficiency and Marginal Cost Pricing

An important benchmark by which policies relating to water supply may be judged is the contribution those policies make toward economic efficiency. An efficient policy may be defined roughly as one which maximizes the net benefits accruing to a community from a given course of action, with no consideration paid to the way in which those benefits are distributed within the community. A proposition stemming from this definition is that the price of any service or commodity supplied by a public body should be equated to the cost of producing an additional unit of it, or, in other words, to its marginal or incremental cost. If consumers are willing to pay a price that exceeds marginal cost, it means that they place a value on the marginal unit consumed at least as great as the cost to the rest of society of producing that unit; output and consumption should therefore be expanded when system capacity is reached. If, on the other hand, the market clearing price is less than marginal cost, it can be assumed that there is oversupply of the commodity: the cost of additional output exceeds the benefits.

Whether or not a policy is thought to contribute to a movement toward efficiency will, of course, depend upon the community whose benefits the analyst is interested in maximizing. Having determined the relevant target group of people, he must distinguish between purely accounting costs and real (or economic) costs incurred by that group. The former costs, which might include repayment of past loans, simply represent a transfer of income within the community. Efficiency in resource allocation dictates that these "sunk costs" be ignored for pricing purposes, for they represent no net loss, or avoidable cost, to society as a whole. On the other hand, the resources employed in the construction and operation of a particular project represent, at the time of employment, real costs in terms of opportunities foregone elsewhere. The price charged for the good or service concerned should clearly incorporate recovery of such costs if they are incurred as a result of additional consumption.

The principle outlined here is straightforward. There are a number of difficulties, however, regarding both its practicality and its desirability that surround its implementation. Other problems such as capital indivisibility, financial constraints, and the use of shadow values, arise in all applications of marginal cost-pricing principles; while important, they are not peculiarly rural water supply problems and are only briefly discussed in this section. The specific problems of measuring water consumption and of supplying the rural poor are dealt with separately.

Capital Indivisibility

The foregoing remarks suggest that a distinction should be made, for water supply pricing purposes, between those costs that are a function of consumption and those that are not. Ambiguity in the definition of marginal cost arises where capital indivisibility (or "lumpiness") is present, for, with respect to consumption, costs will be marginal at some times and nonmarginal at others.[1] For example, if the safe yield of a reservoir is less than fully utilized, the only costs immediately attributable to additional consumption are certain additional operating and maintenance costs. These represent short-run marginal costs. Long-run marginal costs, on the other hand, refer to the sum of short-run marginal costs and marginal capacity costs; the latter are defined as the cost of extending capacity—for example, building a new reservoir—to accommodate an additional unit of consumption.

Now that we have two definitions of marginal cost, one applicable in the short run and the other in the long run, what happens to the rule that price should equal marginal cost? Strictly interpreted, the rule requires that price should equal short-run marginal cost when capacity is less than fully utilized, but if demand increases so that existing capacity becomes fully utilized, price should be raised to

---

1. Certain other costs are not marginal *with respect to consumption*. These may include "consumer costs" such as meter reading and billing, certain managerial overheads, and so on.

ration existing capacity. This procedure should continue up to the point where consumers reveal their willingness to pay a price equal to short-run marginal cost plus the annual equivalent [2] of marginal capacity cost. At this stage, that is, where price equals annual equivalent long-run marginal cost, investment in capacity is justified. Once the investment has been carried out, however, price should fall again to short-run marginal cost, for the only real costs (or opportunity costs, in terms of alternative benefits forgone) are then operating costs. Price therefore, plays the roles of (a) obtaining efficient utilization of resources when operating at less than full capacity, and (b) providing a signal to invest.

Problems associated with strict marginal cost pricing, as just described, are particularly apparent in the presence of capital indivisibility, a condition typical of water supply projects, where productive capacity is often installed to meet demands for a number of years hence. Initial costs of constructing reservoirs and laying connecting mains are usually very high in relation to operating and maintenance costs. Strict marginal cost pricing in these circumstances would entail significant fluctuations in price, a source of considerable uncertainty for consumers, which would create particular problems for planning long-term investment in facilities complementary to, or competitive with, water consumption. Exploitation of groundwater—the primary source for rural systems—often gives rise to less difficulty in this respect; in the economist's jargon, the long-run marginal cost curve is frequently relatively "smooth." Even where it is technologically possible to extend capacity in fairly small increments, however, fluctuations in the availability of finance may mean that capacity is extended in large lumps. This issue is particularly important in developing countries, where large backlogs in supply may be remedied and excess capacity created at the same time.

2. The annual equivalent A of a lump sum expenditure E is here defined as:

$$A = \frac{Ei(1+i)^n}{(1+i)^n - 1},$$

where i is the rate of interest and n is the expected useful life of the project. Any demand period could be chosen, but an annual one is obviously convenient. Note that if demand is expected to continue growing, willingness to pay a price equal to annual equivalent long-run marginal cost by consumers in the first year would imply willingness to do so over the rest of the designated useful life of the asset. If not, it simply means that the useful life has been estimated incorrectly.

One solution—necessarily an imperfect one—to this problem is to define marginal cost more broadly, and to set price equal to the average unit cost of incremental output. Average incremental costs can be calculated by dividing the discounted value of future supply costs by the (similarly discounted) amount of additional water to be produced. In practice, any version of marginal cost pricing has to be approximate, and ultimately some averaging of costs over a range of output is always required. Average incremental cost pricing will be theoretically less desirable the greater the degree of capital indivisibility, for while capacity remains idle, price will be in excess of the currently relevant marginal cost. However, in view of the difficulties inherent in any system requiring fluctuating prices,[3] this method appears to be the best practicable approximation to optimal pricing that can be achieved in the water supply field, and is the one that, in general, we recommend.

The characteristic of capital indivisibility is demonstrated in an extreme form by a distribution network: prior to its inception it is by definition a marginal cost and, presumably, is a function of the expected consumption of those benefiting from it. It is, however, normally designed to meet demands placed upon it for many years hence, during which time additional consumption by existing consumers is responsible for negligible additional distribution capacity costs. The pure marginalist approach would suggest that the price charged for this element of a water undertaking's services should also be negligible. It has to be financed somehow, though, and the case is illustrative of the conflict often encountered between economic efficiency and financial requirements.

Financial Viability and Economic Efficiency

Marginal cost pricing results in financial losses for an enterprise when average costs are falling, that is, when marginal cost is less than average cost. This situation could be temporary, arising, for example, where there was excess capacity and price was equated to short-run marginal cost. It might also be a situation of some permanence, even if there were perfect capital divisibility, if long-run average costs

---

3. The political difficulties of changing prices for water supply are well known. Fluctuating prices are also unsatisfactory in that they will not provide adequate signals to consumers about long-term water supply costs and therefore will not encourage optimal investment in water using (or saving) equipment by domestic or industrial users.

continued to decline and price were equated to long-run marginal cost. If there were lumpiness, a price equal to average incremental cost would, in these circumstances, also result in loss-making. On the other hand, if long-run average costs were rising, financial surpluses would be generated.[4]

Any surplus resulting from the application of marginal cost pricing could conceivably be used to defray other public expenditures, or to avoid taxation, and only limited distributional or resource allocation problems would arise. Loss-making, on the other hand, may be attacked on the grounds that those who benefit should pay for a service, even though the expenditure of real resources might have taken place in the past. Indeed, the possibility that efficient resource allocation could require subsidy from those in society who do not directly benefit from the good supplied should lead the analyst to examine with care the often multiple objectives of a pricing policy. Thus, if a clear conflict of interest exists among various groups in society, the benefits of overall economic efficiency must be weighed against those of income redistribution.

Loss-making may also entail certain drawbacks from an efficiency standpoint. First, the accounting losses have to be made good somehow, and it will often be difficult to achieve the necessary transfer of real income without creating distortions of consumer or producer's choice as severe as those encountered in departing from marginal cost pricing. Second, the financial discipline and organizational autonomy resulting from financial viability are often necessary to ensure efficient operation of the undertaking concerned.

Solutions to this dilemma have been proposed which have usually tried to obtain the best of both worlds: the resource allocation advantages of marginal cost pricing on the one hand and the avoidance of financial loss-making on the other. There are, in fact, many variations on a common theme, the simplest of which is a two-part tariff where a water consumer would pay a sum per thousand gallons consumed equal to marginal cost, plus a lump sum covering nonmarginal "sunk costs" and consumer costs. In this way, as long as liability

---

4. This may not, in view of the extreme shortage of public funds in most developing countries, appear to be a problem. Politically, however, it may be, since it is often advocated that public utilities should avoid making large profits. If so, the optimal strategy might be to set price equal to marginal cost, and allow consumers to have a rebate, which does not vary according to the amount they consume.

to the lump sum payment does not deter anyone from consuming the system's water altogether, optimal allocation may be achieved. Similarly, efficient allocation may theoretically result from the activities of the imaginary "perfectly discriminating monopolist," who charges each consumer a price equal to the maximum the consumer would pay, right on down to the consumer who places a value on water equal to its marginal cost. Although such omniscience is rare, this general approach, popularly known as charging "what the traffic will bear," is often employed to finance water supply: for example, industrial consumers may be charged higher prices than domestic consumers. Even if these methods succeed in achieving efficiency in the short run, however, the investment decision still cannot be signalled without price fluctuations if capital indivisibility is present.

The Second-Best Problem and Shadow Pricing

Another difficulty encountered in applying marginal cost pricing to the provision of water supplies is known as the second-best problem. What may appear at first sight to be a step in the direction of economic efficiency (for example, setting a price equal to marginal cost, or indeed, of introducing a pricing mechanism where none hitherto existed) may not be an improvement at all should inefficient conditions prevail in other sectors of the economy. Optimality in any one sector might require a price greater or less than marginal cost to counter such inefficiencies.

In practice, in any economy in which there is a good deal of competition, it has to be assumed as a rough and ready principle that elsewhere goods and services are sold at prices that in general approximate their long-run marginal costs. If not, the difficulties of adjusting for all imperfections would lead to the nihilistic conclusion that there are, after all, no empirical grounds for preferring any one set of pricing rules over any other. Where, however, goods or services that are in direct competition with (or are complementary to) the service in question are priced in a way that diverges sharply from the standard set for the water supply or sewage disposal system, it may be necessary and feasible to make some adjustment. If prices of resources employed in constructing and operating water supplies diverge from their long-run marginal cost to society, shadow prices should ideally be placed upon them in evaluating the real cost to society of the expenditure. Thus, labor that would otherwise be unemployed might be valued near zero (that is, at its opportunity cost) even though, due to market imperfection, it is able to command a wage rate in excess of the minimum amount needed to attract it; foreign exchange costs should be valued at their natural market rate; interest rates should reflect the social opportunity cost of capital, and so on. Adjustments of this nature are necessary if the ultimate consumer is to be faced with a price for water that reflects the true economic cost his consumption entails.

Relevance of Pricing Theory for Village Water Supply

The theoretically ideal pricing and investment rules discussed above are generally somewhat removed from the methods actually used to finance and determine the value of municipal and rural water supplies in both the developed and developing world. Water authorities are normally reluctant to make use of price as a means of achieving an efficient allocation of resources, the inefficiencies generated by failure to adhere to marginal cost pricing rules being extreme when the means of implementation (that is, metering) do not exist.

The Benefits and Costs of Pricing: Existing Consumers

Where the cost to a consumer does not vary with consumption, he will continue to use water up to the point where the value to him of the last unit consumed is zero. At this point the net economic loss will be the relevant marginal cost—which, when system capacity is less than fully utilized, will equal short-run marginal cost. Inefficiency is particularly evident when, at the current level of consumption, existing capacity is on the verge of full utilization, and for some reason rationing by price is not feasible. In these circumstances, the decisionmaker is faced with the choice of permitting shortages and allocating water by nonprice means or of extending capacity. Rationing by physical or administrative means is generally accepted as being unsatisfactory as a permanent policy, although it has become the norm in many developing countries. As a public utility, a water undertaking should be able to supply water to those willing to pay for it; and as we have noted, health hazards may arise from intermittent supplies. There are also theoretical objections: nonprice rationing is a necessarily arbitrary device and can rarely be administered in accordance with the value of the benefits derived from the services rendered. It is therefore inefficient in allocating resources in the short run, and offers no guidance for the investment decision.

The policy usually preferred by decisionmakers in the water supply and sewerage sector is automatically to increase capacity when existing capacity approaches full utilization. In other words, at this point, more capacity is deemed to be required. Clearly, in the absence of a signal to invest, such as a willingness of consumers to pay a price equal to marginal cost, it can rarely be certain that the value of the additional consumption—or usage—made possible by the investment will exceed the costs thereby incurred.

Where significant budgetary constraints are lacking, a failure to employ pricing and a reliance upon the "requirements" approach will almost certainly result in overinvestment. But when guidance of the pricing mechanism is not available, budgetary constraints may prevail when, in terms of the costs and benefits of a given project, they should not. Either way, inefficiency is likely to follow.

Unfortunately, implementation of use-related pricing (that is, through metering) for water supply is a costly exercise, and its introduction or continuation should ideally be subject to cost-benefit analysis. Briefly, the benefits of metering are the cost-savings brought about by reducing consumption. Savings may be achieved by deferring investment as well as by reducing annual operating and maintenance costs. To determine whether the investment in metering is worthwhile,[5] the present worth of these savings should be compared with the present worth of initial and annual costs of metering, plus the reduction in the value of water consumed.[6] Because the reduction in consumption likely to result from metering is normally highly conjectural, one way to approach the problem is to

---

5. For details, see Appendix D and J. J. Warford, "Water Requirements: The Investment Decision in the Water Supply Industry," in *Public Enterprise*, ed. Ralph Turvey (New York: Penguin Books, 1968). Note that our concern should be with *real* as opposed to purely monetary costs, so it is irrelevant to argue that, because of expected inflation, to delay investment is to incur greater costs in the future. Real costs are defined solely in terms of resources used up: general price increases therefore should not affect the calculation, although if they were known, relative price changes should.

6. This would be roughly equal to the product of half the expected reduction in consumption and the price per gallon that is charged when metering is introduced.

ask the question, what percentage reduction in consumption would justify the introduction of metering? If extreme values result from such a calculation, it is easy to make a judgment as to whether or not metering is justified; if not, at least the worst excesses of installing or not installing meters may be avoided.

The case for metering industrial consumers in urban and many rural areas is usually not a matter for serious dispute; the cost of metering is normally insignificant in relation to the cost of water consumed. The real question is whether or not to meter domestic and small commercial consumers,[7] and here the need for some sort of cost-benefit calculation is clear. Despite the lack of hard empirical evidence, the water supply industry usually argues that, although metering will reduce recorded per capita consumption, changes in price, once meters have been installed, generally appear to have an insignificant effect on consumption. This apparent paradox is conventionally explained in two ways. First, universal metering reveals discrepancies between the quantity of water going into supply and that actually received on consumers' premises. Such discrepancies, revealing the extent of leakage from the mains and of illegal connections, at once facilitate and provide an incentive for the improvement by water authorities of waste prevention methods, for waste outside of registered consumers' premises would, prior to metering, have been recorded as domestic consumption. Metering would therefore bring about a permanent reduction in annual wastage, a condition that would obviously remain unaffected by subsequent price changes. Second is the argument that metering will encourage individuals to reduce the amount of water wasted on their premises, but once having made this adjustment, their demand for water remains relatively inelastic. Intuitively both arguments would seem to be valid.

There are a number of special problems, reflected in both the cost and benefit sides of the calculation, which suggest that metering will rarely be appropriate for residential and commercial consumers in rural areas. The costs of metering will tend to be relatively high, for meter reading and maintenance will be more costly because of lower population density (particularly a population wealthy enough

---

7. Since a utility manager will be more concerned with financial viability than with optimal resource allocation he may prefer that metering should be extended only to poorer properties rather than to more valuable ones. This attitude would typically be encountered where a progressive property tax is currently employed to finance water supply.

to have household connections). Furthermore, in smaller communities the meter reader may be under greater social pressure to under-record consumption. On the benefit side, consumption tends to be lower in rural areas where people are poorer and do not have water-using appliances or adequate means of disposing of wastewater. The potential gains from conservation of water are therefore limited. Exceptions of course exist: the lower density of population may mean that more water is used for garden watering or for livestock; where this is so, metering is a more viable proposition.

Central to the problem of metering, however, is that, because of low incomes in rural areas, the appropriate source of supply may not be household connections but rather communal standposts or wells with hand pumps. Although in these circumstances metering, in the normal sense of the term, may not be an appropriate means of influencing consumption, principles similar to those outlined above should be applied to the decision to use a village or water board employee to supervise the dispensing of water from standposts, or to sell the concession to an individual. These methods are frequently used in urban areas of developing countries where standpost supplies are provided, although somewhat less so in rural areas. Where they are used, selection of the means of control is sometimes based on financial considerations, rather than on a comparison of economic costs and benefits, as described above. This is not always so, however, for conservation of water and the prevention of vandalism to taps—which presumably should be defined in cost-benefit terms— are often cited as the reason for employee control of taps or sale of concession.

Kenya provides an interesting example of a case in which water vendors (water kiosk operators) in a number of rural villages serve the multiple functions of generating a small amount of revenue from public taps, of limiting public tap water wastage, and of protecting the taps from vandalism. In several regions of the country, villagers had not been paying the small monthly tax which was to be used to help operate and maintain their local water supply systems.
financially very costly and physically almost im-
many of the public standposts because of fre-
lism on taps, drainage facilities, protective fences,
esult, in a few areas the public standposts were
vendor operations in which a licensed vendor
d rate for the metered standpost water and sells
(debe) at a fee slightly higher than he pays. The

difference between the kiosk operator's buying and selling price does not have to be large because most of the rural kiosks are operated by the wife or children of the vendor, and their opportunity cost is low. The result of the switch to kiosks is that vandalism has been greatly reduced (the tap and meter are locked up when not in use), a small amount of revenue has been generated, and the rate at which people have applied for house connections has increased. (Some people presumably feel that, if they are going to have to pay for water, it might as well be convenient water.) A drawback to the system, however, is the inability of some kiosk operators to retain for any period of time the revenues collected from water sales, thereby forcing the water authority to collect its sales revenues daily from the kiosk operators, a rather costly alternative.

New Consumers or Communities

The previous section dealt with consumers who currently have a supply of water, and who may or may not be charged on the basis of the amount they actually consume. The question of pricing as an indicator of project benefit takes on a different complexion when related to the problem of deciding whether individual households or communities, hitherto relying on private sources of supply, should be supplied from a public system. Here, by definition, direct ex ante observation of the willingness of individual consumers to pay is not possible. We would also argue that the questionnaire approach to estimating individuals' willingness to pay has been shown to be virtually useless.

As far as new communities are concerned, the approach to this problem should be twofold. First, as an example, in India and in many Latin American countries, the necessary qualification for supply should be a community contribution, say of 20 to 30 percent of initial project costs. Where the smaller villages are concerned, this contribution may be a reasonable indication of the value placed upon the project; the larger or less democratic the village, and the more activities that it carries on as a community, the less this proxy can be relied upon.

This screening device should be supplemented, as far as possible, by analysis of other communities in the country in terms of the observed willingness of their inhabitants to pay for water (clearly such analysis should be extended to administrative and technical aspects). The greater the variation in the economic, cultural, and climatic conditions of the villages concerned, and the smaller the sample of such villages, the harder will be the task of estimating willingness to pay in those areas as yet unserved. Even in these circumstances, however, this discipline is valuable for policymakers in determining investment priorities, and there is no real alternative to the procedure.

A somewhat similar approach should be followed in deciding on whether or not to extend service to new consumers in areas currently served. As far as household connections are concerned, there is no real problem—individual willingness to pay for connection can easily be demonstrated. Where the issue is whether or not to extend standposts into a new area of a community, there would be no problem if (a) the consumers concerned had cultural and economic characteristics fairly similar to those in other parts of the community (or in other communities) who currently had standpost supplies; and (b) if those currently served were able to demonstrate willingness to pay by the means described in the foregoing section. Where these conditions do not exist, little guidance is available to the policymaker as to the economic merits of the investment, and a method of trial and error is his only course of action.

The Problem of Geographically Uniform Tariffs

A particularly important application of the incremental cost-pricing principle is to be found in the establishment of a charging policy for nationwide or statewide water boards, which may serve hundreds of different communities. The question at issue, one highly relevant for village water supplies, is how one should respond to what seems to be a mounting pressure for geographically uniform prices. This pressure is important, not only because of the strength of the emotional appeals for uniform water rates, but also because of the wide variations in costs of supply within relatively small geographical areas.

The observed tendency toward uniformity results in part from the growing recognition that, in the interest of operational efficiency, particularly where skilled manpower is at a premium, consolidation of the management of water authorities into large regional, state, or countrywide water boards is often desirable. For no sound reason—except to some extent in those cases in which the water board is set up to permit a grid system to be established where at least marginal production costs will tend to greater geographical uniformity—the replacement of a number of small water authorities by one water board often involves the replacement of many different pricing policies by one uniform tariff schedule.

Another explanation for the trend toward increasing uniformity is the improvement in communications which allows residents of remote communities to become aware of the prices that consumers in other parts of the country are being asked to pay for water. Parallel to those arguments which have been heard in the past regarding variations in water charges within cities and which have been successful in eliminating surcharges for consumers who live on hillsides or in the less densely populated suburbs, it is alleged that only a uniform rate of charge is equitable. Because, it is said, a gallon of water is a gallon of water wherever it is supplied, a village should not be penalized if supplying it with water happens to be relatively expensive.

There are many examples one can cite of the unfortunate effects of uniform water pricing on land use. In one African country in which uniform water charges are in force, a brewery was located in an area where existing water supplies were of a sufficiently high quality but capacity was on the verge of full utilization. Although additional water could readily have been supplied, its extremely high fluoride content meant that it could not be used for brewing beer, and treating it would have been very costly. Convenient sources of low fluoride water soon ran out, and the brewery eventually closed down, to be reopened at a later date only when high-cost water was transported from many miles away. The initial brewery-location decision in this case was most inefficient, and stemmed in effect from a failure to levy charges for water (of an acceptable quality) that reflected incremental costs.

Aside from their direct impact on locational choice, if prices reflected the incremental costs of supply in different areas, a valuable discipline might be imposed on regional or urban planners. In the same African country, a number of development areas, or "growth poles," have been designated. As uniform water charges are levied throughout the country, the choice of industrial location is not influenced by the cost of water. Unfortunately, the incremental costs of water for many of the growth poles are not known even by the planners. If industry expects to be faced with costs which vary according to geographical location, it would make inquiries as to expected water or other charges, thereby forcing planners to carry out the necessary cost estimates, and indirectly to improve the efficiency of their plans.[8]

Paradoxically, the geographically uniform water rate is also frequently the cause of further adjustments to tariff structures that are unwarranted by variations in cost. One argument used in developing countries to defend the uniform rate is the necessity to ensure that the poor obtain water, based on the assumptions, first, that economies of scale and of population density mean that urban areas are the cheapest to supply on a per capita basis; and, second, that the smaller the community, the poorer the people. Whereas, for a given standard of service, the first assumption will usually be true (see the discussion on scale economies in Chapter 4), there are, as has been previously discussed, some problems in blindly accepting the second assumption. Given the goal of providing cheap water to poor people, the geographically uniform tariff is usually associated with an increasing block rate in which the more one consumes, the higher the price paid for incremental consumption. In efficiency terms this might produce the worst of both worlds: between villages, prices are uniform when costs vary; within villages, there are variations in price which do not reflect cost differences. Moreover, quite apart from the allocative inefficiency of the increasing block rate, it may also have adverse income distributional consequences.

Although the adjustment is designed to take advantage of the presumed positive income elasticity of demand for water, the final

---

8. Some idea of the extent of cross-subsidization that may be involved in setting geographically uniform water rates can be gained from a study of the cost of supplying a rural community in England. The cost of water mains alone was $7,000 per house, which at the time was about the mean value of houses in the area. Yet water revenues were estimated at about $50 per house annually, an amount that in the water board area as a whole was sufficient to cover accounting costs. This prompted the Ministry of Housing and Local Government, then responsible for the administration of subsidies for rural water supply, to ask whether or not it would be cheaper to relocate families rather than to continue to supply them with expensive services—not only water but also transportation and other utilities. Estimates were made of the net savings that would result from relocation and implications for pricing and administration were drawn (see J. J. Warford, *The South Atcham Scheme,* report submitted to the Minister of Housing and Local Government [London: Her Majesty's Stationery Office, 1969]). Relocation of rural populations would probably be more of a feasible alternative in developing countries, where sunk infrastructure costs are not as great.

outcome may still be the effective subsidization of relatively high-income rural consumers by low-income urban slum dwellers. Moreover, even within an urban or village area, the increasing block rate may be regressive in its effect, a fact illustrated by another brewery example—this time in a small South American community. As the largest water consumer in the community, the brewery also paid the highest per unit price for water, much higher than even the wealthiest residential consumer. It is probable that the higher price for water was reflected in higher beer prices, and because beer formed a relatively high proportion of the expenditure of low-income groups in the village, this policy was probably regressive.

If, where variations in price are administratively feasible, uniform pricing is chosen instead to achieve certain objectives, such as maximization of the number of consumers or extension of supply to low-income groups, a form of price discrimination is in effect being practiced. In common with most other discriminatory pricing schemes, this approach is likely to yield an inefficient allocation of resources and to result in inefficient locational decisions. Indeed, the uniform-charges policy is such a cumbersome instrument that it will only be by chance that the intended objectives are in fact realized. It is a perfect illustration of the difficulties which arise from not using cost as a basis for establishing water tariffs.

Other Methods of Regulating Consumption

Where direct regulation of consumption by price is ruled out, a variety of methods may still be called upon by water authorities to conserve water. Some of these allow consumers' willingness to pay for water to be revealed, albeit indirectly, and therefore have the characteristic of a pricing policy. Others rely on legal or social pressure, or on physical restrictions. Some examples follow.

Individual House Reservoirs. The rural water supply program in Argentina makes use of a system of individual house water tanks, or reservoirs, both to regulate the flow of water and to charge according to the volume of water consumed. A cement tank sitting on top of each house has a small hole through which the water flows, taking a considerable time to fill up the tank. The inhabitants of the house can use the water in whatever quantity they want until the tank is empty. Generally, the water users ration their consumption over the period of a day, so that the tank is never quite dry except perhaps in the evening. The tank can then refill throughout the night.

180 § PROGRAM PLANNING

People pay different water charges according to whether they want tank inlets (orifices) rated at 300, 500, 800, or 1,000 liters. The tanks, or cement house reservoirs, come in two sizes: 300 and 500 liters. The 300-liter tank serves the 300- and 500-liter inlets (the orifice is larger so that the tank refills more rapidly for a 500-liter inlet); the 500-liter tank serves the 800- and 1,000-liter inlets. The price charged for water varies by village but, in general, the monthly water rate for the 300-liter inlet is approximately 1 to 2 percent of the monthly income of the water consumers. This device therefore acts as a means of pricing and regulation of consumption and is probably much cheaper than metering.

The one potential danger of a system like this, however, is that, since all water consumers have roof tanks, there may be the temptation at some future date to provide users with intermittent service. Such an event could result in a marked deterioration in the health benefits of the system.

Flat Rates, with Rules about Consumption. In many countries a flat monthly rate is charged for each house connection, with rules about how the water may be used. The rules sometimes specify that only the family cow, horse, and chickens may be watered with the potable water, or that certain plants or trees that consume a lot of water cannot be grown near the water tap. Often the wasting of water is prohibited (failing to turn the tap off), and the village water committee, or council, has the right to disconnect people's water supply either for water wastage or nonpayment of water bills.

In areas where some of the residents desire to water their livestock during dry seasons, there may be communal animal-watering stations, or residents may be allowed to purchase an extra water outlet and have it installed near their residence so that they can water their livestock there. In the case of communal livestock-watering stations, water might be provided free or each resident might have to pay a monthly fee for the right to water livestock. Where the resident acquires an additional outlet to water his livestock he usually has to pay a rate approximately equal to what he would have to pay for another individual house connection. In countries that have financially viable water supply programs, and that charge for water, the monthly flat fee water rate for house connections rarely exceeds 5 percent of estimated monthly income. Several forms of price discrimination, in addition to that based solely on quantity of water consumed, are also generally practiced. For example, in a number of countries most rural household users are charged a flat rate, whereas any large users in the village (village industry, and so on) are metered. Also the use of outlets for livestock watering, or for gardens, can be charged at a higher or lower rate than the household rate. In some areas of Kenya, for example, the domestic rate is set in an attempt to cover both fixed and variable costs whereas the cattle rate is supposed to cover only variable pumping costs.[9]

In most countries, different rates are charged to families that use public fountains, or standposts, than to those that have house connections. Those with house connections have to pay not only an initial connection fee but also a higher monthly charge than those who use public fountains. In many instances, despite the greater cost of house connections, the proportion of the village with house connections increases fairly rapidly through time. Real incomes increase and there seems to be a demonstration effect existing: as people begin to perceive the advantages of having a house connection they somehow manage to save the money necessary to acquire and maintain one. The trend is sometimes reinforced (as in several Latin American countries) by the closure of public fountains after a certain percentage of the village has house connections, leaving the remainder little alternative but to connect also, or to purchase water from neighbors.

In some countries and cultures the collection of monthly flat-rate water charges is difficult. Generally, arrears seem to be less of a problem in Central and South America than in some portions of Africa where water is viewed as a special gift from God and therefore always free. Head taxes or house taxes for water in some rural areas of both East Africa and West Africa have been quite unsatisfactory, with collection rates of less than 20 percent.

Social Pressure and Physical Restrictions. When a flat-rate water fee is instituted, water wastage can, in some countries and cultures, be a problem. There are essentially two means of dealing with this problem: community moral suasion and the installation of flow-limiting devices. Throughout much of Latin America and in some areas in Asia, country officials claim that community moral suasion has been sufficient to keep water wastage within acceptable limits. A village water committee, or village council, attempts to police the

---

9. I. D. Carruthers, *Rural Water Investment in Kenya: Impact and Economics of Community Water Supply* (London: University of London, Wye College, 1972).

water wastage problem, and if anyone persists in not turning off the tap he is either barred from using the public fountains, his house connection is disconnected, or a flow-limiting device is installed at his residence.

In addition to fears that the reservoir may run dry and that pumping costs will increase, the problem of drainage is a factor inducing the water committee and the water system users to act against water wasters. In most rural areas improved drainage does not exist and, as a result, wastewater can become small pools of stagnant water and mud.

In those cases where for reasons of location, culture, education, or habit it is projected that it will be difficult to induce the population to refrain from wasting water, or where the source of supply is small relative to potential demand, it might be necessary to install flow-limiting devices on all nonmetered outlets in the system. Besides the Argentina house-reservoir system for limiting flow and setting price, there seem to be a number of different flow-limiting devices functioning throughout the world. A small-diameter pipe or a pipe with a small orifice appears to be the most common means of limiting house connection wastage. In this case, even if the tap is left open twenty-four hours a day (it usually is when filling containers) wastage will not be great. Unfortunately, consumers eventually either enlarge the orifice or remove it altogether.

Public standposts with some form of spring-loaded tap are also relatively common.[10] But villagers are usually quite ingenious at inventing means to tie open the tap, or somehow to fault the spring mechanism. A variation of the spring-loaded tap is a gravity-operated public standpost tap used in several states in India. This tap dispenses water when the mouthpiece is lifted and stops when the mouthpiece is released. The problem again is that it is relatively easy to wedge the mouthpiece permanently open with a stick, rock, or piece of wire. These taps also seem to be subject to above-average leakage.

More sophisticated self-closing taps are also in use, but on a more limited scale. Among the various types are the fordilla valve, Aquatrol valve, Tylor "Waste Not" valve, and the Tropicale device.

---

10. For a description of the physical and technical aspects of various types of public standposts and wastage control devices used on public standposts, see C. A. deVlieger and others, "Drinking Water Supply by Public Hydrants in Developing Countries," draft final report (The Hague, Voorburg: WHO International Reference Centre for Community Water Supply, October 1975).

These are generally constructed using some form of piston or plunger which automatically shuts off the water after a liter or two has been dispensed.

If the objective of the flow-limiting device is to reduce wastage but not to reduce beneficial consumption significantly, fordilla-type valves are probably an acceptable solution. This depends, however, almost entirely on the amount of maintenance they require. A number of favorable reports on their usage are available, including one from Asunción, Paraguay,[11] and one from St. Lucia.[12] Imitations of the fordilla-type valve, manufactured locally, have been used in other places, however, and problems of leakage and breakage have been significant. Also, the use of a sophisticated flow-limiting device may increase the per user construction cost of the distribution system and will certainly require more specialized maintenance personnel. This increased system cost must of course be compared with the savings in production and capacity costs achievable by the use of a flow limiter.

An economically and financially cheaper, and less sophisticated, version of a flow-limiting device is a crank-operated water paddle wheel which has been used on public standposts in some areas of both Nigeria and Cameroon. It consists of a small reservoir tank in which the water level is maintained by a float mechanism. Water is splashed from this tank into a receiving funnel by turning a crank attached to a form of paddle wheel at the water level inside the tank. When properly maintained the device seems to function reasonably well; it does not dispense water except when the crank is being turned, is made locally, and takes a relatively low level of skill to maintain and repair. The problem is that paddle wheel bearings tend to wear out, and crank handles tend to be stolen, and if the wheel is not maintained regularly very little water can be dispensed.

Another wastage-limiting device for public standposts that makes use of a reservoir and float mechanism operates essentially as a siphoning tank for water (used in Gabon and Cameroon). In this case, on the outside of a tank there is a nipple connected to a fixed

---

11. E. K. G. Borjesson and Carlos M. Bobeda, "New Concept in Water Service for Developing Countries," *Journal of the American Water Works Association* 56, no. 7 (1964):853–62.

12. Gladwin O. Unrau, "Individual Household Water Supplies in Rural St. Lucia as a Control Measure against Schistosoma Mansoni" (New York: The Rockefeller Foundation, 1974).

tube extending inside the tank down into the water. Each water consumer brings his own plastic tube which is inserted over the outside nipple. The consumer then sucks on the tube until water begins to flow. The disadvantage with this means of dispensing water is that little children, who enjoy making gurgling noises, have a considerable propensity to blow into the nipples, thus contaminating the water. Also, the tubes used by individual consumers tend to become contaminated rapidly.

In areas where water pressure is low, or water supply intermittent, a handpump sitting on top of an underground reservoir or cistern has proven useful. Of course another means of limiting water consumption is the conscious provision of intermittent water service to users. Although this procedure could cut down on water production and storage costs, it also undoubtedly reduces the potential benefits of the system. People tend to use other water sources when the system is not operating, thereby negating much of the health benefits of the system. Furthermore, wastewater can seep into the distribution lines when they are not under pressure. This would not only compromise the quality of the water the system provides but could occasion the system's being the vehicle for the spread of disease. Finally, intermittent service in some instances actually increases water use. This is the case if, during the period the water is flowing, people fill all available containers whether or not the water is eventually used. They might do this because of an uncertainty about when the water will be turned on again.

The Willingness- and Ability-to-Pay Criterion

There are a number of arguments against relying entirely upon the willingness of consumers to pay as a criterion for supplying them with water. These include consideration of external benefits, the extent of consumer knowledge, and the ability to pay.

Externalities, Consumer Knowledge, and Ability to Pay

An external benefit that might result from the consumption of potable water is that the health of X might improve because he makes use of an improved supply, and as a consequence X may not infect Y, whose future health would also improve. However, since X would not take the health of Y into account in his decision to consume potable water, his willingness to pay would tend to understate the benefits that would accrue to the community as a whole. Another argument is simply that the villagers may not understand (like the rest of us) the relationship between improved water supply and health: the assumption of a well-informed consumer is essential if normative judgments are to be made about the expression of his willingness to pay.

Apart from the issues of externality and consumer information, both of which are primarily relevant to the health question, the major criticism of the willingness-to-pay criterion is that, if strictly enforced, it would effectively mean that large numbers of people would never, or at least would not for many years, obtain adequate water supplies. To be a useful concept, willingness to pay has to assume an ability to pay. As noted earlier, the combination of low per capita incomes and higher per capita costs (for a given quality of service) in rural areas constitutes a formidable obstacle to improvement in the rural water supply field. Any rapid expansion of service to the rural poor requires that the willingness-to-pay criterion be modified to allow low-income groups to obtain at least a basic supply of water for minimum health needs. In practice, therefore, subsidy might be necessary, and current practice in this regard is described below.

Financial Subsidies and Ability to Pay: Current Practice

We have observed that many different methods of charging for water are used in developing countries, but in most countries it is fairly clear that rural consumers normally pay less than average system costs, and frequently even fail to cover operation and maintenance costs. In fact, the WHO data presented in Tables 7.1 and 7.2 show that, of those rural programs surveyed, well over half require only partial payment, or no payment at all, toward system operation and maintenance costs.

Since the primary rationale for subsidization of rural water supply is the lack of the beneficiaries' ability to pay, two questions should be investigated: the average real income of the population and the amount of that income that can be spent on water. Money income may be very different from real income in rural areas, primarily because of the prevalence of subsistence agriculture. With little or no reliable data available on either money or real income in rural villages, the estimation of the real income of rural populations is an extremely difficult task.

Table 7.1. Patterns of User Participation in Covering Cost of Urban Water Supply and Sewers
(Number of countries)

World Health Organization region	Operation, maintenance, and capital repayment		Operation, maintenance, and partial capital repayment		Operation and maintenance only		Partial operation and maintenance		No payment	
	Water	Sewer	Water	Sewer	Water	Sewer	Water	Sewer	Water	Sewer
Africa	14	2	6	5	1	4	7	4	1	3
Central and South America	14	6	10	9	8	6	9	8	—[a]	4
Eastern Mediterranean	5	2	8	4	8	2	11	4	1	2
Algeria, Morocco, Turkey	—[a]	—[a]	1	1	2	1	—[a]	—[a]	1	—[a]
Southeast Asia	2	1	2	1	3	1	3	3	—[a]	4
Western Pacific	3	2	3	—[a]	—[a]	1	3	1	—[a]	4
Total	38	13	30	20	22	15	33	20	3	17

a. Nil or magnitude negligible.
Source: Same as Table 1.1, p. 753.

Table 7.2. Patterns of User Participation in Covering Costs of Rural Water Supply
(Number of countries)

World Health Organization region	Operation, maintenance, and capital repayment	Operation, maintenance, and partial capital repayment	Operation and maintenance only	Partial operation and maintenance	No payment
Africa	2	4	6	11	10
Central and South America	3	9	7	11	4
Eastern Mediterranean	1	2	7	12	9
Algeria, Morocco, Turkey	—a	—a	1	—a	2
Southeast Asia	—a	2	2	3	5
Western Pacific	1	2	1	1	4
Total	7	19	24	38	34

a. Nil or magnitude negligible.
Source: Same as Table 1.1, p. 753.

Even if the real income level was known there is the second question: What amount of a family's real income *can* be spent on water? A frequently used rule-of-thumb reply is that a rural near-subsistence family should never have to spend more than about 5 percent of its income for water. This 5 percent-of-income figure is usually more than most urban dwellers pay for the water they consume from the public system. Table 7.3 presents very tentative estimates of the percent of household income spent for water in twelve selected cities in developing countries. According to these estimates, it may be seen that the lowest income group pays about 5 percent of household income only in São Paulo and Lima and more than 5 percent in Addis Ababa, Manila, and Nairobi. In the remaining seven cities the figure is considerably less than 5 percent.

There are several reasons, however, why any reliance on an arbitrary 5 percent of income rule as an "appropriate maximum percentage" is fraught with hazards. Clearly, the "appropriate percentage" will be determined in large measure by the degree of monetization of the local economy, the cost of other essential items, and so on. Furthermore, who is to decide what the word "appropriate" means in each case? Who decides that the villager should give up an additional three glasses of beer a week and one pair of

Table 7.3. Estimated Monthly Water Charges as a Percentage of Estimated Monthly Income, by Income Group, Twelve Selected Cities

City	Income group (and consumption category by liters)				
	Lowest 20 percent (7,000)	Second 20 percent (15,000)	Third 20 percent (27,000)	Fourth 20 percent (36,000)	Upper 20 percent (40,000)
Addis Ababa (1972)	8.70	7.89	7.70	6.17	2.46
Ahmedabad (1971)	4.25	4.28	10.53	11.70	27.19
Bogotá (1971)	0.67	0.70	1.04	0.83	1.51
Bangkok (1972)	0.49	1.12	2.19	2.02	0.86
Cartegena (1971)	0.97	0.84	1.23	1.25	0.62
Kingston (1971)	1.76	3.04	6.05	3.75	0.81
Lima (1971)	4.96	2.34	1.25	1.41	0.56
Manila (1970)	9.27	1.67	1.65	1.50	0.72
Mexico City (1970)	0.41	0.33	0.38	0.29	0.17
Nairobi (1970)	6.80	5.51	6.00	3.93	1.88
São Paulo (1970)	4.71	2.28	3.35	2.85	0.90
Seoul (1972)	0.36	0.32	0.55	0.61	0.49

Note: Water charges are estimated from tariff schedules and estimated water consumption figures for households in the individual cities. Income is the estimated monthly income of households.
Source: Computed by Kenneth Hubbell from survey data.

shoes each year in order to pay a monthly water charge that covers total cost, or that is equal to marginal cost?

Even if a villager can pay for water, he may not be willing to alter his current expenditure pattern, or reduce his slight savings each month, in order to improve the quantity or quality of water he and his family consume. If this is the case, there are two alternatives available to the water supply authorities once they have decided that the villager needs, and will be provided with, an improved water supply. First, they can attempt to alter the villager's perception of the "value" to him and his family of a better water supply. There are various means by which this might be done, but generally they involve some form of demonstration or education program acquainting the villager with the more obvious benefits of improved water and sanitation. If this education function is successful, the villager will then perceive greater benefits from the improved water supply or sanitation system, value the improved system more highly, and therefore be willing to pay a higher price for it.

The second alternative is for the water supply authorities to subsidize the village system, using the rationale that the unrealized or unperceived benefits which accrue to the villagers, together with the benefits external to the villagers but which accrue to society as a whole, make the subsidy worthwhile.

A few countries, particularly in Latin America, have attempted to gather information on the ability to pay of village dwellers by undertaking so-called social, or socioeconomic, surveys of villages. These surveys generally have consisted of little more than forms on which a casual observer documents his impressions of a village after visiting it for an hour or two. Several of the more elaborate surveys have contained a sometimes lengthy set of questions essentially asking villagers about their income and what price they could (or would be willing to) pay for the water supply system that was probably going to be installed. Questionnaire approaches such as these almost always produce very low estimates of ability and willingness to pay. This result is not surprising, as it amounts to approaching a group of individuals, strongly hinting that they are going to receive a certain good, and then asking if they would prefer to (or could) pay a high price or a low price for that good.

A few more rigorous case studies have been undertaken attempting to determine the amount a given population at a specific point in time can pay for water.[13] Studies such as these, however, are expensive to carry out, and it is difficult to generalize about their specific results. Even if generalization were possible, there would still be problems of implicit, subjective judgments.

Given the difficulties described, we have particular doubts as to the practical relevance of the concept of ability to pay in arriving at a judgment about willingness to do so. There is much evidence that even where consumers are wealthy, they often refuse to pay or otherwise cause difficulties for a water authority which is attempting to introduce or increase water charges. This leads us to suggest that the only way in practice to address this issue is, rather than to conduct elaborate, assumptive socioeconomic surveys, to "test the market" by the gradual introduction of new tariff policies, and then to observe consumer reaction before deciding to increase those charges or to expand capacity.

13. See, for example, Pan American Health Organization, "Rural Water Supply Services, Community Financing," Special Meeting of Ministers of Health of the Americas, Buenos Aires, 14–18 October 1968, Working Documents, 1969, Official Document no. 90 (Washington, D.C., 1969); and José A. Chico Romero, "Financing of Water Supply Programs for Rural Communities in El Salvador," *Boletín de la Oficina Sanitaria Panamericana* 69, no. 2 (1970): 141–46.

proaches have also been recommended. One knowledgeable observer (only partly in jest) opined that a low cost way, as good as any to judge the economic state of a village, is to watch what the inhabitants are drinking. He contended that the relative quality (and cost) of the alcoholic beverages consumed usually gives a reliable indication of whether or not the village has the ability (not the willingness) to pay for water.

The general lack of any hard evidence on ability (and willingness) to pay has resulted in the politically expedient assumption, which has been made in most developing countries, that the rural population cannot pay the full cost of water. As noted earlier, in a number of Asian and Latin American countries, the beneficiary village is expected to make only a partial contribution of between 10 and 30 percent to construction costs, and to pay only for the operation and maintenance of the system. Experience in these countries suggests that this is a minimum prerequisite for program viability. In a few countries, however, rural consumers do not pay at all. These countries argue that potable water is a basic human right, irrespective of ability to pay, and as a result the national government should completely subsidize the rural water supply program from national general revenues. Tanzania and Zambia provide good examples of this philosophy, although their neighbor, Kenya, does not generally subscribe to it.

The most prominent or frequently stated rule of thumb about an acceptable minimum a village should be required to pay to be eligible to receive an improved water supply system in the first place is that the village should at least be able to cover ongoing operation and maintenance expenses. This principle probably has as its base a form of administrative rationality in that it simplifies local accounting, and it bestows upon the villagers the psychological satisfaction of paying for what they can see is taking place. In addition, there is the financial consideration that capital funds are relatively easy to budget, get grants for, and so on, whereas adequate funds for operation and maintenance tend to be more difficult to generate from central government sources. From an economic point of view, however, if the villagers are to be partially subsidized, it makes no difference whether the subsidy occurs for their operating expenses or for the capital costs of the project. A capital costs–operating costs dichotomy for purposes of subsidy can hardly affect the magnitude of the health and economic benefits the villagers receive from the project.

Part Four | *Summary*

8 | Conclusions and Recommendations

ACHIEVEMENT OF THE UNITED NATIONS Development Decade targets described in Chapter 1 is clearly a task beyond the capability of many countries. In an absolute sense, however, the targets themselves are modest, and in many regions of the developing world represent the beginning of a long and arduous campaign to improve the lot of rural populations. In these pages we have surveyed the problem in its magnitude, examining its economic, social, technical, financial, and administrative aspects. Summarized below are our major conclusions and recommendations.

Population to Be Served

1. A number of factors can be considered in choosing who should benefit from a rural water supply and sanitation program. The program may have many objectives, such as improved health, economic development, real income redistribution, influencing migration patterns, and so on. Water supply and sanitation development policies should be determined by these objectives, subject to resource constraints, rather than by an arbitrary dichotomy between so-called urban and rural programs. There is no universal definition of the terms "rural" and "urban" which fits all developing countries and all of the possible objectives of water supply investment.

2. The more dispersed the population to be served, the less likely is a water supply system to be financially viable, and properly maintained, not only because of lower per capita village income but also because average system costs, for a given standard of service, will be higher.
3. It is possible that water supply systems together with improved sanitation and other complementary investment programs could slow rural-to-urban migration rates. There is little evidence, however, that, in the short run, a rural water supply program, by itself, will have any effect on migration. In fact, in the long run, if the water supply program resulted in a healthier, more potentially productive rural population, the lack of rural employment opportunities could cause an increase in the flow of population into urban areas.
4. Although the short-run migration effects of a rural water supply and sanitation program are doubtful, it is more likely that potable water supply systems can be used to encourage, over a period of time, the grouping of dispersed populations into more economically viable village units.

Economic Development

5. Although a potable water supply for residents of a village may be a necessary condition for significant economic development, it is clearly not sufficient—even as a catalyst—to achieve this objective.
6. Concentrating water supply and sanitation investment in rural growth points will tend to increase the long-run economic development impact of the investment.
7. A strategy of assigning the highest priority for improved water supply and sanitation to the smaller, poorer, and least educated rural villages is a high cost and extremely risky venture. These villages generally have higher per capita construction costs, and have difficulty contributing financial resources to construction, or levying charges adequate to cover even operation and maintenance expenses.
8. Investing in complementary programs (health education, crop improvement, feeder roads, marketing information, and so on) will increase the probability that the water supply and sanitation

program will have an economic development impact on an area.
9. If in semiarid regions or in areas with a dry season a village water supply system is designed to include the provision that livestock can be watered and small gardens irrigated, the probability that the system will have a signficant economic impact is substantially increased.
10. Underemployment is a common characteristic of rural areas in developing countries. Together with the frequently observed overvaluation of local currency, this condition points to the need to shadow price inputs in order that, in terms of real resources, the least-cost means of construction and operation is selected. Shadow-pricing exercises themselves are costly, however, and an educational problem exists in persuading the relevant authorities, contractors, and consultants to apply economic analysis to investment decisions. Furthermore, the financial consequences of using shadow pricing may prove unpalatable to the water supply or relevant fiscal authority.

Health-Related Benefits

11. The review of the twenty-eight empirical studies (see Appendix A) that examine the relation between the quantity and quality of water consumed, sanitary facilities, and the level of various water and sanitation-associated diseases, provides some evidence that more and better water and better sanitary facilities are associated with better health.
12. The empirical health studies also suggest that the degree of improvement in health to be expected in any given population depends on the level of health in the first place, the economic state, cultural habits, educational level, the general physical environment including adequate means of waste disposal, and income level. Because of the interdependence of these factors, in two different villages identical water supply improvements can have significantly different results.
13. In many rural areas of developing countries unskilled labor is abundant and is greatly underemployed. A rural water supply and sanitation program, designed solely to improve the health of the labor force, may therefore increase the extent to which there

is an oversupply of labor but have very little impact on economic output and earnings.

14. Most studies have shown that water and sanitation-related health improvements are much greater among children, who are not members of the labor force. Consequently, with respect to rural localities in which income-generating work may be found, estimates of increased income generation brought about by water supply-induced health improvements must take into account both the age distribution and the distribution of skills among the population.

15. There is some evidence, with regard to waterborne diseases such as typhoid and cholera, that improved sanitation is, in the long run, more effective and less expensive than vaccination. In a more general sense, preventive medicine is usually more cost effective than curative medicine, and water supply and sanitation are key elements of preventive medicine.

16. There are several different methods by which changes in mortality and morbidity rates can be valued. The most workable seems to be to discount any changes in expected lifetime earnings resulting from water supply and sanitation-induced better health. This method has the defect of the dubious assumption that the economic output of humans reflects the value of life and health.

17. Factors that affect benefits also affect costs of a project. One approach to the cost-health improvement problem is to formulate it in terms of the question: what amount of improvement in the major disease rates (valued either qualitatively or in income terms) would it take to make a given investment (and the level of service implied by that investment) worthwhile?

18. Studies of the association between health and water supply and sanitation allowing an accurate prediction of health (and economic) improvements under a variety of circumstances have not been carried out. The primary reasons for this failure are (a) that social, economic, and physical conditions vary greatly among target populations, precluding accurate generalizations; (b) that the sampling problems and problems of uncontrollable exogenous factors greatly increase the probability of significant errors in the results; and (c) that the water supply-health relationship is highly collinear with a variety of economic, environmental, social, and cultural factors, the effects of which are difficult, if not impossible, to isolate.

Redistribution of Income

19. Investments in rural water supply systems and sanitation facilities in developing countries are sometimes claimed to be a useful means of redistributing real income from higher income urban areas to lower income rural areas. The assumptions are that most of the real resources used in the rural water supply program would have been allocated to, and consumed in, urban areas; that the rural water supply program would not use resources otherwise consumed by low income, urban-slum dwellers; and that subsidization would be a feature of the financing plan.
20. If redistribution of income is one of the goals of the water supply and sanitation program, a national or regional water board with responsibility for urban and rural supplies may be in the best position to charge higher water tariffs to middle and upper income urban dwellers in order to subsidize lower income, urban-slum and rural dwellers. Such a water board would in effect be using water charges as a tax.
21. Redistribution of real income in a developing country may be accomplished through the water supply and sanitation sector by serving both rural villages and urban slums. Indeed, it is possible that meeting increasing urban water supply needs should take precedence over rural programs if a failure to do so requires that urban water supplies be furnished on an intermittent basis. Consequent wastewater seepage could turn a water distribution system into a vehicle for the transmission of disease. Eliminating intermittent water service is frequently of primary benefit to the lower income groups; for only middle and upper income groups have private storage tanks, or the money to install pumps to suck water from the main. Intermittent service in a rural village, it should be noted, might not be quite as undesirable from a health point of view because there will normally be no sewerage lines from which seepage can occur.
22. The income distribution case for financing rural water supply systems and sanitation programs is not as straightforward as is generally thought. In many countries, the wealthier villages receive priority in obtaining water supply because of their political influence, their greater awareness of the benefits of clean water, and the greater chance that their systems will operate efficiently. Furthermore, from a health and income distribution point of view, many higher income rural villages are prob-

ably less in need of assistance than the urban slums, where alternative sources of supply and means of disposal are less available, where greater population density may encourage communicable disease, and where, moreover, subsidies can be generated from higher income users in the larger metropolitan system.

System Design

23. In the design and construction of a rural water supply project, or a means of waste disposal, technology should be kept as simple as possible, so that local operators will be able to operate and maintain the system for long periods of time in the absence of a qualified engineer.
24. The design capacity of rural water supply systems should be at least partially dependent upon the presence of economies of scale and the relevant discount rate. In most instances, community needs for a period of not longer than six to ten years provide a reasonable design capacity.
25. The quality-of-service or design criteria for a rural water system should depend primarily on the system's desired goals. Whether or not village residents should have house connections or public standposts is part of the overall quality-of-service question and should be decided by considering (a) the quantity of water the villagers should consume to meet minimum health standards, and (b) the expressed demands of water consumers to pay for more convenient house installations.
26. There are economies of scale associated with water supply construction and, for equivalent levels of service, per capita costs of urban systems will usually be lower than for rural. Per capita costs of rural water supply installations, however, can be less than urban installations because per capita consumption may be less, and the quality of water service, lower. Investment programs should be specific in detailing the standards of service being sought, in order that misunderstandings by budgetary and national planning authorities may be avoided.

Administration and Finance

27. The major problem associated with providing water supplies in rural areas of developing countries relates to the operation and

maintenance of systems. It is difficult to find villages where the systems are working precisely as planned (both technically and financially), and it is common to find even relatively new systems which are not functioning at all.

28. Assigning a high priority for water service to villages able to pay a user fee at least sufficient to cover operation and maintenance expenses, and enthusiastic about receiving improved water, increases the probability that the water supply systems will remain operational for a significant period of time.

29. There is some evidence that villages tend to value their water systems more highly, make better use of the systems, and operate and maintain them more efficiently when they have contributed resources (labor or money) to help cover construction costs, and are paying user fees which at least cover operation and maintenance expenses.

30. Encouraging villages to contribute free labor to the construction of their piped water supply systems can lower both the economic and financial costs of the systems and can stimulate the rural population to take pride in their systems. Numerous instances, however, have been reported where difficulties with the reliability of the free labor force have more than negated any financial savings. In general, a community's contribution of free labor must be encouraged and closely supervised by a capable community water supply promoter, and any work he does to encourage and supervise the free labor should be counted as one of the costs of the labor.

31. There is some evidence that a community water supply and sanitation program that requires a contribution (labor or money) from village populations may be used as a catalyst to stimulate a community organizational infrastructure which will continue to function after the water supply project has been completed.

32. The level of education and skills existing among the rural population is one of the major factors to consider in determining whether or not the operation and maintenance phase of the program should have a national, regional, or local administrative base. When village systems are turned over to low income, relatively uneducated local authorities to operate, the probability of system failure is high. Many failures, however, have been accompanied by a reluctance on the part of central water authorities to use their best men for the highly important function

of training village operating personnel. In cases where it is decided that system operation and maintenance must be handled on a highly centralized basis, it is desirable at least to set up local village advisory committees so that local populations feel the water systems are their own and will take pride in seeing the systems operate properly.

33. To achieve efficient management and avoid duplication of effort, the national rural water supply and sanitation program should be under the control of, or be coordinated by, one national or regional agency. The specific agency to be in charge (an independent water board, ministry of public works, national planning or rural development authority, ministry of agriculture, etc.) should depend on the major goals of the program.

34. There are several advantages of combining urban and rural water supply systems under one semiautonomous water board. In particular, such a board could (a) provide a more stable source of revenue to subsidize (if necessary) rural operation and maintenance expenses, and (b) assure a greater availability of experienced engineers to supervise and provide technical assistance for operation and maintenance.

35. To increase the probability that permanent health and economic benefits will occur, the water supply and sanitation program should provide for the training of pump or system operators, bill collectors, and community promoters. An educational program for villagers focusing on good sanitation and water-use habits and on any village gardening or livestock watering potential of the system should also be provided.

36. An output-oriented, bonus incentive system for local and regional employees of the water supply program might be of value in increasing the probability that the continuing goals of the program are met at the local level.

Long-Term Strategy

37. Although the economic impact of investments in village water supply and sanitation cannot adequately be measured by standard benefit-cost techniques, allocation of resources to the sector is essentially an economic problem, the satisfactory solution of which requires somehow that project benefits be compared with project costs prior to making final investment decisions.

38. Doubtless it will be necessary to continue to rely heavily on rule-of-thumb tests for project desirability—such as convenience and quality of existing supplies, community development potential, and so on—but the real hope for rapid advancement in the sector is to place increasing reliance upon consumers' willingness to pay for the services they consume. Otherwise, since budgetary authorities cannot be presented with estimates of the economic benefits of investments in the sector, it is likely that economically justified projects will be rejected. Furthermore, potential beneficiaries from the extension of existing systems should be given the opportunity to demonstrate the direct value to them by the price they pay. Thus, even in relatively poor rural areas, people may prefer to have, and to pay for, a water supply, than to have none at all.

39. The principle, therefore, should be that those who can afford to pay the full (marginal) cost of water supply and sanitation facilities should be asked to do so. For water supply this rule will typically mean that house connections should be provided only to those who pay for the full cost of both connection and water actually consumed. Where house connections exist and metering is in force it may, however, be desirable to modify the principle so that an initial supply, the minimum for basic health needs, is provided at a low subsidized rate. Similarly, it may be desirable to finance standpost supply so that consumption is not reduced to an extent detrimental to public health. Where metering is not used, it is important that any flat-rate charge for water supply or sanitation facilities should be known as such, so that the principle of payment is established in the consumer's mind. A policy of full payment for all but the minimum basic supply is essential if expanding rural water supply and sanitation programs are not to produce an overwhelming fiscal burden on poor countries.

40. For those households too poor to pay for basic supply, the willingness-to-pay criterion is, by definition, ruled out. There is no precise way, however, to determine who should fall into this category, and it is fairly clear that in this regard "socioeconomic surveys" undertaken before project formulation constitute little improvement over the rule-of-thumb judgments normally employed by sanitary engineers. Moreover, such surveys have been shown to be of little assistance in determining pricing policy. Observation of consumer reaction to the introduction of water

charges or increases in existing charges generally provides the only useful evidence for this purpose.

41. In those circumstances in which the willingness-to-pay criterion has to be rejected, there is currently no scientific procedure for making investment decisions, including those about project ranking. Efforts should therefore be concentrated on ensuring that all consumers who are judged to have passed a defined threshold of poverty should be charged, whether by metering or not, the full economic cost their consumption entails. Implementation of such a policy is absolutely essential if significant progress is to be made in extending water supply and sanitation facilities to rural communities in the developing world.

Appendixes

A | Improved Water Supply and Sanitation: Studies of Its Impact on Health

Studies of Diarrheal Disease

CAUSES OF DIARRHEA CAN BE classified as bacterial, parasitic, and viral.[1] *Shigellae, Salmonellae,* and enteropathogenic *Escherichia coli* are the etiological agents of bacterially caused diarrhea, whereas various parasites including helminths are the parasitic agents. Diarrhea may also accompany various diseases of viral origin.

Perhaps one of the most interesting descriptions of some of the characteristics of diarrheal disease and of problems associated with controlling it is contained in the following passage from Wall and Keeve:

> The disease is a clinical syndrome, like the common cold, with distinguishable regular symptoms, but mostly indistinguishable infecting agents. Aside from the traditional water-related diseases caused by the bacteria *Shigella* and *Salmonella,* and cholera, which typically produce diarrhea, the syndrome remains inscrutable. There is no universally accepted definition of diarrhea. It is at best a complex of symptoms. Intensive worldwide studies have produced no bacterial cause, yet the disease acts as though it was due to some contagious agent, possibly viral as well as bacterial, but no definitive answer exists. An intensive

1. World Health Organization, "Summary Report on Diarrhoeal Diseases Studies in Seven Developing Countries over a Five-Year Period, 1960–1965" (Geneva, 1966).

two-year study of the life history of bacterial flora of the infant's gut from birth failed to explain most diarrheal episodes.

Even though diarrheal disease is present in all populations, its incidence, prevalence, severity, and fatality vary greatly by area of the world, by level of modernization, by season, by socioeconomic status, and by age group. In many areas of the world, the less developed areas, diarrheal disease is the single largest cause of death and illness. This much is known despite woefully inadequate vital statistics on morbidity and mortality. But much remains unknown, particularly about effective and economic control of the disease.[2]

The following studies on the relation between diarrheal disease and water supply are concerned essentially with bacteria-related causes of diarrhea.[3]

1. Helen Moore and others, "Diarrheal Disease Studies in Costa Rica," 1965–1966.

This study was undertaken to determine why gastrointestinal disease is the leading known cause of death in Costa Rica. Researchers examined general sanitary conditions, rectal swabs, stool specimens, fly populations, and the bacteria content of water supplies, meat, milk, and animals for a cross-section of the population. The conclusion was that piped water was important in reducing infections with enteropathogenic bacteria but was not greatly effective in reducing diarrheal morbidity or parasite infestation. Moore stated that "had a larger proportion of the diarrhea cases been of bacterial etiology, an effect on diarrhea morbidity might also have been visible." However, high rates of *Ascaris* infestation were noted with a lack of toilet facilities.

2. Arthur C. Hollister, Jr., and others, "Influence of Water Availability on *Shigella* Prevalence in Children of Farm Labor Families," 1955.

This test for *Shigella* involved between one-half and two-thirds of all children ten years and under in California, U.S.A., farm labor

---

2. John W. Wall and J. Phillip Keeve, "Water Supply, Diarrheal Disease, and Nutrition: A Survey of the Literature and Recommendations for Research," draft working paper (Washington, D.C.: World Bank, September 1974).

3. Full citations of case studies are listed in the bibliography.

camps. *Shigella* was found in 1.6 percent of those living in cabins with inside water faucets, showers (tubs), or toilets, 3.0 percent of those living in cabins with inside water faucets but with all other facilities communal, and 5.8 percent of those living in cabins with no inside water or other facilities. The researchers then examined a selected group, part of which had no inside facilities and part of which had only an inside faucet. (Both subgroups had approximately the same number of people per shower and per toilet, and approximately the same volume of flies and garbage.) The availability of water for personal hygiene made a great difference; only 1.2 percent of the group with indoor water had the disease while 5.9 percent of those without an indoor faucet were infected.

3. Leland J. McCabe and T. W. Haines, "Diarrheal Disease Control by Improved Human Excreta Disposal," 1957.

In 1952 a program was undertaken to upgrade the facilities for human excreta disposal in Boston, Georgia, U.S.A. Borehole privies were improved and expanded in 178 cases. This study showed a decrease in fly breeding in privies but no change in the number of flies. In eighteen months, however, following the improvements, there were significantly fewer *Shigella* infections in children under ten years of age.

4. D. J. Schliessmann and others, *Relationship of Environmental Factors to the Occurrence of Enteric Diseases in Areas of Eastern Kentucky,* 1958.

This was a study of conditions in seven mining camp areas of eastern Kentucky, U.S.A., from 1955 to 1957. Diarrheal disease rates were measured monthly by taking rectal swabs of preschool children. The presence of parasites was determined by the examination of stool specimens collected semi-annually from all age groups. Fly abundance and local water quality were also measured. The results of the study were that (a) *Shigella* and parasites were found most frequently in children from the area with the poorest sanitation; (b) people with piped water inside their houses but a privy outside had two times as much enteric disease, two times as much disease caused by *Shigella,* and three times as much disease caused by *Ascaris* as those with piped water and inside flush toilets; (c) *Ascaris* infestation was three times as high in people whose water supply was outside the house; (d) disease caused by *Shigella* was 5 percent lower in children who lived in homes with an indoor water supply; (e) rates of *Shigella* and *Ascaris* diseases were two to three times greater in people from homes without baths than with baths; (f) no association of disease rates with quality of drinking water was observed; (g) housefly abundance was not significantly correlated with morbidity or *Shigella* prevalence; and (h) the ratio of "summer" diarrhea to "winter" diarrhea for the years 1955 and 1956 was approximately two to one.

The authors concluded that the results of the study strongly support the premise that the incidence of acute infectious diarrheal disease may be reduced significantly through selective modification of specific environmental factors within communities without regard to etiological or sociological differences.

5. James Watt and others, "Diarrheal Diseases in Fresno County, California," 1953.

This was primarily a cross-section study of a sample of migrant farmers living under different types of conditions in Fresno County, California, U.S.A. Results showed that *Shigella* disease rates were lowest in housing projects with plumbing in each house, next lowest in the same type of housing but where the occupants had a lower socioeconomic level, higher in housing with no indoor plumbing but fewer than fifteen people per water outlet, and highest in housing with no indoor plumbing and with more than fifteen people per water outlet. A general conclusion was offered that if *Shigella* were eliminated, diarrheal diseases would be reduced by approximately two-thirds.

6. A. Rubenstein and others, "Effect of Improved Sanitary Facilities on Infant Diarrhea in a Hopi Village," 1969.

A Hopi Indian village in Arizona, U.S.A., was divided into two parts: an upper area in which indoor plumbing was installed and a lower area which was left unchanged. An examination of the health of infants was made "from hospital records" for both areas of the village both before and after the plumbing installations. The results showed that the average number of visits to the hospital per child in his first year of life declined in the upper village from 2.0 visits before indoor plumbing to 0.85 after indoor plumbing. At the same time the rate in the lower village was declining from 3.1 to 2.6. The decline in the upper village was statistically significant at the 0.05 level. The decline in the lower village was not.

Several problems with the study were noted. There seemed to be basic political and social differences between the two parts of the village which might influence the illness of infants; there was no control for breast feeding; many lower village mothers seemed reluctant to seek hospital assistance; and there was no record of who had refrigerators.

7. Miguel Kourany and Manuel Vásquez, "Housing and Certain Socioenvironmental Factors and Prevalence of Enteropathogenic Bacteria among Infants with Diarrheal Disease in Panama," 1969.

Cross-section data were collected from a sample of parents and from the National Census Bureau on housing, plumbing, sewage systems, number of plumbing outlets, the availability of running water, and diarrheal disease in infants. The general conclusion was that, as general sanitation increased, the rate of enteropathogenic *E. coli, Shigella,* and *Salmonella* infections decreased. Other variables which were found to be associated with diarrheal disease were the health habits of the people (negative) and the density of the (urban) population (positive).

8. William H. Stewart and others, "IV. Diarrheal Disease Control Studies: Relationship of Certain Environmental Factors to the Prevalence of *Shigella* Infection," 1955.

Researchers examined data on 28,000 rectal swab cultures from children in southwest Georgia, U.S.A. The data were grouped in four categories: poor, fair, good, or very good sanitation depending upon (a) location and type of water, (b) type of excreta disposal, (c) fly densities and potentials for fly population, (d) aesthetic quality of the house and surroundings, and (e) structural quality of the house. Among the conclusions of the study were the findings that (a) *Shigella* infection rates in a neighborhood vary with the proportion of poor housing; (b) infection rates were higher where water was least available for personal hygiene (the *availability of water* for washing purposes must now be considered along with *purity of water* in any diarrheal disease control program); (c) infection rates were significantly higher for premises with water sources "far from the house," regardless of whether it was well or city water.

9. World Health Organization, "Report of a Survey of Diarrhoeal Diseases in Mauritius," 1960.

On a cross-section basis, several samples of children and their families were physically examined and rectal swab cultures were taken. The following were among the conclusions of the examinations: (a) greater diarrheal infection rates were found among those who had a less readily available water supply; (b) there was less diarrhea among those using municipal water; (c) occurrences of malnutrition and gastroenteritis were independent (not related); and (d) diarrhea occurs in children who are both over and under the average height and weight.

10. World Health Organization, "Studies on Diarrhoeal Diseases," Venezuela, 1965.

Two villages were surveyed and briefly monitored. One, Pompanito, was given an improved water system that 100 percent of the population could use. The other, Monay, was essentially tank-truck supported. In Pompanito, 70 house connections and 22 standposts were set up. Generally the water was good at the source and in the distribution system but became contaminated in the house during storage. In Monay, the water was contaminated at the source. Some regular bathing was possible in Pompanito but not in Monay. Study results showed that diarrhea was "significantly" lower in Pompanito after the water system was introduced, while at the same time there was no significant change in diarrhea rates in Monay. Diarrhea was also found to be more prominent among the children.

11. World Health Organization, "Studies on Diarrhoeal Diseases in Venezuela," follow-up report, 1966.

This was a follow-up study of the above two villages and of several other areas. It included the collection of data on diarrhea cases (monthly), fly counts (biweekly), meteorological data (monthly), and water supply. Among the conclusions were that (a) the area with the worst sanitation had the highest diarrhea rates; (b) the incidence of flies and diarrhea is dependent on climatological conditions (more infections after rain); (c) contact, not flies, seems to be the way diarrhea spreads; (d) children with diarrhea checked at health centers had one or more of the following: parasitic infection, trichuriasis, infections caused by *Balantidium coli* and *Entamoeba histolytica,* and lambliasis; (e) the areas examined with the worst sanitation had the highest mortality rates.

12. World Health Organization, "Report of Studies on Diarrhoeal Diseases," Sudan, 1966.

This study attempted to compare two population groups which differed especially in their environmental sanitation. Among information collected were cross-section data on family size, housing, economic status, and sanitation as well as general information on diarrhea infections and specific information on rectal swabs. Among the conclusions were that (a) it took about twice as long to recover from a spell of diarrhea if the person had a lower standard of living; (b) most diarrhea occurred in children one to two years old; (c) zeers (porous water storage jars used by families) tended to be contaminated; (d) people who had unsanitary privies tended to have more diarrhea; (e) there was no correlation found between diarrhea cases and family ownership of animals; (f) the amount of water used was inversely correlated with diarrhea infections.

13. World Health Organization, "Report on Study of Diarrhoeal Diseases in Egypt," 1961.

Several villages were examined and a variety of socioeconomic and diarrheal infection data were collected on a cross-section basis. No results were drawn from a correlation of diarrhea with literacy, privy conditions, showers, animal availability, or water supply. General conclusions were that (a) sanitation and education were the long-run solution to the diarrhea problem; (b) diarrhea was most prevalent in the zero to two years age group; (c) diarrheal disease was a very great problem in the areas examined.

14. World Health Organization, "Summary Report on Diarrhoeal Diseases Studies in Seven Developing Countries over a Five-Year Period, 1960–1965," 1966.

Between 1960 and 1965, surveys on diarrheal diseases were carried out in Mauritius, Sudan, United Arab Republic (UAR), Sri Lanka, Iran, East Pakistan, and Venezuela. This document summarizes the studies abstracted above as items 9, 10, 12, and 13, as well as the studies that took place in Sri Lanka, Iran and East Pakistan, and which were essentially cross-sectional in nature. Among the general conclusions of the studies were that (a) "with the availability of water the rate of reported diarrhea was found to decrease. A similar decrease in the isolation rate of *Shigellae* was evident. The trend of the figures was always in the same direction. Differences between the reporting rates of diarrhea in water-supplied and nonwater-supplied areas were statistically significant in the UAR and Iran. Differences in the isolation rates of *Shigellae* in the UAR and Venezuela were also statistically significant." (b) "The availability of water definitely influenced the incidence of diarrhea. However, in all areas with basic sanitation, where a piped-water supply was available, diarrhea rates were reduced but still remained at a high level. This indicates that such a facility alone. without complete sanitation, was of little benefit to the population in so far as reducing the incidence of diarrhea was concerned." (c) "Provision of a piped-water supply to a community with only basic sanitation led to a statistically significant reduction of diarrhea and rates for *Shigellae* and *Balantidium coli*. However, in all countries where investigations were made, the real reduction was very little and of limited practical importance. Likewise, provision of complete sanitation resulted in a statistically significant reduction in the rates of diarrhea, *Shigellae,* and so on, especially in the diarrhea rate, which was so low that it strongly indicated the practical importance of complete sanitation." (d) " For areas with high and low fly counts diarrhea rates were found to be the same. However, after a subdivision of all houses into groups having water and sanitary facilities and those having none, a statistically significant reduction of diarrhea was noted in the better homes. The availability of simple privies, as we noted in several countries, did not add anything to the solution of the problem. Because many of these were unsanitary they proved, in fact, to have a statistically significant adverse effect."

The studies of the seven countries also revealed that children, especially those under three years of age, had by far the highest diarrheal incidence rates.

15. Gilbert F. White and others, *Drawers of Water: Domestic Water Use in East Africa,* 1972.

Information on disease patterns at several sites in East Africa was collected by an interviewer through a questionnaire, by examination of excreta specimens, and by other "specific" investigations. A significantly higher rate of diarrhea was found in families without piped water. Also, diarrheal diseases were both common and severe, especially in children, in all areas lacking a piped water supply. White also observed instances in which low income households withdrew an average of 30 liters of water per capita daily if they were provided with connections near the house; but if water had to be carried from points away from the house, consumption fell to a mean of 15 liters per capita daily. With carried water, consumption tended to be higher where the source was within 150 feet of the household.

16. Melvin H. Goodwin and others, "Observations of Familial Occurrence of Diarrhea and Enteric Pathogens," 1966.

Sample families in Arizona, U.S.A., were visited weekly by a nurse who collected information on general illnesses and personal hygiene, and who collected stool specimens. The families in the sample were similar in that each had a newborn infant and at least two other children under five years of age, and all had a piped water supply, water heaters, waterborne sewage systems, and refrigerators. The study concluded that, in general, crowding and socioeconomic conditions were unimportant factors in the occurrence of diarrhea-causing pathogens. An awareness of and an appreciation for personal hygiene, however, are necessary in order to reap the health benefits from sanitary facilities.

Studies of Several Diseases Including Skin and Diarrheal Diseases

17. U.S. Department of Health, Education, and Welfare, "Health Program Evaluation: Impact Study of the Indian Sanitation Facilities Construction Act," 1968.

Researchers chose six Indian communities in Arizona, U.S.A., and collected information on morbidity and mortality before, during, and after the installation of sanitary facilities in twenty homes in each community. The study lasted six years and was concerned with skin and enteric diseases. The combined disease rates were slightly higher in the "before" phase of the study for the people who were to receive sanitation facilities than for the people who did not receive sanitation facilities. After sanitary facilities were installed in the selected groups of homes, the disease rates became significantly lower. It was conjectured that the installation of sanitary facilities has a greater impact through disease containment than through prevention. Houses receiving more facilities (more than one indoor faucet, a sanitary privy, a shower or bath) showed the greatest improvement in health. Incidence of skin disease decreased during installation of facilities but increased again later in the period. It was suspected that without proper education on use and operation and maintenance of the facilities, the health benefits deteriorated.

18. "Rural Water Supply and Sanitation Scheme in Pharenda Block of District Gorakhpur," Uttar Pradesh, India, n.d.

Piped water was installed for 34 percent of the population in eleven villages. For three years thereafter the morbidity rates for several diseases were calculated in two of the villages. A general decrease was reported in diarrhea, dysentery, typhoid, scabies, trachoma, and conjunctivitis over the 1966–1968 period for the two villages. Similar results were reported in a comparable study dealing with seven villages in the Banki Block of District Barabanki, Uttar Pradesh, between 1965 and 1968.

19. K. W. H. Fenwick, "The Short Term Effects of a Pilot Environmental Health Project in Rural Africa: The Zaina Scheme Reassessed After Four Years," 1966.

Two communities in Kenya were surveyed in both 1961 and 1965. The communities were similar until an environmental sanitation program was introduced into one of them (Zaina) in 1962. The program included chlorinated water piped to all houses, storage tanks for livestock on farms, drainage pipes for irrigation, concrete latrine slabs for homes, privies and showers in schools, and a public laundry unit, drinking fountain, and aqua privy in the village. Health was surveyed by a nurse who visited most houses in Zaina and the control area twice a month from March to September. Data were gathered on respiratory, gastrointestinal, and childhood diseases as well as general morbidity and mortality. The "health-related" results of the study were somewhat mixed. Morbidity incidence, prevalence, and duration rates showed a general decline in Zaina for infants and children under twelve years of age while there was a slight increase in the control area. Morbidity incidence and prevalence rates were generally lower in both areas in 1965 for people thirteen years and over. Diarrheal disease rates were higher in the control area in 1965 than in Zaina.

The birth rate stayed constant in Zaina but decreased slightly in the control area from 1961 to 1965. The fertility rate increased in Zaina but did not significantly increase in the control area. The infant mortality rate dropped in Zaina and in the control area. The crude death rate dropped in both areas. In 1965 worm infestation (*Ascaris lumbricoides* was the most common) was found to be six times more common in the control area than in Zaina.

Study results may have been affected by such matters as drier weather in 1965, difficulties in getting equal responses in both areas, sampling and data problems associated with the nonprofessional field staff, and changes in exogenous factors.

Studies Dealing with Cholera

20. World Health Organization, "Strategy of Cholera Control," 1971.

Between 1968 and 1970 the Philippines Cholera Committee undertook a study of four communities which, at the beginning of the study period, were similar in size, geographic characteristics and demographic composition. The following sanitary changes were made in the communities: the water supply was improved in one community, the water supply and waste disposal in the second, and waste disposal alone in the third. The last community, with poor water supply and waste disposal, was left unimproved as a control. The population of each community was about 750 to 800. The general objective of the study was to test the effect of improved water supply and/or improved waste disposal on cholera incidence.

Study results showed that in the three communities where either water, waste disposal, or both were improved there was between a 69.6 and 71.3 percent reduction in the incidence of cholera. All three communities had significantly lower incidence rates than the control community. The study concluded that "improvements in water supply or waste disposal facilities, or a combination of both, can produce a significant reduction in the cholera incidence in a community. Furthermore, infections that gain access to such communities show less tendency to spread and produce secondary cases. The incidence of infections in the three communities with sanitary improvements, however, showed no significant differences. Apparently, only a certain level of reduction in cholera incidence by sanitary measures is obtainable, beyond which any further sanitary improvements give only small returns."

21. J. C. Azurín and M. Alvero, "Field Evaluation of Environmental Sanitation Measures against Cholera," 1974.

This study is a follow-up to the Philippine cholera study (no. 20 above) and presents two additional years of data. The results of the total five-year study are summarized in Tables A.1 and A.2. The stated conclusion of Azurín and Alvero is "that the provision of sanitary facilities for human waste disposal can reduce the incidence of cholera by as much as 68%, while the provision of a safe water supply can decrease it by 73%. Where both toilets and water supplies are provided, the incidence can be reduced by as much as 76%."

22. K. Subrahmanyan, "Note on the Importance of Environmental Sanitation in the Campaign Against Cholera," 1951.

In India in the late 1940s, borehole wells were dug for several villages, a limited number of latrines were installed, and an attempt was made to educate the local populations on the need to use clean water and latrines. After examining the short-run effects of the improvements in sanitation, it was concluded that there was notably

Table A.1. **Relation between Sanitation and Cholera in Bacolod City, Philippines, 1968–72**

Community	Sanitation category	1968	1969	1970	1971	1972	Total
	Number of bacteriologically confirmed cholera infections						
West Visayan	Control	31	44	64	14	18	171
Dawis	Water	10	19	9	5	7	50
Magsungay	Toilets	13	17	10	10	8	58
Sibucao	Toilets and water	17	5	12	7	0	41
Total		71	85	95	36	33	320
	Incidence rates per 1,000 population						
West Visayan	Control	41.7	59.2	86.1	18.8	24.2	230.2
Dawis	Water	12.4	23.7	11.2	6.2	8.7	62.3
Magsungay	Toilets	16.5	21.6	12.7	12.7	10.2	73.7
Sibucao	Toilets and water	22.5	6.6	15.9	9.3	0	54.2
	Effectiveness of sanitation measures (percent)						
West Visayan	Control	—	—	—	—	—	—
Dawis	Water	70.2	60.0	87.0	66.9	64.0	72.9
Magsungay	Toilets	60.4	63.5	85.2	32.5	58.0	68.0
Sibucao	Toilets and water	46.1	88.8	81.6	50.5	100.0	76.4

Source: J. C. Azurín and M. Alvero, "Field Evaluation of Environmental Sanitation Measures against Cholera," 1974.

less cholera in districts that had sanitation programs, and that the death rate from cholera was less in towns with piped water than in areas of the districts without piped water.

Studies Dealing with Schistosomiasis (Bilharziasis)

It has been claimed that schistosomiasis (bilharziasis) is the "greatest unconquered parasitic disease now afflicting men and animals."[4] Schistosomiasis is a disease that affects inhabitants of rural areas and results primarily from a lack of sanitary facilities. The life cycle of the parasitic worm or schistosome includes periods of development in both people and snails. The life cycle can be interrupted by keeping people away from snail-infested waters, by providing filtered drinking water, by providing sanitary waste disposal for people so that eggs passed by those who are infected will not

4. John M. Weir, "The Unconquered Plague," *The Rockefeller Foundation Quarterly* 2(1969):4–23.

reach open water and develop into host snails, and by killing the snail population of the area. Tentative studies to date have shown that the first three alternatives seem to be the most efficient and perhaps the cheapest.[5]

23. Francine M. Siegel, "Schistosomiasis Hematobia in Preschool Children of Ibadan, Nigeria," 1968.

In this cross-section study, 100 single and multifamily houses in one section of Ibadan were chosen at random. A total of 279 preschool children resided in these houses. During the rainy season information was gathered on (a) the number of preschool children passing ova of *Schistosoma haematobium* in urine, (b) which houses were located on the river, (c) which houses were located more than 150 yards from the river, or were more than three houses away from the river, and (d) which houses had public water sources and which had private sources. The study results showed that (a) the prevalence of *Schistosoma haematobium* ova was significantly greater in the area closest to the river, and (b) the rate of infection differed by the source of water: 5 percent of the children without private water taps were passing ova while 20.9 percent of the children in houses without private taps were passing ova.

24. Frederico S. Barbosa and others, "Control of Schistosomiasis Mansoni in a Small North East Brazilian Community," 1971.

This study took place between 1960 and 1969 in a small Brazilian village with a population slightly over 1,000. Between 1960 and 1961 an initial sample was taken in which sanitary standards and the prevalence and morbidity of schistosomiasis were recorded. A health education program was introduced in 1963, and in 1964 construction began on household latrines, a central building with sinks, showers, latrines, and drinking water taps, and on nine dug wells and hand pumps distributed throughout the village. Between 1963 and 1968 the village was afforded some medical attention, health education, a monthly examination of snails, a check of small mammals, periodic inspections of the sanitary facilities installed, and periodic fecal examination. Fecal examinations were made in three similar small villages in 1963 and in 1969 in order to provide nonproject control data for the experiment.

5. R. J. Pitchford, "Findings in Relation to Schistosome Transmission in the Field Following the Introduction of Various Control Measures," *South African Medical Journal* 40, (8 October 1966 supplement):1–16.

Table A.2. Frequency of Introduction of Cholera Infection into Four Communities, Bacolod City, Philippines, 1968–1972

Community	Sanitation category	Number of times infection was introduced	Number of introductions that spread	Percentage of introductions that spread	Number of cases involved in spread	Average number of cases per spread
West Visayan	Control	31	22	71	162	7.4
Dawis	Water	24	12	50	38	3.2
Magsungay	Toilets	26	13	50	45	3.5
Sibucao	Toilets and water	17	9	53	33	3.7

Source: Same as Table A.1.

The results showed a significant decline in human infection rates in the project area and in two of the three control areas. It was concluded that there was a general decline in infection because of improvement in social and economic conditions between 1961 and 1968. It was further concluded that the more dramatic reduction in infections in the project area was a direct result of the sanitation and education program. It was suggested that "the successful degree of control achieved in the project area was mainly due to prevention of contact of the people with the infected waters."

25. R. J. Pitchford, "Further Observations on Bilharzia Control in the Eastern Transvaal," 1970.

This study took place on a large, irrigated farm in South Africa. Between 2,000 and 3,000 Bantu were housed in five villages on the farm. In 1959 construction work started on a system to provide piped water on a communal basis for domestic purposes, on swimming facilities with clean water, and on a system to reduce or prevent access to potentially dangerous (snail-infested) water in the vicinity of the villages. Construction was completed in the 1963–1964 period. The objective of the program was to provide the population with reasonably unpolluted water, adequate for domestic and recreational purposes, at a reasonable cost. The study found that there was a gradual decrease of *Schistosoma haematobium* and *Schistosoma mansoni* infection rates in schoolchildren during the period 1959 to 1968. For children between five and nine years of age the *Schistosoma haematobium* infection rate dropped from 75 percent in 1959 to 41 percent in 1968, while it dropped from 92 to 56 percent for children ten to nineteen years old over the period. The *Schistosoma mansoni* infection rate dropped from 68 to 51 percent and from 85 to 71 percent from the two age groups over the same period.

26. P. Jordan and others, "Control of *Schistosoma Mansoni* Transmission by Provision of Domestic Water Supplies in St. Lucia; A Preliminary Report," 1974.

Individual household water supplies in which wastage was controlled by the use of fordilla valves was provided during the 1970–1972 period in five rural settlements (total population approximately 2,000) of the Riche Fond Valley, St. Lucia, where *Schistosoma mansoni* is endemic. The five settlements were also provided with public laundry-shower units and shallow swimming pools. There was one laundry tub and one shower per 12.5 houses. Six other settlements in the same valley, provided with a public standpipe water system in 1969, served as a comparison area. The six comparison settlements, also having a combined population of approximately 2,000, had access to sixteen public standpipes spaced at about 350-meter intervals along a main road. Tentative study results showed that "before control, all indices of (*Schistosoma mansoni*) infection were slightly greater in the household water supply (HWS) area, but the pattern of change from year to year was the same as in the comparison area. By 1973, all indices of infection had fallen in the HWS area, and all had increased and were then higher in the comparison area. In cohorts (groups) of children of ages 0 to 13 who had been followed two years prior to control (1968–70), the percentage infected increased significantly in both areas. When similarly aged cohorts were followed from 1971 to 1973, a significant increase in the percentage of children infected occurred in the comparison area but there was no increase in the HWS area."

Studies on Child Mortality

27. Ruth R. Puffer and others, *Inter-American Investigation of Mortality in Childhood,* 1971.

This report represents the beginning of an effort to collect health data on childhood mortality in fifteen areas of Central and South America. Although water supply was not the specific focus of the report, the effect of water was noted in an aggregate sense as follows: "The central cities and other areas with limited water supplies, especially Recife, Resistencia, and San Salvador are the ones with excessive mortality of children under 5 years of age. In contrast, Kingston and Santiago, with water supplies available to high proportions of homes, have low death rates. Cali and the other cities in Colombia, however, with water provided to a high proportion of homes have intermediate positions in mortality. Thus the provision of water does not appear to have the same inverse correlation for these areas as presented in the 'Progress Report, June 1970.' Within Brazil the inverse relationship is noted and, likewise, when urban and rural areas in projects are studied. In Figure 70 the relationship between availability of piped water and death rates is presented for the rural areas and corresponding cities of four projects. In these, an inverse relationship can be observed between mortality and availability of piped water."

The study also states that "Death rates in childhood are usually higher in rural areas than in cities and water supplies in the rural areas are available for much smaller proportions of the population."

28. Robert E. Jarrett, "Environmental Factors and Childhood Mortality," 1970.

This study is part of the "Progress Report, June 1970" referred to in the PAHO report (no. 27 above). It is essentially a cross-section examination in which some least-squares regression analysis is used, and it generally shows somewhat more statistical analysis than did the 1971 report. Among the conclusions are the following: (a) a strong negative correlation between childhood deaths and the use of piped water, (b) a strong negative correlation between childhood deaths and the use of flush toilets, (c) a quantifiable relationship between access to piped water and flush toilets and childhood mortality. It was also suggested that the "total access" to piped water is a better indicator of mortality than is piped water inside or outside dwellings.

B | The "Health-State" Approach to Project Evaluation

THIS ILLUSTRATION [1] OF THE HEALTH-STATE approach, introduced in Chapter 2, assumes that an individual lives in a community where two diseases are endemic, schistosomiasis and cholera. Assume also that medical opinion provides a life prognosis (indicated in Table B.1) that is divided into four health states depending on whether or not the average villager contracts the diseases or lives a healthy life. ("Healthy" here may be taken as relative to schistosomiasis or cholera.) Now assume that a water treatment plant is introduced which reduces the probability of schistosomiasis from 0.06 to 0.02 and reduces the probability of cholera from 0.05 to 0.01. Extrapolating from Table B.1 the expected life prognosis becomes:

Health state	Duration (days)
Well-being	17,800
Discomfort	1,045
Minor disability	515
Major disability	525

and the benefit of the investment is represented by a so-called

---

1. The authors are indebted to Morton Lane for summarizing much of the following material on, and constructing the community water supply illustration of an application of, the Fanshel and Bush approach.

Table B.1. Simulated Life Prognosis in Village with Endemic Schistosomiasis and Cholera
(Days)

Health state	Individuals with:			Life expectancy
	Good health (probability =0.89)	Schistosomiasis (probability =0.06)	Cholera (probability =0.05)	
Well-being	18,000	14,500	6,000	17,190
Discomfort	1,000	3,000	1,500	1,145
Minor disability	500	1,000	1,000	555
Major disabilitly	500	500	3,000	625
Life total	20,000	19,000	11,500	19,515

health-state vector which is the difference between the two expected prognoses.

Health state	Duration (days)
Well-being	+610
Discomfort	−100
Minor disability	− 40
Major disability	−100
Life	370

Under ideal conditions, any investment project can be represented by this kind of health-state benefit vector. Of course, to make the approach operational it is necessary to get professional medical opinion about the prognosis for a particular disease in a particular area both with and without the investment. Although physicians are familiar with diagnosis, they may be less able to offer explicit prognosis for patients many of whom undoubtedly have multiple infections. This is particularly true if the physicians are required to predict the medical effects in terms of health states and probabilities.

One effort to assist in this task is to divide the population into medically similar cohorts. As was discussed in Chapter 2, the prognosis for schistosomiasis, diarrhea, and many other water-associated diseases is markedly different for the young than for the mature. Prognosis could therefore be collected for children under five, say, and separately for mature groups and people over sixty. The results would then be added after weighting by the size of respective cohorts, and after translating into the so-called health-state benefit vectors.

Two assumptions are necessary in order to aggregate the health-benefit vectors of different cohorts. The first is that a day of "physical well-being" is valuable equally now as in the future. The second is that the community is indifferent between days of well-being or pain in any of the cohorts. Each assumption is certainly equitable, in the sense that it does not discriminate between one section of the community and another, but each assumption is also questionable. Certain villagers may prefer to give up some well-being in their early years in order to receive more in their old age. Others may prefer to get as much physical well-being as they can, while they can. Similarly, many communities would prefer to spend money treating the young rather than the old, and others clearly demonstrate a preference for the health of males above that of females. These communities contradict either the assumptions of indifference between cohorts, or of time indifference.

Where there is evidence to suggest a particular preference ordering, weights should be added to each of the cohort's health-state benefit vectors before aggregating them. These weights may be difficult to obtain, and there may be good operational reasons for proceeding with the assumptions of indifference. It is important, however, to remember that assumptions are made and that the results are not value free.

If assumptions are made relating to the two above factors, any water supply or sanitation investment program may be reduced to a single health-benefit vector as illustrated above. It remains then to reduce this vector to a single index for comparison with alternate medical programs. Here it is legitimate to observe that the health states may be ordered, or ranked, in a way that corresponds to the ordering as determined by most rational individuals. For these purposes it can be assumed that physical well-being is preferred to discomfort, which is preferred to major disability and so on. There will be pathological exceptions to this ordering, such as that of hypochondriacs, but for most people in any community the health states can probably be ordered in a reasonable manner.

Fanshel and Bush suggest that any weighting system which preserves the ordering can be used to define a Health Status Index. They suggest that an exponential weighting function would do this, and they derive the following set of weights for their example of eleven health states: [2]

---

2. Anyone who has recently had a toothache, which would seem to place him in the discomfort category, might argue that the exponential weighting

State	Weight
Well-being	1.000
Dissatisfaction	0.9961
Discomfort	0.9922
Minor disability	0.9844
Major disability	0.9687
Disability	0.9375
Confinement	0.875
Confinement, bedridden	0.5
Isolation	0.15
Coma	0.0
Death	0.0

These weights would be multiplied by the benefit vector to determine the program's Health Status Index.

A sample calculation of the Index, again using an exponential weighting function, for the four-state village water supply example might look like that in Table B.2. This Health Status Index (374.53) could then be divided by the per capita cost of the village water supply project and the resulting HSI/cost ratio could be used in comparison with other HSI/cost ratios derived for water supply projects in other villages, or with ratios derived for other medical programs or sanitation improvements in the same village, in other villages, or in cities. The program or projects with the largest HSI/cost ratios would then be implemented as the most "cost effective" of the alternatives examined.

The HSI approach is appealing on the surface but there are practical problems inhibiting its implementation. At first glance, it appears to have some theoretic consistency that is lacking in many other approaches, but its major problem is that it depends heavily on at least two assumptions implicit in the analysis, and on others implicit in the weighting function chosen for the health states.

With regard to the weighting function, it is difficult to dispute that the ordering of health states is monotonic. It is quite easy to devise any number of weighting functions that preserve this monotonicity. It can be shown, however, that the most cost-effective program is not invariant against the weighting function chosen. Hence the optimal health program is still indeterminate if there is any dispute about the proper weighting function to be used.

---

function does not effectively separate him far enough from the perfect well-being score of 1.000.

Table B.2. Derivation of Village Water Supply Health Status Index [a]

State	Prognosis	Weight	Product
Well-being	+610	1.0	610
Discomfort	−100	0.9922	−99.22
Minor disability	−40	0.9844	−39.38
Major disability	−100	0.9687	−96.87
Health Status Index			374.53

a. For method of derivation, see accompanying text.

Ideally, the weighting function should be chosen so that it does indeed represent informed community preferences. The traditional medium through which a community expresses its preferences, however, is its expenditure of resources, and this points us back to an economic analysis.

C | *Economies of Scale: Regression Analysis of U.S. Waterworks Data*

ANALYSIS OF U.S. WATERWORKS data was carried out on a stratified random sample of 77 American Water Works Association (AWWA) water utilities. The sample was drawn from those utilities whose retail population served equaled total population served in 1960. So that a sufficient number of larger utilities would be included in the examination, the sample was stratified by size of utility. Variables collected or constructed for each utility were as follows:

$P =$ Retail population served
$G =$ Million gallons [1] produced
$D_1 = 1$ if 50 percent or more of the water is purchased wholesale by the utility, 0 if less than 50 percent is purchased
$D_2 = 1$ if 100 percent of the water is from the utilities' own sources, and 75 percent or more is derived from surface sources, 0 if other
$D_3 = 1$ if 100 percent of the water is from the utilities' own sources and 75 percent or more is derived from ground sources, 0 if other
$D_4 =$ No treatment of the water required
$\% \Delta P =$ Percentage change in population between 1950 and 1960 for the city in which the utility is located, if the retail

---

1. One gallon equals 3.785 liters.

population served in 1960 was approximately equal to the 1960 city population. If the retail population served was significantly larger than the city population, the information entered was the percentage change in population between 1950 and 1960 in the Standard Metropolitan Statistical Area (SMSA) in which the utility was located.

$AC =$ Utility expenses for operation, maintenance, and administration purposes

$TC = AC$ plus expenses for interest payments, debt reserves, bonds retired, and depreciation reserves

The equations which were estimated were the linear additive form of the following:

(1) $AC/G = f(P, P^2, D_1, D_2, D_3, D_4)$
(2) $AC/G = f(G, G^2, D_1, D_2, D_3, D_4)$
(3) $AC/P = f(P, P^2, D_1, D_2, D_3, D_4)$
(4) $AC/P = f(G, G^2, D_1, D_2, D_3, D_4)$
(5) $AC/G = f(P, D_1, D_2, D_3, D_4)$
(6) $AC/G = f(G, D_1, D_2, D_3, D_4)$
(7) $AC/P = f(P, D_1, D_2, D_3, D_4)$
(8) $AC/P = f(G, D_1, D_2, D_3, D_4)$
(9) $TC/G = f(P, P^2, D_1, D_2, D_3, D_4, \%\Delta P)$
(10) $TC/G = f(G, G^2, D_1, D_2, D_3, D_4, \%\Delta P)$
(11) $TC/P = f(P, P^2, D_1, D_2, D_3, D_4, \%\Delta P)$
(12) $TC/P = f(G, G^2, D_1, D_2, D_3, D_4, \%\Delta P)$
(13) $TC/G = f(P, D_1, D_2, D_3, D_4)$
(14) $TC/G = f(G, D_1, D_2, D_3, D_4)$
(15) $TC/P = f(P, D_1, D_2, D_3, D_4)$
(16) $TC/P = f(G, D_1, D_2, D_3, D_4)$

For equations (5) through (8) and (13) through (16), all variables were transformed into their natural log equivalents before estimating the linear additive regressions. Before taking the logs of the dummy variables for those equations, the dummy variables were transformed by the addition of the constant 1, making them of the magnitude 1 and 2 rather than 0 and 1.

With regard to the variables specified in the regression analysis, population served was selected as a proxy for output in one-half of the equations, and gallons of water produced was the proxy for output in the other half. The output variable squared was also included in eight of the equations in an attempt to search, on the cost-output plane, for a possible parabolic relationship which, if found, could signify diseconomies of scale after an optimum utility size was reached. A statistical result of the form $AC/G = a - b_1 G + b_2 G^2$ where a, b_1, and b_2 are the estimates of the parameters and where b_1 is much larger than b_2 would give a U-shaped average cost curve where economies and diseconomies of scale exist at different levels of output.

The dummy variables were introduced into the analysis in an attempt to control for differences in source-related costs of water which might, for regional or historical reasons, be related to city size in the United States. The initial hypothesis with regard to the four dummy variables was that they should all be negatively related to costs. D_1 should be negatively related; because of the way the data were collected and tabulated, the amount paid by the utilities for water purchased is not included in either AC or TC. Therefore, other things being equal, AC and TC should be lower for utilities which purchase a substantial proportion of their water. D_2 and D_3 are included to reflect the possible presence of utilities that have adequate supplies of relatively cheap water from one source. Utilities making significant use of both ground and surface sources are presumed to include those that are using their cheapest source of water to its capacity and have moved on to a higher cost source. D_4 is included because it was observed that there were several utilities in the population that, for one reason or another, do not have to treat the water they produce.

Finally, the percentage change in population variable was included in four of the average total cost regressions to account for the possibility that utilities which had expanded relatively rapidly in recent years could have disproportionately high debt service and depreciation costs.

Two additional variables which were crude proxies for population density (miles of distribution and transmission lines per capita, and population density per square mile in the city or SMSA) were included initially in several of the regressions, in an attempt to examine for possible cost economies related to population density. These, however, were omitted from the final analysis when it was found that they contributed nothing in a statistical sense.

The eight regressions estimated in a log form represent an attempt to examine something other than a linear additive relationship between costs and size. Essentially, the log regressions give equations of the form:

$$\text{Average cost} = a(\text{Output})^b,$$

where a is a constant and b is the elasticity of output with respect to cost. If there are cost economies of scale one would expect b to be less than 0.

Table C.1 presents the results of the sixteen regressions. It can be seen that, in general, less than 30 percent of the variation in the cost variables is explained. Furthermore, when costs are measured on a per capita basis, or when output is measured in terms of population, the results are not as satisfactory as when gallons of water produced is used as the output proxy.

In total, the regressions do, however, present strong evidence supporting the existence of economies of scale in the provision of water supply. The sign of the output variable is in all cases negative, and in all of the regressions where gallons is the output proxy, output is statistically significant at the 0.05 level. G^2 and P^2 always have a positive sign, but they are never statistically significant at the 0.05 level. G^2 is significant, however, at the 0.10 level in regressions (2) and (10), giving at least weak support to the possibility that the rate of decline in costs per gallon of output slows as the utility increases in size.[2]

---

2. J. L. Ford and J. J. Warford, "Cost Functions for the Water Industry," *Journal of Industrial Economics* 18, no. 1 (1969):53–63. Ford and Warford carried out a set of regressions with a somewhat similar objective on 1965 data for the water supply industry in England and Wales. Although most of their results were inconclusive, they provide some evidence to support the existence of economies of scale with respect to quantity of water supplied.

Table C.1. Selected Regressions, Examining Cost Economies of Scale in the Provision of Water Supplies, United States, 1960

Dependent variable	Equation number	Independent variables			
		a	P	P^2	G
AC/G	(1)	278.20	−484119 (0.211964)	0.000461 [b] (0.000313)	......
	(2)	284.04	......	......	−10.4128 (4.1052)
AC/P	(3)	11.511	−0.009197 [b] (0.010126)	0.000005 [b] (0.000015)	......
	(4)	11.589	......	......	−0.186543 [c] (0.198733)
AC/G [c]	(5)	5.6683	−0.116581 (0.033588)	......	......
	(6)	6.5118	......	......	−0.132878 (0.029923)
AC/P [c]	(7)	2.4917	−0.073032 (0.029683)	......	......
	(8)	2.2847	......	......	−0.057352 (0.027976)
TC/G	(9)	361.82	−0.619249 (0.309095)	0.000670 [b] (0.000457)	......
	(10)	369.15	......	......	−13.1230 (5.9903)
TC/P	(11)	15.881	−0.011496 [b] (0.014940)	0.000011 [b] (0.000022)	......
	(12)	15.879	......	......	−0.000970 [b] (0.006120)
TC/G [c]	(13)	5.9273	−0.067392 [a] (0.035181)	......	......
	(14)	6.5589	......	......	−0.094812 (0.031653)
TC/P [c]	(15)	2.7473	−0.021680 [b] (0.031157)	......	......
	(16)	2.6927	......	......	−0.011315 [b] (0.029078)

Note: Standard errors are shown in parentheses below the regression coefficients. Definitions of symbols are in the text.

a. Not significant at the 0.05 level but significant at the 0.10 level.

(Table continues on the following page.)

Table C.1 (*continued*)

Dependent variable	Equation number	Independent variables		
		G^2	D_1	D_2
AC/G	(1)	......	−118.891	−130.562
			(36.827)	(31.249)
	(2)	0.193935 [a]	−123.216	−135.655
		(0.102588)	(36.635)	(31.144)
AC/P	(3)	......	−2.12531 [b]	−4.63777
			(1.75937)	(1.49294)
	(4)	0.002762 [c]	−2.18304 [b]	−4.73455
		(0.004966)	(1.77354)	(1.50771)
AC/G [c]	(5)	......	−0.751565	−0.928849
			(0.361294)	(0.308498)
	(6)	......	−0.769425	−0.899603
			(0.345695)	(0.295374)
AC/P [c]	(7)	......	−0.431689 [b]	−0.789577
			(0.323207)	(0.272628)
	(8)	......	−0.431689 [b]	−0.785374
				(0.276160)
TC/G	(9)	......	−138.231	−143.815
			(54.104)	(45.566)
	(10)	0.257917 [b]	−143.473	−149.864
		(0.149669)	(52.829)	(45.535)
TC/P	(11)	......	−3.44251 [b]	−5.26870
			(2.61509)	(2.20242)
	(12)	0.003098 [b]	−3.45022 [b]	−5.32269
		(0.007312)	(2.6969)	(2.21960)
TC/G [c]	(13)	......	−0.615630 [b]	−0.816519
			(0.378432)	(0.323131)
	(14)	......	−0.628046 [a]	−0.789798
			(0.365688)	(0.312457)
TC/P [c]	(15)	......	−0.516438 [b]	−0.659388
			(0.335140)	(0.287038)
	(16)	......	−0.518204 [b]	−0.661254
			(0.335939)	(0.287038)

b. Not significant at the 0.10 level.
c. For equations (5) through (8) and (13) through (16), all variables are transformed into their natural log equivalents before estimating the linear additive regression.

Table C.1 (*continued*)

Dependent variable	Equation number	Independent variables			
		D_3	D_4	%ΔP	R^2
AC/G	(1)	−140.716 (33.691)	−52.9167 [a] (29.89001)	. . . . . .	0.30055
	(2)	−146.259 (33.649)	−52.5687 [a] (29.5961)	. . . . . .	0.31384
AC/P	(3)	−5.66709 (1.60956)	−1.20151 [b] (1.42797)	. . . . . .	0.23796
	(4)	−5.74498 (1.62899)	−1.19188 [b] (1.43275)	. . . . . .	0.23241
AC/G [c]	(5)	−1.03120 (0.32960)	−0.676162 (0.296208)	. . . . . .	0.28165
	(6)	−1.04848 (0.31532)	−0.597423 (0.283122)	. . . . . .	0.34241
AC/P [c]	(7)	−1.00497 (0.29128)	−0.1866569 [b] (0.261767)	. . . . . .	0.23175
	(8)	−0.995673 (0.294815)	−0.142617 [b] (0.264705)	. . . . . .	0.21284
TC/G	(9)	−180.392 (49.406)	−80.6440 [a] (43.6139)	0.165499 [b] (0.126404)	0.24944
	(10)	−187.166 (49.347)	−80.1160 [a] (43.2034)	0.162269 [b] (0.125279)	0.26307
TC/P	(11)	−7.89802 (2.38803)	−1.04516 [b] (2.10804)	−0.000962 [b] (0.006110)	0.18389
	(12)	−7.91654 (2.41074)	−1.02227 [b] (2.11059)	−0.000970 [b] (0.006120)	0.18144
TC/G [c]	(13)	−1.05747 (0.34524)	−0.745874 (0.310258)	. . . . . .	0.22715
	(14)	−1.08144 (0.33356)	−0.696621 (0.299497)	. . . . . .	0.27839
TC/P [c]	(15)	−1.04698 (0.30575)	−0.166856 [b] (0.274766)	. . . . . .	0.18149
	(16)	−1.03979 (0.30643)	−0.154994 [b] (0.275132)	. . . . . .	0.17767

D | *The Metering Decision*

THE DECISION ON WHETHER to meter the consumption of individual consumers should be subjected to cost-benefit analysis. The costs of metering consist of the purchase and installation of the meter and subsequent maintenance, reading, and billing costs. Benefits arise if metering induces consumers to waste less water, thereby permitting savings in production costs to be achieved. In addition, by providing better information to the water supply authorities, metering may facilitate detection of losses from the distribution system, and therefore effect savings. As an offset to these benefits, however, the reduction in water used by a consumer may involve some loss to him; because price is raised from zero (at the margin) to some positive figure, the benefits of water used for purposes which have a unit value of between zero and the new price will be lost; indeed the additional cost of metering could, if care is not taken, preclude many lower income families from having any access at all to piped water.

In most cases the metering decision can be made by comparing the present worth (or annual equivalent) of metering costs with the present worth (or annual equivalent) of the resultant benefits, that is, production cost savings *less* the value of foregone consumption. Inasmuch as we can rarely say with any confidence how large a reduction in consumption would follow the introduction of metering, the best way to deal with the problem is to ask, with respect to any particular category of consumer, the following questions: What reduction in consumption would be sufficient to justify metering? Is that reduction in consumption likely to result?

Following is an illustration of the way in which the metering decision should be approached. Although the cost and consumption data are based on an actual case study in a large Asian city, the same principles may be followed in evaluating schemes for rationing water by any of the means open to village water supply operations. These might range from a system of intermittent supplies to the sale of water by the bucket from standposts.

The costs of metering per connection were estimated as follows:

Item	Cost
Purchase of ½-inch meter	27.50
Installation	2.50
Ancillary equipment	.50
Total cost of connection	30.50
Annual cost (maintenance, reading)	3.50
Total annual cost (assuming a discount rate of 10 percent and a life of five years)	11.54

In the city being studied, marginal water production and waste disposal costs were estimated at 5.82 cents per thousand gallons.[1] Given an annual metering cost of $11.54, the reduction in water production per connection necessary to achieve equivalent savings in costs would be about 550 gallons a day. Total current production was estimated at 62.89 million gallons a day; with connections (including commercial) totalling 90,000, production per connection was 698 gallons a day. On average, therefore, metering would have had to reduce production by about 80 percent to be worthwhile. Clearly for most consumers this would be unlikely, but it does not follow that metering should be abandoned altogether. What it does mean is that careful analysis is a necessary prelude to deciding which category of consumer should be metered.

The foregoing comparison does not include the loss to consumers resulting from the reduction in consumption that follows metering, which may be estimated using either of the following extreme assumptions: first, that reduction in the flow of water to a consumer's premises has no cost (that is, water would otherwise have been put to

---

1. One gallon equals 3.785 liters.

no useful purpose, and no costs—for example, repair of plumbing fixtures—are incurred in restricting waste because of metering); and, second, that the demand for water, after the adjustment due to metering, is perfectly inelastic in the price range between zero and the metered rate.[2] In other words, price changes, once meters have been installed, have no effect on consumption.

Another feasible assumption, however, is that metering results in a loss to the consumer that can be approximated by a function which relates quantity consumed linearly to price. Algebraically the metering decision in this case requires that the reduction in consumption R be estimated which equates the present worth of metering costs M with the present worth of the benefits $S-V$ where S is savings in production costs and V is the value of water that is now foregone.[3] Both S and V are a function of R, that is:

$S = cR$, and
$V = \frac{1}{2} pR$ [4]

where c is marginal production cost and p is price of metered consumption. If $M = (S - V)$, then:

$$R = \left(\frac{M}{c - \frac{p}{2}} \right).$$

Having estimated a value of R which equates the present worth of metering costs and benefits, a judgment then has to be exercised as to whether the estimated R is likely to be greater or less than the actual R. Clearly, the assumption that is made about the value of water lost to the consumer as a result of metering could be critical to the decision. If, for example, price equals marginal cost (that is,

---

2. The distinction implied in these assumptions between water wasted and water used is an important one, and may help to justify the seemingly paradoxical conclusion reached by many water authorities that, while metering may have a salutary effect on water production, subsequent price changes have a relatively small effect.

3. A parallel calculation should be made for any savings in production costs from improved detection of losses from the distribution system. Because remedies for detected leaks are not costless, it should be interpreted as the net savings from metering that accrue to the water supply authorities.

4. Because of the assumption of linearity, the value of water that would have been consumed in the absence of metering (the area under the demand curve) is one-half the product of price and the reduction in quantity consumed.

$c=p$) and linearity between pre- and postmetering rates of consumption is assumed, an offset of 50 percent of the savings in production costs would result, and R would have to be twice as great as if reduction in production is costless and demand thereafter inelastic. Indeed, application to the results quoted above would require a reduction in consumption of 1,110 gallons per connection—about 60 percent more than the average amount currently consumed.

To conduct the above analysis more thoroughly, further information is required on both the benefits and on the costs of metering. One necessary task is the analysis of water use by type of consumer. The general objective of this analysis would be to rank types of consumers in the order of the priority they should receive in the metering program, and to determine a cutoff point below which metering would not be worthwhile. The impact of metering, and therefore the relationship between metering costs and potential benefits presumably varies according to category of consumer. It may be necessary to distinguish not simply individual, commercial, and residential usage but also subcategories. For example, distinctions might be made between residential consumers according to whether or not they are connected to the sewerage system or have septic tanks, or whether or not they have gardens. It is possible that the present definition of consumer categories is not appropriate for this purpose. The compulsory metering of commercial or new residential properties, for example, may be less useful than compulsory metering of all residential properties with a garden area exceeding a certain size.

This analysis should include not only comparison of aggregate consumption in premises with and without metering, but also the more difficult task of trying to determine the type of water use by various categories of consumer. This information may allow some judgment to be made about the extent to which metering may inhibit wastage, rather than actual use of water, and thereby provide some indication as to the nature of the demand curve for water. For example, if water is running to waste simply because a consumer is too lazy to turn a tap off, it can reasonably be assumed that the loss to him of reducing that amount of flow by metering is zero.

It may be of special interest, therefore, to determine the seasonal pattern of water consumption. Thus, during the summer peak period, a given reduction in aggregate consumption will achieve greater production cost savings than an equivalent reduction during the winter season. Moreover, it is likely that summertime activities such as lawn watering and dust damping may be more responsive to metering (or price changes) than uses of water for drinking and washing. To take account of the seasonal complication, a range of values for R_o and R_p should be estimated which satisfy the equation:

$$R_o(c_o-[p_o/2])+R_p(c_p-[p_p/2])=M,$$

where subscripts $_o$ and $_p$ refer to the offpeak and peak periods respectively and, as before, judgment is exercised as to their likelihood.

Bibliography

"Accelerated Rural Development Manual for Domestic Water Resources Development Planning." Bangkok: Office of Accelerated Rural Development, 1971.

Acurio, Guido. "Agua Potable Rural Perú." Report to Rural Water of Peru, Lima, October 1969.

Afifi, Hamdy H., and V. Lewis Bassie. *Water Pricing Theory and Practice in Illinois*. Urbana: University of Illinois, Bureau of Economic and Business Research, 1969.

Almquist, Frederick O. A. "Domestic Water Suppy in East Pakistan." *Journal of the American Water Works Association* 59, no. 2 (1967): 156–62.

Alonso, William. "The Economics of Urban Size." Center for Planning and Research Development Working Paper no. 138. Berkeley: University of California, 1970.

Altouney, Edward Gregory. *The Role of Uncertainties in the Economic Evaluation of Water Resources Projects*. Report EEP-7. Stanford, Calif.: Stanford University, August 1968.

Anderson, Robert S. "People and Water in Rural Bangladesh (1972–1973)." Vancouver, Can.: University of British Columbia, Dept. of Anthropology and Sociology, July 1974.

Appalachian Regional Commission. *Appalachia*. Washington, D.C., May 1969, pp. 14–15.

Arensburg, Conrad Maynadier, and Arthur H. Niehoff. *Introducing Social Change*. Chicago: Aldine Publishing Co., 1964.

Arrow, Kenneth J. "Criteria for Social Investment." *Water Resources Research* 1 (January 1965):1–8.

Associazione per lo sviluppo dell'industria nel Mezzogiorno. "Ricerca sui coste d'insediamento." Rome, 1967.
Athikomrungsarit, Charnvit. "Benefits and Costs of Providing Potable Water to Small Communities in Thailand." Master's thesis no. 566, Asian Institute of Technology, Bangkok, 1971.
Atkins, Callis H. "Global Water Supply Development." *Journal of the American Water Works Association* 61, no. 1 (1969):49–51.
———. "Some Economic Aspects of Sanitation Programs in Rural Areas and Small Towns." Paper presented to the Expert Committee on Environmental Sanitation (WHO/Env. San./56). Geneva: World Health Organization, n.d.
Azpurúa, Pedro Pablo. "Water Supply Management in Latin America." *Journal of the American Water Works Association* 60, no. 6 (1968): 743–45.
———, Celestino Martínez, and Pedro F. Millán Ruiz. "The Caracas Water Utility: Overall Appraisal." *Journal of the American Water Works Association* 63, no. 2 (1971):72–78.
———, and Germán Rovati. "Future Water Demand of Caracas, Venezuela." *Journal of the American Water Works Association* 59, no. 1 (1967):13–19.
Azurín, J. C. and M. Alvero. "Field Evaluation of Environmental Sanitation Measures Against Cholera." *Bulletin of the World Health Organization* 51, no. 1 (1974):19–26.
Bagchi, S. C., Y. S. Murty, and B. G. Prasad. "A Study of Water Supply in Rural Health Center, Sarojini Nagar, Lucknow District." *Indian Journal of Medical Sciences* 16 (December 1962):1048–62.
Bahl, Roy W., Stephen P. Coelen, and Jeremy J. Warford. "Land Value Increments as a Measure of the Net Benefits of Urban Water Supply Projects in Developing Countries: Theory and Measurement." Paper presented at the Taxation Resources and Economic Development Conference, Madison, Wisconsin, 1972.
Baker, Timothy D. "Problems in Measuring the Influence of Economic Levels on Morbidity." *American Journal of Public Health* 56, no. 3 (1966):499–507.
Barbosa, Frederico S., Raimundo Pinto, and Otamires A. Souza. "Control of Schistosomiasis Mansoni in a Small North East Brazilian Community." *Transactions of the Royal Society of Tropical Medicine and Hygiene* 65, no. 2 (1971):206–13.
Barlow, Robin. "The Economic Effects of Malaria Eradication." *American Economic Review* 57, no. 2 (1967):130–48.
Bartone, Carl R. "Cost-Effectiveness Model for Establishing Investment Priorities for Water and Sewage Projects in Guayas River Basin." Lima: Pan American Health Organization, 1972.
Bateman, G. H. *A Bibliography of Low-Cost Water Technologies.* 2d ed. London: Intermediate Technology Development Group, 1971.

Bertsch, Howard. "Administration of Rural Water Supply Program." *Journal of the American Water Works Association* 58, no. 8 (1966): 977–82.

Bhaskaran, T. R., C. R. Das, S. De, and I. Radhakrishnan. "Chlorination of Unfiltered Water Supply as an Interim Measure for Control of Cholera in Calcutta." In *Problems in Water Treatment*. Magpur, India: Central Public Health Engineering Research Institute, 1965.

Boring, John R., III, W. T. Martin, and L. M. Elliott. "Isolation of *Salmonella typhi-murium* from Municipal Water, Riverside, California, 1965." *American Journal of Epidemiology* 93, no. 1 (1971):49–54.

Borjesson, E. K. G., and Carlos M. Bobeda. "New Concept in Water Service for Developing Countries." *Journal of the American Water Works Association* 56, no. 7 (1964):853–62.

Bradley, David J. "Health Problems of Water Management." *Journal of Tropical Medicine and Hygiene* 73 (November 1970):286–91.

———. "Infective Disease and Domestic Water Supplies." In *Water Supply*, edited by G. Tschannerl. BRALUP Research Paper no. 20. Dar es Salaam: University of Dar es Salaam, 1971.

———. "Water Supplies—the Consequences of Change." In *Human Rights in Health*. CIBA Foundation Symposium no. 23, new series. Edited by Katherine Elliot and Julie Knight. New York and London: Associated Scientific Publishers, 1974.

"Breakthrough on Rural Water District Planning." *Water Well Journal* 25 (October 1971):25–28.

Bruno, M. "The Optimal Selection of Export Promoting and Import Substituting Projects." In *Planning External Sector: Techniques, Problems and Policies* (ST/TAO/SER.C/91). New York: United Nations, 1967.

Burki, Shahid Jared, and Shahid Yusuf. "Population: Exploring the Food-Fertility Link." *Finance and Development* 12, no. 4 (1975):29–32.

Burton, Ian, and Terence R. Lee. "Community Water Supplies and Economic Development: The Scale and Timing of Investment." Inter-Regional Seminar on Integration of Community Water Supply into Planning of Economic Development, Geneva, 19–28 September 1967 (CWS/WP/67.8). Geneva: World Health Organization, 1967.

Burton, Ian, Yves Maystre, and Emanuel Idelovitch. *Technology Assessment Research Priorities for Water Supply and Sanitation in Developing Countries*. Ottawa: International Development Research Centre, 1973.

Buzo, Z. J. "Design and Construction of Rural Community Water Supply Systems." WHO Regional Seminar on Rural Water Supply, Khon Kaen, Thailand, 4–14 March 1970.

———. "Personnel Training for Rural Community Water Supply Programmes." WHO Regional Seminar on Rural Water Supply, Khon Kaen, Thailand, 4–14 March 1970.

Cairo, Tito H. *Acueductos Rurales en República Dominicana.* Dominican Republic: Instituto Nacional de Aguas Potables y Alcantarillados, August 1974.

Cameron, Gordon C. *Regional Economic Development: The Federal Role.* Washington, D.C.: Resources for the Future, 1970.

Carruthers, I. D. "Assessing the Contribution of Rural Water Investment to Development." *East African Journal of Rural Development* 3, no. 2: pp. 96–110.

———. "Cost-Benefit Analysis and Agricultural Development—A Comment on Current Practice." *Farm Economist* 12, no. 2 (1971):107–11.

———. *Rural Water Investment in Kenya: Impact and Economics of Community Water Supply.* London: University of London, Wye College, 1972.

Chico Romero, José A. "Financing of Water Supply Programs for Rural Communities in El Salvador." *Boletín de la Oficina Sanitaria Panamericana* 69, no. 2 (1970):141–46.

Coles, G. C., and H. Mann. "Schistosomiasis and Water Works Practice in Uganda." *East African Medical Journal* 48 (January 1971):40–43.

Costopoulos, J. M. "Water Supply and Public Health." Paper presented at International Conference on Water for Peace, 23–31 May 1967, Washington, D.C.

Cox, P. Thomas, C. Wilford Grover, and Bernard Siskin. "Effect of Water Resource Investment on Economic Growth." *Water Resources Research* 7 (February 1971):32–38.

Craun, Gunther F., and Leland J. McCabe. "Review of the Causes of Waterborne-Disease Outbreaks." *Journal of the American Water Works Association* 65, no. 1 (1973):74–84.

Cvjetanović, B. Sanitation versus Vaccination in Cholera Control: Cost-Effect and Cost-Benefit Aspects. In "Strategy of Cholera Control" (BD/Cholera/71.1). Geneva: World Health Organization, 1971.

———, B. Grab, and K. Uemura. "Epidemiological Model of Typhoid Fever and Its Use in the Planning and Evaluation of Antityphoid Immunization and Sanitation Programmes." *Bulletin of the World Health Organization* 45, no. 1 (1971):53–75.

Dajani, Jarir S. "Cost Studies of Urban Public Services." *Land Economics* 49, no. 4 (1973):479–83.

———, and Robert S. Gennell. "Economic Guidelines for Public Utilities Planning." Journal of the Urban Planning and Development Division, *Proceedings of the American Society of Civil Engineers* 99, UP2, no. 9977 (1973):171–82.

Dalton, G. E., and R. N. Parker. *Agriculture in South East Ghana.* Vol. 2. Special Studies. Reading, U.K.: University of Reading, 1973.

Dasgupta, Ajit K., and D. W. Pearce. *Cost-Benefit Analysis: Theory and Practice.* New York: Barnes and Noble, 1973.

deGreiff, Beatriz. "First Stage of Planar Project." Washington, D.C.: George Washington University, Dept. of Economics, Spring 1971.

Dejene, Tekola, and Scott E. Smith. *Experiences in Rural Development: A Selected Annotated Bibliography in Planning, Implementing, and Evaluating Rural Development in Africa.* OCC Paper no. 1. Washington, D.C.: American Council on Education, Overseas Liaison Committee, 1973.

deVlieger, C. A., A. R. Manuel, G. A. Vierstra, and M. C. Onlandvan Schendelen. "Drinking Water Supply by Public Hydrants in Developing Countries." Draft final report. The Hague (Voorburg): WHO International Reference Centre for Community Water Supply, 1975.

Dieterich, Bernd H., and John M. Henderson. *Urban Water Supply Conditions and Needs in Seventy-Five Developing Countries.* Public Health Papers no. 23. Geneva: World Health Organization, 1963.

Donaldson, David. "The Point of the Lance—The Construction Resident on Overseas Construction." Paper presented at the Engineers with International Responsibilities Workshop, American Water Works Association, June 1971, Denver, Colorado.

———. "Progress in the Rural Water Programs of Latin America (1961–1971)." Washington, D.C.: Pan American Health Organization, January 1973.

———. "Rural Water Supplies in Developing Countries." *Water Resources Bulletin* 8 (1972):391–8.

———. "Water for the Rural Community." *Gazette* 6, no.1–2 (1974): 2–9. Washington, D.C.: Pan American Health Organization.

Dooley, Delmer J., ed. "The Near East Foundation Program of Rural Development in the Varimin Plains of Iran 1946–1959." New York: Near East Foundation, 1969.

Downing, Paul B. *The Economics of Urban Sewage Disposal.* New York: Praeger, 1969.

Dublin, Louis I. *The Money Value of a Man.* Rev. ed. New York: Ronald Press, 1946.

"The Economics of Water Supply and Control. III: Canada, Egypt, Denmark." *International Journal of Agrarian Affairs* 15 (January 1961).

"The Economics of Water Supply and Control. II: Jordan, Iran, Peru, Poland." *International Journal of Agrarian Affairs* 14 (July 1960).

"The Economics of Water Supply and Control. I: Norway, Portugal, U.S.A., Lebanon." *International Journal of Agrarian Affairs* 13 (June 1959).

"The Economics of Water Supply and Control. IV: Pakistan, India." *International Journal of Agrarian Affairs* 17 (October 1963).

Eighmy, Thomas H. "Rural Periodic Markets and the Extension of an

Urban System: a Western Nigeria Example." *Economic Geography* 48, no. 3 (1972): 299–315.

Enke, Stephen. "The Gains to India from Population Control: Some Money Measures and Incentive Schemes." *Review of Economics and Statistics* 42 (May 1960):175–81.

———. "The Economic Aspects of Slowing Population Growth." *Economic Journal* 76 (March 1966):44–56.

———. "Economic Consequences of Rapid Population Growth." *Economic Journal* 81 (December 1971):800–11.

Fair, Gordon M., and Daniel A. Okun. *Water and Wastewater Engineering*, 2 vols. New York: John Wiley, 1966.

Fanshel, S., and J. W. Bush. "A Health-Status Index and Its Application to Health-Services Outcomes." *Operations Research* 18 (1970): 1021–66.

Farooq, M. "A Possible Approach to the Evaluation of the Economic Burden Imposed on a Community by Schistosomiasis." *Annals of Tropical Medicine and Parasitology* 57 (September 1963):323–31.

———. "Medical and Economic Importance of Schistosomiasis." *Journal of Tropical Medicine and Hygiene* 67 (May 1964):105–12.

Feachem, Richard G. *Domestic Water Use in the New Guinea Highlands: The Case of the Raiapu Enga.* Water Research Laboratory Report no. 132. Manly Vale, N.S.W., Australia: University of New South Wales, 1973.

———. "Faecal Coliforms and Faecal Streptococci in Streams in the New Guinea Highlands." *Water Research* 8 (1974):367–74.

———. "Water Supplies for Low-Income Communities in Developing Countries." Journal of the Environmental Engineering Division, *Proceedings of the American Society of Civil Engineers,* 101, no. EE5 (1975):687–702.

Fein, Rashi. *Economics of Mental Illness.* New York: Basic Books, 1958.

Fenwick, K. W. H. "The Short Term Effects of a Pilot Environmental Health Project in Rural Africa: The Zaina Scheme Reassessed after Four Years." Nyeri, Central Province, Kenya: Ministry of Health, 1966.

"Flush Latrine Program." Uttar Pradesh, India: Local Self-Government Engineering Department, n.d.

Ford, J. L., and J. J. Warford. "Cost Functions for the Water Industry." *Journal of Industrial Ecoiomics* 18, no. 1 (1969):53–63.

Frankel, Richard J. "Research on Rural Community Water Supply at the Asian Institute of Technology, Bangkok." Paper presented at the WHO Regional Seminar on Rural Water Supply, Khon Kaen, Thailand, 4–14, March 1970.

———. "An Evaluation of the Effectiveness of the Community Potable Water Project in Northeast Thailand: Final Report." Bangkok: Asian Institute of Technology, 1973.

———, and P. Shouvanaberakul. "Demand for Water in Small Communities of Northeast Thailand." Bangkok: Asian Institute of Technology, n.d.

Frederiksen, Harald. "Consequences of Mortality Trends in Ceylon" and "Malaria Control and Population Pressure in Ceylon." In *Readings on Population*, edited by David M. Heer. Englewood Cliffs, N.J.: Prentice-Hall, 1968.

Ghana, Ministry of Health, Environmental Health Division. "Water Supplies and Water-Borne Diseases in Ghana." Accra, 1970.

Ginn, H. W., M. W. Corey, and E. J. Middlebrooks. "Design Parameters for Rural Water Distribution Systems." *Journal of the American Water Works Association* 58, no. 12 (1966):1595–1602.

Goodwin, Melvin H., Gorey J. Love, Don C. Mackel, and Rudolf G. Wanner. "Observations of Familial Occurrence of Diarrhea and Enteric Pathogens." *American Journal of Epidemiology* 84, no. 2 (1966):268–81.

Gopalakrishnan, Chennat. "Water Transfer and Economic Development." *Water Resources Bulletin* 4 (June 1968):45–48.

Gordon, J. E., "Acute Diarrheal Disease." *American Journal of the Medical Sciences* 248 (September 1964):345–65.

Gramiccia, G., P. A. Stevens, M. Faghih, B. Janbakhsh, and F. A. Arjomand. "Comprehensive Report and Evaluation of Work and Results of Arthropod-Borne Diseases Control Project in Iran for Years 1953–1955." Tehran: Ministry of Health, Institute of Malariology and Parasitology, 31 December 1955.

Greenwood, Michael J. "Research on Internal Migration in the United States: A Survey." *Journal of Economic Literature* 13, no. 2 (1975): 397–433.

Gremliza, F. G. L. "A Method for Measuring the Quality of Village Conditions in Less Developed Rural Areas." *American Journal of Public Health* 55, no. 1 (1965):107–15.

Grossman, Michael. "On the Concept of Health Capital and the Demand for Health." *Journal of Political Economy* 80 (March–April 1972): 223–55.

Grover, Brian. "Harvesting Precipitation for Community Water Supplies." Master's thesis, University of Manitoba, April 1971.

Gysi, Marshall. "The Effect of Price on Long Run Water Supply Benefits and Costs." *Water Resources Bulletin* 7 (June 1971):521–28.

Hale, J., and T. R. Jacobi. "Report on Community Water Supply for Ethiopia." Geneva: World Health Organization, Regional Office for the Eastern Mediterranean, July–September 1968.

Hamilton, Henry R., D. H. Owens, T. E. Carrol, A. R. Gunn, and B. A. Gilmore. *Bibliography on Socio-Economic Aspects of Water Resources*. Prepared at the Office of Water Resources Research, Washington, D.C. Columbus, Ohio: Battelle Memorial Institute, 1966.

Hansen, Niles M., ed. *Growth Centers in Regional Economic Development.* New York: Free Press, 1972.

Harris, Robert R. "A Summary of Guidelines and Criteria for Water Supplies in Developing Countries." *Journal of the American Water Works Association* 62, no. 9 (1970):561–62.

Heer, David M., and Dean O. Smith. "Mortality Level, Desired Family Size and Population Increase." *Demography* 5 (1968):104–21.

Heijnen, J. D., and D. Conyers. "Impact Studies of Rural Water Supply." In *Water Supply*, edited by G. Tschannerl. BRALUP Research Paper no. 20. Dar es Salaam: University of Dar es Salaam, 1971.

Henderson, J. M. *Report on Global Urban Water Supply Program Costs in Developing Nations.* Washington, D.C.: International Cooperation Administration, 1961.

Herrara, Felipe. "Nationalism and Urbanization in Latin America." *Ekistics* 32 (1971):369–73.

Herrick, Bruce, and Ricardo Morán. "Declining Birth Rates in Chile: Their Effects on Output, Education, Health, and Housing." *Tempo*, April 1972. Santa Barbara, Calif.: General Electric Company.

Herrington, P. R., and J. C. Tate. "Water Consumption in England and Wales: An Economic Analysis." Leicester, U.K.: University of Leicester, 1971.

Hirshleifer, Jack, James C. DeHaven, and Jerome W. Milliman. *Water Supply: Economics, Technology and Policy.* Chicago: University of Chicago Press, 1960.

Hite, James C., and Eugene A. Laurent. "Empirical Study of Economic-Ecological Linkages in a Coastal Area." *Water Resources Research* 7 (October 1971):1070–78.

Hollister, Arthur C., Jr., Dorothy Beck, Alan M. Gittelsohn, and Emmarie C. Hemphill. "Influence of Water Availability on *Shigella* Prevalence in Children of Farm Labor Families." *American Journal of Public Health 45*, no. 3 (1955):354–62 (English). *Sanitary Engineering* 7 (January 1955):23–33 (Spanish).

Holloway, J. M. "Development of Rural Water Supplies in Tanzania." *Proceedings of Institution of Civil Engineers* 45 (April 1970):641–60.

Hoover, Edgar M. *An Introduction to Regional Economics.* New York: Alfred A. Knopf, 1971.

Howe, Charles W. *Benefit-Cost Analysis for Water System Planning.* Water Resources Monograph no. 2. Washington, D.C.: American Geophysical Union, 1971.

Hudson, James. "Lītānī River of Lebanon: An Example of Middle Eastern Water Development." *Middle East Journal* 25 (Winter 1971): 1–14.

Huisman, L. "Treatment Methods for Water Supplies in Rural Areas of

Developing Countries." The Hague (Voorburg): WHO International Reference Centre for Community Water Supply, October 1975.

Intermediate Technology Development Group Ltd. "The Introduction of Rainwater Catchment Tanks and Micro-Irrigation to Botswana." London, September 1969.

Isard, Walter, and Robert E. Coughlin. *Municipal Costs and Revenues Resulting from Community Growth.* Wellesley, Mass.: Chandler-Davis Publishing Co., 1957.

―――, and John H. Cumberland, eds. *Conference on Regional Economic Development.* Conference held at Bellagio, Italy, July 1960. Paris: Organization for European Economic Cooperation, European Productivity Agency, 1961.

Jackson, Sarah. *Economically Appropriate Technologies for Developing Countries: A Summary.* Washington, D.C.: Overseas Development Council, 1972.

Jarrett, Robert E. "Environmental Factors and Childhood Mortality." Washington, D.C.: Pan American Health Organization and World Health Organization, 1970.

Johnson, James E. " 'Jash' Self-Help Program in Jordan." Eighth annual report. Amman: Near East Foundation, April 1967.

―――. "Rural Resources Development Program for Jordan." Amman: Near East Foundation, 1967.

Jordan, P., Lilian Woodstock, Gladwin O. Unrau, and J. A. Cook. "Control of *Schistosoma Mansoni* Transmission by Provision of Domestic Water Supplies in St. Lucia; A Preliminary Report." New York: The Rockefeller Foundation, 1974.

Kally, Elisha. "Determination of Water Supply Investment Priorities in Developing Countries." *Journal of the American Water Works Association* 57, no. 8 (1965):955–64.

Kawata, Kazuyoshi. "Providing a Safe Water Supply in the African Bush." *Public Health Reports* 82 (December 1967):1057–62.

Ketcham, David L. "End of Tour Report on Malagasy Republic." New York: Near East Foundation, 1968.

Khorev, B. "What Kind of City Is Needed?" *Literaturnaya gazeta* 14 (1969), reported in *The Current Digest of the Soviet Press* 21, no. 14 (23 April 1969).

Klarman, Herbert E. *The Economics of Health.* New York: Columbia University Press, 1965.

―――. "Present Status of Cost-Benefit Analysis in the Health Field." *American Journal of Public Health* 57, no. 11 (1967):1948–53.

―――. "Syphilis Control Program." In *Measuring Benefits of Government Investments,* edited by Robert Dorfman. Studies of Government Finance. Washington, D.C.: Brookings Institution, 1965.

Kneese, Allen V. "The Quality of Water and Economic Development." *Boletín de la Oficina Sanitaria Panamericana* 69 (July 1970):36–49.

―――, and Blair T. Bower. *Managing Water Quality: Economics, Technology, Institutions.* Baltimore: Johns Hopkins University Press, 1968.

Kourany, Miguel, and Manual A. Vásquez. "Housing and Certain Socioenvironmental Factors and Prevalence of Enteropathogenic Bacteria among Infants with Diarrheal Disease in Panama." *American Journal of Tropical Medicine and Hygiene* 18, no. 6 (1969):936–41.

Krishnaswami, S. K. "Health Aspects of Water Quality." *American Journal of Public Health* 61, no. 11 (1971):2259–68.

Krueger, Anne O. "Some Economic Costs of Exchange Control: The Turkish Case." *Journal of Political Economy* 74 (October 1966): 466–80.

Kuznets, Simon S. *Modern Economic Growth: Rate, Structure, and Spread.* New Haven: Yale University Press, 1966.

Lamanna, Carl. "Public Health Microbiological Needs in Underdeveloped Nations." *American Journal of Public Health* 56, no. 2 (1966):243–53.

Lauria, Donald T. *Interim Report on the Optimal Design of Small Water Supplies in Developing Countries.* Chapel Hill: University of North Carolina, Dept. of Environmental Sciences and Engineering, School of Public Health, 1971.

―――. *Planning Small Water Supplies in Developing Countries.* Final report submitted to the U.S., Agency for International Development, Office of Health. Chapel Hill: University of North Carolina, Dept. of Environmental Sciences and Engineering, School of Public Health, 1972.

Lee, Terence R. *Residential Water Demand and Economic Development.* Dept. of Geography Research Publication no. 2. Toronto: University of Toronto Press, 1969.

Leibenstein, Harvey. "Pitfalls in Benefit-Cost Analysis of Birth Prevention." *Population Studies* 23 (July 1969):161–70.

Leopold, Luna B.; Frank E. Clarke, Bruce B. Hanshaw, and James R. Balsley. "A Procedure for Evaluating Environmental Impact." *Geological Survey Circular 645.* Washington, D.C.: U.S., Geological Survey, 1971.

Levy, Mildred B., and Walter Wadycki. "Lifetime versus One-Year Migration in Venezuela." *Journal of Regional Science* 12 (December 1972): 407–15.

Lieberman, Morton W., and John T. Robinson. "Report on an Inspection of Potable Water Supply Installation in Peru." New York: United Nations, February 1965.

Linaweaver, F. P. *A Study of Residential Water Use.* A report prepared by Johns Hopkins University, Dept. of Environmental Engineering

Science, for U.S. Dept. of Housing and Urban Development. Washington, D.C.: Government Printing Office, 1967.

Little, Ian M.D., and James A. Mirrlees. *Manual of Industrial Project Analysis*. Vol. 2. *Social Cost-Benefit Analysis*. Development Centre Studies. Paris: Organization for Economic Cooperation and Development 1969.

Logan, John A. "The Quantitative Relationships between Community Water Supplies and Economic Development." *International Review of Tropical Medicine* 2 (1963):27–40.

———. "The International Municipal Water Supply Program: A Health and Economic Appraisal." *American Journal of Tropical Medicine and Hygiene* 9 (September 1960):469–76.

Lowry, Ira S. *Migration and Metropolitan Growth: Two Analytical Models*. San Francisco: Chandler Publishing Co., 1966.

Maass, Arthur A., and David C. Major. "The Objectives of Water Policy and Related Institutional Problems." United Nations Panel of Experts on Water Resources Development Policies, Buenos Aires, June 1970.

Maass, Arthur A., Maynard M. Hufschmidt, Robert Dorfman, Harold A. Thomas, Stephen A. Marglin, and Gordon Fair. *Design of Water Resource Systems*. Cambridge, Mass.: Harvard University Press, 1962.

Mabogunje, Alvin L. "Manufacturing and the Geography of Development in Tropical Africa." *Economic Geography* 49, no. 1 (1973): 1–20.

McCabe, De Soto B. "Water and Wastewater Systems to Combat Cholera in East Pakistan." *Journal Water Pollution Control Federation* 42 (November 1970):1968–81.

McCabe, Leland J., and T. W. Haines. "Diarrheal Disease Control by Improved Human Excreta Disposal." *Public Health Reports* 72 (October 1957):921–28.

McCabe, Leland J., James M. Synons, Roger D. Lee, and Gordon G. Robeck. "Survey of Community Water Supply Systems." *Journal of the American Water Works Association* 62, no. 11 (1970):670–87.

McConnell, Charles B. "Bilharziasis Pilot Control Project, February 1969 to February 1971, Dezful, Iran." New York: Near East Foundation, 1971.

McJunkin, Frederick E. *Community Water Supply in Developing Countries*. U.S. Agency for International Development, with the U.S. Public Health Service, Office of International Health. Chapel Hill, N.C. 1969.

———. *Engineering Measures for Control of Schistosomiasis*. Washington, D.C.: U.S., Agency for International Development, 1970.

McKim, Wayne. "The Periodic Market System in Northeastern Ghana." *Economic Geography* 48, no. 3 (1972):333–44.

Mahler, Halfdan. "Health Strategies in a Changing World." *WHO Chronicle* 29, no. 6 (1975):212.
Malenbaum, Wilfred. "Health and Productivity in Poor Areas." In *Empirical Studies in Health Economics,* edited by Herbert Klarman. Baltimore: Johns Hopkins University Press, 1970.
Mandelmann, E. "Malta: A Many-Sided Health Program." *World Health,* August 1968, pp. 28–35.
Manne, Alan S., ed. *Investments for Capacity Expansion: Size, Location, and Time Phasing.* Cambridge, Mass.: M.I.T. Press, 1967.
Marglin, Stephen A. *Public Investment Criteria; Benefit-Cost Analysis for Planned Economic Growth.* Cambridge, Mass.: M.I.T. Press, 1967.
Marshall, Carter L. "The Relationship Between Trachoma and Piped Water in a Developing Area." *Archives of Environmental Health* 17 (August 1968):215–20.
———. "Some Exercises in Social Ecology: Health, Disease and Modernization in the Ryukyu Islands." In *The Careless Technology,* edited by M. Taghi Farvar and J. P. Milton. New York: Natural History Press, 1972.
Mendenhall, Ralph L. " 'Jash' Self-Help Program in Jordan." Tenth annual report. New York: Near East Foundation, 1969.
Miller, Arthur P. *Water and Man's Health.* AID Community Water Supply Technical Series 5. Washington, D.C.: U.S., Agency for International Development, 1962.
Mishan, Edward J. *Cost-Benefit Analysis: An Introduction.* New York: Praeger, 1971.
———. "Evaluation of Life and Limb: A Theoretical Approach." *Journal of Political Economy* 79 (July–August 1971):687–705.
Mobasheri, Fereiderun. *Economic Evaluation of Water Resources Development Projects in a Development Economy.* Water Resources Center Contribution no. 126. Berkeley: University of California, 1968.
Molina, Gustavo, and Ilana Freda Noam. "Indicators of Health, Economy and Culture in Puerto Rico and Latin America." *American Journal of Public Health* 54, no. 8 (1964):1191–1206.
Moore, G. T., W. M. Cross, and D. McGuire. "Epidemic Giardiasis at a Ski Resort." *New England Journal of Medicine* 281 (1969):402–7.
Moore, Helen A., Enrique de la Cruz, and Oscar Vargas-Mendez. "Diarrheal Disease Studies in Costa Rica: I. Plan and Methods of Investigation." *American Journal of Public Health* 56, no. 2 (1966): 276–86.
———. "Diarrheal Disease Studies in Costa Rica: III. Morbidity and Mortality from Diarrhea." *American Journal of Epidemiology* 82, no. 2 (1965):143–61.
———. "Diarrheal Disease Studies in Costa Rica: IV. The Influence of Sanitation Upon the Prevalence of Intestinal Infection and Diarrheal

Disease." *American Journal of Epidemiology* 82, no. 2 (1965):162–84.

———, and Flora I. Perez. "Diarrheal Disease Studies in Costa Rica: II. The Prevalence of Certain Enteric Organisms and Their Relationship to Diarrhea." *American Journal of Public Health* 56, no. 3 (1966):442–51.

Morfitt, R. P., & Associates. "A Non-Conventional Mass Approach to Rural Village Water Projects." A report to the Pan American Health Organization, Corvallis, Ore., 1969.

Morse, R. "Costs of Urban Infrastructure as Related to City Size in Developing Countries: India Case Study." Stanford, Calif.: Stanford Research Institute, 1968.

Mushkin, Selma. "Health As An Investment." *Journal of Political Economy* 70 (October 1962 supplement):129–57.

———, and B. A. Weisbrod. "Investment in Health—Lifetime Health Expenditures on the 1960 Work Force." *Kyklos* 16 (1963):583–98.

Nathan Consortium for Sector Studies. "The Design and the Costs of New Water Supply Systems." Prepared for the Ministry of Finance and Economy Planning, Accra, April 1970.

Niehoff, Arthur H., ed. *A Casebook of Social Change.* Chicago: Aldine Publishing Co., 1966.

Okun, Daniel A. *The Community Water Supply Program of the Agency for International Development.* Washington, D.C.: U.S., Dept. of State, February 1965.

———. "Planning for Water Supply Development." *American Journal of Public Health* 54, no. 6 (1964): 900–7.

Ostrom, Vincent, and Elinor Ostrom. "Legal and Political Conditions of Water Resource Development." *Land Economics* 48 (February 1972):1–14.

Palmer, Juan R., Aída Z. Colón, Frederick F. Ferguson, and William R. Jobin, "The Control of Schistosomiasis in Patillas, Puerto Rico." Boletín de la Asociación Médica Puertoriqueña 62 (May 1970): 156–60.

Pan American Health Organization. *Community Water Supply and Sewage Disposal Programs in Latin America and Caribbean Countries.* ES Technical Series 5. Washington, D.C.: Dept. of Engineering and Environmental Sciences, 1969.

———. *Facts on Health Progress 1971, Goals in the Charter of Punta del Este.* Scientific Publications no. 227. Washington, D.C., 1971.

———. *Man-Environmental Relationships in the 1970's.* Washington, D.C., August 1971.

———. *Reported Cases of Notifiable Diseases in the Americas, 1968.* Scientific Publications no. 233. Washington, D.C., 1971.

———. "Rural Water Supply Services Community Financing." Special meeting of the Ministers of Health of the Americas, Buenos Aires,

14–18 October 1968. Working Documents, 1969. Official Document no. 90. Washington, D.C., 1969.

"Paraguay: Water for a Thirsty City." *World Health,* July–August 1960, p. 27.

Patchick, Paul F. "Management of a Foreign Water-Resources Research Project." *Water Resources Bulletin* 4, no. 3 (1968):44–57.

Pelaez, Emmanuel. "Philippine Water Resources Development and Its Problems." *Economic Research Journal* 15 (March 1969):249–53.

Pescod, M. B. "Sludge Handling and Disposal in Tropical Developing Countries." *Water Pollution Control Federation Journal* 43 (April 1971):555–70.

———, and Daniel A. Okun, eds. *Water Supply and Wastewater Disposal in Developing Countries, Proceedings.* Bangkok: Asian Institute of Technology, 1971.

Pineo, Charles S. "Community Water Supply and Sewage Disposal Situation and Needs in Latin America and Other Areas of the Developing World." Paper presented at the XIV Interamerican Sanitary Engineering Congress, 4–9 August 1974, Mexico City.

Pitchford, R. J. "Findings in Relation to Schistosome Transmission in the Field Following the Introduction of Various Control Measures." *South African Medical Journal* 40 (8 October 1966, supplement): 1–16.

———. "Further Observations on Bilharzia Control in the Eastern Transvaal." *South African Medical Journal* 44 (18 April 1970): 475–77.

Pontes, Luíz Augusto de Lima, and Carlos Roberto Minervino Ramos. "Preliminary Study of Investment Cost-Benefit in Urban Sanitation." Paper presented at the Sixth Brazilian Congress and Sanitary Engineering, São Paulo, 17–22 January 1971, and XII Interamerican Congress of Sanitary Engineering, Caracas, 23–29 August 1970.

Prest, A. R., and R. Turvey. "Cost-Benefit Analysis." *Economic Journal* 75 (December 1965):683–735.

Proctor, J. H., ed. *Building Ujamaa Villages in Tanzania.* Studies in Political Science no. 2. Dar es Salaam: University of Dar es Salaam, 1971.

Puffer, Ruth Rice, and Carlos V. Serrano. *Patterns of Mortality in Childhood.* Scientific Publication PAHO 262. Washington, D.C.: Pan American Health Organization, 1973.

———, and Ann Dillon. *Inter-American Investigation of Mortality in Childhood.* Provisional report. Washington, D.C.: Pan American Health Organization, September 1971.

Pyatt, Edwin F., and Peter P. Rogers. "On Estimating Benefit-Cost Ratios for Water Supply Investments." *American Journal of Public Health* 52 (October 1962):1729–42.

———, and Hassan Sheikh. "Benefit-Cost Analysis for Municipal Water Supplies." *Land Economics* 40 (November 1964):444–49.
Redford, Arthur. *Labour Migration in England, 1800–1850*. New York: A. M. Kelley, 1968.
Rees, Judith. "Domestic Water Supply." In *Infrastructure Problems of the Cities of Developing Countries*. New York: The Ford Foundation, 1971.
Rice, Dorothy. *Estimating the Cost of Illness*. Health Economics Series no. 6. Washington, D.C.: U.S., Dept. of Health, Education, and Welfare, May 1966.
———, and Barbara S. Cooper. "The Economic Value of Human Life." *American Journal of Public Health* 57 (November 1967):1954–66.
Richardson, Harry W. *The Economics of Urban Size*. Lexington, Mass.: D. C. Heath and Co., 1973.
Riddell, Barry J., and Milton E. Harvey. "The Urban System in the Migration Process: An Evaluation of Step-Wise Migration in Sierra Leone." *Economic Geography* 48 (July 1972):270–83.
Ripman, H. *Water Use and Economic Development*. Paper presented at International Conference on Water for Peace, 23–31 May 1967, Washington, D.C.
Riverside County, California, Department of Health. "A Waterborne Epidemic of Salmonellosis in Riverside, California, 1965." A collaborative report. *American Journal of Epidemiology* 93 (1971):33–48.
Robertson, Robert L. "Economic Effects of Personal Health Services: Work Loss in a Public School Teacher Population." *American Journal of Public Health* 61, no. 1 (1971):30–45.
Robinson, Warren C., and David E. Horlacher. "Population Growth and Economic Welfare." *Reports on Population/Family Planning* 6. New York: The Population Council, February 1971.
Rosenfeld, P. L. *Schistosomiasis Transmission Model*. Washington, D.C.: U.S., Agency for International Development, 1975.
Rosser, R., and V. Watts. "The Measure of Hospital Output." Paper presented to the Operational Research Society Conference, September 1971, Lancaster, U.K.
Rubenstein, A., J. Boyle, C. L. Odoroff, and S. J. Kunitz. "Effect of Improved Sanitary Facilities on Infant Diarrhea in a Hopi Village." *Public Health Reports* 84 (December 1969):1093–97.
Ruíz, Aldelmo. "Efforts of U.S. Agency for International Development to Supply Water to People of Yemen." *Journal of the American Water Works Association* 58, no. 10 (1966):1247–59.
"Rural Water Supply and Sanitation Scheme in Pharenda Block of District Gorakhpur." Uttar Pradesh, India, n.d.
Safilios-Rothschild, Constantina. "Children and Adolescents in Slums and

Shanty-Towns in Developing Countries." New York: United Nations Economic and Social Council, March 1971.

Saunders, Robert J. "Economic Benefits of Potable Water Supplies in Rural Areas of Developing Countries." *Journal of the American Water Works Association* 67, no. 6 (1975):314–17.

———. *Forecasting Water Demand: An Inter- and Intra-Community Study.* Monograph Series. Morgantown: Bureau of Business Research, West Virginia University, 1969.

———. "Population Flows, Spatial Economic Activity, and Urban Areas in Appalachia." *Annals of Regional Science* 5, no. 1 (1971):125–36.

———. "Urban Area Water Consumption: Analysis and Projections." *Quarterly Review of Economics and Business* 9 (Summer 1969):5–20.

———, and J. J. Warford. "Village Water Supply and Sanitation in Less Developed Countries." Public Utilities Dept. Report no. RES 2. Washington, D.C.: World Bank, March 1974.

———, and Ronald Cocari. "Racial Earnings Differentials: Some Economic Factors." *American Journal of Economics and Sociology* 32, no. 3 (1973):225–33.

Schelling, Thomas C. "The Life You Save May Be Your Own." In *Problems in Public Expenditure Analysis,* edited by Samuel B. Chase, Jr. Studies of Government Finance. Washington, D.C.: Brookings Institution, 1968.

Schliessman, D. J. "Diarrhoeal Disease and the Environment." *Bulletin of the World Health Organization* 21, no. 3 (1959):381–86.

———, F. O. Atchley, M. J. Wilcomb, Jr., and L. F. Welch. *Relationship of Environmental Factors to the Occurrence of Enteric Diseases in Areas of Eastern Kentucky.* Public Health Monograph 54. Washington, D.C.: U.S., Dept. of Health, Education, and Welfare, 1958.

Schramm, Gunter, and Robert E. Burt, Jr. *An Analysis of Federal Water Resource Planning and Evaluation Procedures.* Ann Arbor: University of Michigan Press, June 1970.

Scott, Earl P. "The Spatial Structure of Rural Northern Nigeria: Farmers' Periodic Markets, and Villages." *Economic Geography* 48, no. 3 (1972):316–32.

Scrimshaw, Nevin S. "Synergism of Malnutrition and Infection: Evidence from Field Studies in Guatemala." *Journal of the American Medical Association* 212 (8 June 1970):1685–92.

———, Carl E. Taylor, and John E. Gordon. *Interactions of Nutrition and Infection.* WHO Monograph Series no. 57. Geneva: World Health Organization, 1968.

Seidel, Harris F., and E. Robert Baumann. "A Statistical Analysis of Water Works Data for 1955." *Journal of the American Water Works Association* 49, no. 12 (1957):1531–66.

Seidel, Harris F. and J. L. Cleasby. "A Statistical Analysis of Water

Works Data for 1960." *Journal of the American Water Works Association* 58, no. 12 (1966):1507-27.
Sen, R., and B. Jacobs. "Pathogenic Intestinal Organisms in the Unfiltered Water Supply of Calcutta and the Effect of Chlorination." *Indian Journal of Medical Research* 57 (July 1969):1220-27.
Shipman, Harold R. "Policies Affecting the Financing of Urban Water Supply in Developing Countries." International Standing Committee on Problems of Water Supply in Developing Countries. Subject no. 2. Washington, D.C.: World Bank, 1972.
———. "Water Rate Structures in Latin America." *Journal of the American Water Works Association* 59, no. 1 (1967):3-12.
———. "Water Supply Management in Latin America." *Journal of the American Water Works Association* 60, no. 6 (1968):745-48.
———. "Water Supply Problems in Developing Countries." *Journal of the American Water Works Association* 59, no. 7 (1967):767-72.
Siegal, Francine M. "Schistosomiasis Hematobia in Preschool Children of Ibadan, Nigeria." *American Journal of Tropical Medicine and Hygiene* 17, no. 5 (1968):737-42.
Simon, Julian. "The Per-Capita-Income Criterion and Natality Policies in Poor Countries." *Demography* 7 (August 1970):369-78.
———. "The Value of Avoided Births to Underdeveloped Countries." *Population Studies* 23 (March 1969):61-68.
Smith, Courtland L., and Thomas C. Hogg. "Benefits and Beneficiaries: Contrasting Economic and Cultural Distinctions." *Water Resources Bulletin* 7, no. 2 (1971):254-63.
———. "Cultural Aspects of Water Resource Development: Past, Present, Future." *Water Resources Bulletin* 7, no. 3 (1971):652-60.
Snyder, John C. "Population and Disease Control." *American Journal of Tropical Medicine and Hygiene* 21, no. 4 (1972):386-91.
Spruyt, Dirk J., Francis B. Elder, Simon D. Messing, Mary K. Wade, Brook Ryder, Julius S. Price, and Yohannes Tseghe. "Ethiopian Health Center Program—Its Impact on Community Health." *Ethiopian Medical Journal* 5 (July 1967):1-87.
Stander, G. J., and P. G. J. Meiring. "Employing Oxidation Ponds for Low-Cost Sanitation." *Water Pollution Control Federation Journal* 37 (July 1965):1025-33.
Stewart, William H., Leland J. McCabe, Emmarie C. Hemphill, and Thelma DeCapito. "IV. Diarrheal Disease Control Studies, Relationship of Certain Environmental Factors to the Prevalence of *Shigella* Infection." *American Journal of Tropical Medicine and Hygiene* 4 (July 1955):718-24.
Studwick, R. H., and D. Hollinson. "The Zaina Environmental Sanitation Scheme: A Pilot Project in Rural Africa." (WHO/Env. San./135). Geneva: World Health Organization, 1962.

Subrahmanyan, K. "Note on the Importance of Environmental Sanitation in the Campaign Against Cholera." Geneva: World Health Organization, 18 September 1951.

———, T. R. Bhaskaran, and C. C. Sekar. "Studies on Rural Water Supplies." *Indian Journal of Medical Research* 36 (July 1948):211–47.

Taylor, Floyd B. "Functional Design for Effective Operations of Water Supply Systems in Developing Countries." *Journal of the American Water Works Association* 59, no. 2 (1967):150–55.

Taylor, Gary C. *Economic Planning of Water Supply Systems*. Giannini Foundation Research Report no. 291. Berkeley: University of California, 1967.

"Terminal Report of the Community Development Pilot Demonstration in Jordan, 1956–1960." New York: Near East Foundation, 1960.

Turvey, Ralph. *Economic Analysis and Public Enterprises*. Totowa, N.J.: Rowmann and Littlefield, 1971.

———, and J. J. Warford. "Urban Water Supply and Sewerage Pricing." Public Utilities Note no. 11. Washington, D.C.: World Bank, 1974.

Unakul, Somnuek, "Thailand's Rural Community Water Supply Programme." In *Water Supply and Wastewater Disposal in Developing Countries,* edited by M. B. Pescod and D. A. Okun. Bangkok: Asian Institute of Technology, 1971.

United Nations Industrial Development Organization. *Guidelines for Project Evaluation*. (ID/SER.H/2). New York: United Nations, 1972.

United Nations International Children's Fund. UNICEF-WHO Joint Committee on Health Policy. "Assessment of Environmental Sanitation and Rural Water Supply Programmes, Assisted by UNICEF and WHO (1959–1968)." (JC16/UNICEF-WHO/69.2). Geneva, 1969.

United Nations Research Institute for Social Development. "Cost-Benefit Analysis of Social Projects." Report no. 7. A meeting of experts in Rennes, France, 27 September–2 October 1965. Geneva, 1966.

United States, Agency for International Development. "Community Water Supply in Developing Countries." USAID Bibliography Series: Health no. 1. Washington, D.C., 1969.

——— and Ethiopian Ministry of Public Health. "A Study of the Health Impact of a Protected Community Water Supply—Methodology and Baseline Findings." Washington, D.C., December 1965.

———, Office of Science and Technology. "Water Quality Standards and International Development." Washington, D.C., October 1971.

United States, Dept. of Health, Education, and Welfare. "Guidelines and Criteria for Community Water Supplies in the Developing Countries." (PASA TCR 3–67). Rockville, Md.: U.S., Agency for International Development and U.S., Public Health Service, 1969.

———. "Health Program Evaluation: Impact Study of the Indian Sanitation Facilities Construction Act." Prepared by Lawrence Berg and Thomas Mowery, at Tucson, Arizona, 1968.

Unrau, Gladwin O. "Individual Household Water Supplies in Rural St. Lucia as a Control Measure Against Schistosoma Mansoni." New York: The Rockefeller Foundation, 1974.

Van Zijl, W. J. "Studies of Diarrhoeal Diseases in Seven Countries by WHO Diarrhoeal Diseases Advisory Team." *Bulletin of the World Health Organization* 35, no. 2 (1966):249–61.

Wagner, Edmund G., and J. N. Lanoix. *Water Supply for Rural Areas and Small Communities.* WHO Monograph Series no. 42. Geneva: World Health Organization, 1959.

Wagner, Edmund G., and Luis Wannoni. "Anticipated Savings in Venezuela through the Construction of Safe Water Supplies in Rural Areas." (WHO/Env. San. 40). Paper presented to the Expert Committee on Environmental Sanitation, World Health Organization, Geneva, July 1953.

Wall, John W., and J. Phillip Keeve. "Water Supply, Diarrheal Disease, and Nutrition: A Survey of the Literature and Recommendations for Research." Draft working paper. Washington, D.C.: World Bank, September 1974.

Warford, J. J. "A Pricing and Investment Policy for Antigua's Water Supply." *Social and Economic Studies* 16 (June 1967):127–55.

———. "Public Utility Pricing and Urban Land Use Policy in Less Developed Countries." Paper presented at Conference on the Pricing of Local Services and Effects on Urban Spatial Structure at the University of British Columbia, Vancouver, June 1974.

———. "The Role of Economics in Municipal Water Supply: Theory and Practice." Washington, D.C.: World Bank, December 1971.

———. *The South Atcham Scheme.* Report submitted to the Minister of Housing and Local Government. London: Her Majesty's Stationery Office, 1969.

———. "Water Requirements: The Investment Decision in the Water Supply Industry." In *Public Enterprise,* edited by Ralph Turvey. New York: Penguin Books, 1968.

———, and Ralph Turvey. *Lahore Water Supply Tariff Study.* Public Utilities Note 12. Washington, D.C.: World Bank, August 1974.

Warner, Dennis. *The Economics of Rural Water Supply in Tanzania.* Economic Research Bureau Paper 70.19. Dar es Salaam: University College, 1970.

———. "Evaluation Criteria for Village-Level Water Projects in Developing Countries." Report EEP-30. Stanford, Calif.: Stanford University, 1968.

———. "Evaluation of the Development Impact of Rural Water Supply

Projects in East African Villages." Report EEP-50. Stanford, Calif.: Stanford University, 1973.

――――. *A Preliminary Assessment of the Impact of Rural Water Supply Upon Households and Villages.* Dar es Salaam: University College, Economic Research Bureau, 1970.

――――. *Rural Water Supply and Development: A Comparison of Nine Villages in Tanzania.* Economic Research Bureau Paper no. 69.17. Dar es Salaam: University College, 1969.

――――, ed. *Rural Water Supply in East Africa.* Proceedings of the Rural Water Supply Workshop. BRALUP Research Paper no. 11. Dar es Salaam: University College, 1970.

Warner, Dennis, and Jarir S. Dajani. *Water and Sewer Development in Rural America.* Lexington, Mass.: D. C. Heath and Co., 1975.

"Water." *World Health,* May–June 1960, p. 22.

――――. *World Health,* July–August 1964.

Water for Peace. Vol. 1. International Conference on Water for Peace, 23–31 May 1967, Washington, D.C.

Water Supplies and the Socio-Economic Development of a Community. Paris: Société d'Economie et de Mathématique Appliquées, 1968.

Watt, James, A. C. Hollister, M. D. Beck, and E. C. Hemphill. "Diarrheal Diseases in Fresno County, California." *American Journal of Public Health* 43, no. 6 (1953):728–41.

Weibel, S. R., F. R. Dixon, R. B. Weidner, and Leland J. McCabe. "Waterborne-Disease Outbreaks, 1946–1960." *Journal of the American Water Works Association* 56, no. 8 (1964):947–58.

Weir, John M. "The Unconquered Plague." *The Rockefeller Foundation Quarterly* 2 (1969):4–23.

Weisbrod, Burton A. *Economics of Public Health: Measuring the Economic Impact of Diseases.* Philadelphia: University of Pennsylvania Press, 1962.

――――, R. L. Andreano, R. E. Baldwin, E. H. Epstein, and A. C. Kelley. *Disease and Economic Development: The Impact of Parasitic Diseases in St. Lucia.* Madison: University of Wisconsin Press, 1973.

Whetstone, George A. "Water as a Commodity in International Trade." *Water Resources Bulletin* 6 (January–February 1970):65.

White, Anne U., and Chris Seviour. *Rural Water Supply and Sanitation in Less-Developed Countries: A Selected Annotated Bibliography.* Ottawa: International Development Research Centre, 1974.

White, Gilbert F., David J. Bradley, and Anne U. White. *Drawers of Water: Domestic Water Use in East Africa.* Chicago: University of Chicago Press, 1972.

Wiener, Aaron. "Development and Management of Water Supplies under

Conditions of Scarcity of Resources." Tel Aviv: Water Planning for Israel Ltd., April 1964.

Winslow, C. E. A. *The Cost of Sickness and the Price of Health*. WHO Monograph Series no. 7. Geneva: World Health Organization, 1951.

Winton, Elliott F., and Leland J. McCabe. "Studies Relating to Water Mineralization and Health." *Journal of the American Water Works Association* 62, no. 1 (1970):26–30.

———, and R. G. Tardiff. "Nitrate in Drinking Water." *Journal of the American Water Works Association* 63, no. 2 (1971):95–98.

Wittmann, W., A. D. Moodie, and S. A. Fellingham. "An Evaluation of the Relationship Between Nutritional Status and Infection by Means of a Field Study." *South African Medical Journal* 41 (1967):664–82.

Wolff, H. L., W. J. van Zijl, and M. Roy. "Houseflies, the Availability of Water, and Diarrhoeal Diseases." *Bulletin of the World Health Organization* 41, no. 6 (1969):952–59.

Wolman, Abel. "Water Supply and Environmental Health." *Journal of the American Water Works Association* 62, no. 12 (1970):746–49.

———, and Herbert M. Bosch. "Community Water Systems and Their Effect on Health." Paper in report on a United Nations Conference on the Application of Science and Technology for the Benefit of the Less Developed Areas. *Public Health Reports* 78 (April 1963):345–46.

———. "U.S. Water Supply Lessons Applicable to Developing Countries." *Journal of the American Water Works Association* 55, no. 8 (1963):946–56.

Wolman, Abel, and Gilbert F. White, eds. *Water, Health and Society*. Bloomington: Indiana University Press, 1969.

Wollman, Nathaniel. *The Value of Water in Alternative Uses*. Albuquerque: University of New Mexico Press, 1962.

Wood, W. D., and H. F. Campbell. *Cost-Benefit Analysis and the Economics of Investment in Human Resources: An Annotated Bibliography*. Kingston, Ont.: Queen's University, Industrial Relations Centre, 1970.

Wood, W. E. "Cholera Control through Environmental Sanitation: Basic Considerations." (WHO/EH/70.1). Geneva: World Health Organization, 1970.

———. "The Control of Waterborne Epidemics (Including Cholera and Other Enteric Infections) through the Improvement of Community Water Supply." (WHO/CWS/71.1). Geneva: World Health Organization, 1970.

———. "Rural Water Supply and Sanitation Programmes." Draft report. Geneva: World Health Organization, October 1971.

Woolley, P. O., C. A. Perry, and R. N. Eccles. *Syncrisis: the Dynamics of Health. An Analytic Series on the Interactions of Health and Socio-*

economic Development. I: Panama. U.S., Dept. of Health, Education, and Welfare. Washington, D.C.: Government Printing Office, 1970.

World Bank. "Appraisal of a Rural Development Fund Project, Upper Volta." Agricultural Projects Dept. Report PA-127A. Washington, D.C., 16 May 1972.

―――. "Issues in Village Water Supply." Public Utilities Dept. Report no. 793. Washington, D.C., 1975.

―――. "Measurement of the Health Benefits of Investments in Water Supply." Public Utilities Dept. report of an expert panel to the International Bank for Reconstruction and Development. Washington, D.C.: World Bank, December 1975.

―――. "Study of the Substitution of Labor and Equipment in Civil Construction: Phase II Final Report." Working Paper no. 172. Washington, D.C., 1974.

World Health Organization. "Assessment of Environmental Sanitation and Rural Water Supply Programme." Summary Report. Geneva, 1968.

―――. "Community Water Supplies: A Critical Situation." *WHO Chronicle* 23, no. 8 (1969):368.

―――. "Community Water Supplies for the Sudan." *WHO Chronicle* 21, no.8 (1967):359.

―――. "Community Water Supply." Report on a seminar convened by the WHO Regional Office for Africa, Brazzaville, April 1971.

―――. *Community Water Supply.* Technical Report Series no. 420. Geneva, 1969.

―――. "Community Water Supply and Sewage Disposal in Developing Countries (End of 1970)." *World Health Statistics Report,* 26, no. 11 (1973).

―――. "Community Water Supply Programme." Progress report by the Director-General to the Twenty-fifth World Health Assembly. Official Records no. 202 (A25/29). Geneva, 1972.

―――. "Community Water Supply—The Next Ten Years." *WHO Chronicle* 25, no. 2 (1971):70.

―――. "Community Water Systems and Their Effect on Health." *Public Health Reports* 78 (April 1963):345–46.

―――. "Cost of Rural and Village Sanitation in the South-East Asia Region." *WHO Chronicle* 21, no. 7 (1967):309–10.

―――. "Effects of Environmental Health." *WHO Chronicle* 21, no. 10 (1967):442–43.

―――. "General Community Water Supply Problems." Report no. 1. Geneva, November 1971.

―――. "International Conference on Research and Development in Community Water Supply." Report of a Conference at Cavtat,

Dubrovnik, Yugoslavia, 7–14 October 1970. (WHO/CWS/RD/71.4). Geneva, 1971.

———. International Reference Centre for Community Water Supply. *Plastic Pipe in Drinking Water Distribution Practice (Introduction and Bibliography up to 1970)*. Technical Paper no. 1. The Hague (Voorburg), 1971.

———. *International Standards for Drinking Water*. 3d ed. Geneva, 1971.

———. "More and Safer Water for the Developing Countries." *WHO Chronicle* 22, no. 8 (1968):362–71.

———. "The Prevention of Waterborne Viral Infections." *WHO Chronicle* 23, no. 6 (1969):277.

———. "Report on Regional Seminar on Rural Water Supply." Khon Kaen, Thailand, March 1970.

———. "Report of Studies on Diarrhoeal Diseases," WHO Diarrhoeal Diseases Advisory Team in cooperation with the Ministry of Health, Sudan, 20 March–27 June 1966. (WHO/Ent./66.2). Geneva, 1966.

———. "Report of a Survey of Diarrhoeal Diseases in Mauritius." WHO Diarrhoeal Diseases Advisory Team, March–May 1960. (WHO/Ent./66.2). Geneva, 1966.

———. "Report on Study of Diarrhoeal Diseases in Egypt." WHO Diarrhoeal Diseases Advisory Team with the cooperation of the Ministry of Health, United Arab Republic, 1 July–31 October 1961. Geneva, 1961.

———. "Rural Water Supplies in Africa." *WHO Chronicle* 25, no. 11 (1971):524.

———. "Schistosomiasis and Community Water Supplies." Community Water Supply Research and Development Programme, background paper. (WHO/CWS/RD 70.3). Geneva, March 1970.

———. "Second Ten Years of the World Health Organization: Environmental Health—Community Water Supply." *WHO Chronicle* 22, no. 7 (1968):308–9.

———. "Strategy of Cholera Control." Abbreviated proceedings of the WHO Seminar on the Organization of Cholera Control, Manila, 6–9 October 1970. (BD/Cholera/71.1). Geneva, 1971.

———. "Studies on Diarrhoeal Diseases. WHO Diarrhoeal Diseases Advisory Team in cooperation with Dept. of Health, Sri Lanka (Ceylon), 26 February–2 November, 1962. (WHO/Ent./66.4). Geneva, 1966.

———. "Studies on Diarrhoeal Diseases." WHO Diarrhoeal Diseases Advisory Team in cooperation with the Ministry of Health, Venezuela, 7 September 1964–7 July 1965. (WHO/Ent./66.7). Geneva, 1966.

———. "Studies on Diarrhoeal Diseases in Venezuela." Follow-up report on work of WHO Diarrhoeal Diseases Advisory Team in cooperation with Ministry of Health, Caracas. Geneva, 1966.

———. "Summary Report on Diarrhoeal Diseases Studies in Seven Developing Countries over a Five-Year Period, 1960–1965." Geneva, 1966.

———. "Twenty-Fourth World Health Assembly—2." *WHO Chronicle* 25, no. 8 (1971):338–39.

———"Water Supplies for Rural Communities." *WHO Chronicle* 25, no. 8 (1971):376–77.

———. *World Health Statistics Report* 26, no. 11 (1973):750.

———. "The World Health Situation, 1965–1968." *WHO Chronicle* 25, no. 11 (1971):489–97.

Wright, R. A., H. C. Spencer, R. E. Brodsky, and T. M. Vermont. "Giardiasis in Colorado: An Epidemiologic Study." Forthcoming.

Wyckoff, J. B. "Measuring Intangible Benefits—Some Needed Research." *Water Resources Bulletin* 7 (February 1971):11–16.

Yap, Lorene Y. L. "Internal Migration in Less Developed Countries: A Survey of the Literature." Working Paper no. 215. Washington, D.C.: World Bank, September 1975.

Index

Note: Page numbers in italic refer to tables.

Access to service, *4*, 5–13, 18, 19, 25, 78–82, 97, 104, 185, 201; and disease, 205–21
Acurio, Guido, 109n
Addis Ababa, 187
Afifi, Hamdy H., 90n
Africa, 5, 35, 60, 177, 181; construction costs in, 158–159; health and economic output in, 67; system administration in, 145; system supply capacity in, 139. See also East Africa; West Africa
Agriculture, 22, 72, 82, 185
Algeria, 5
Alonso, William, 80n, 81n
Avero, M., 71n, 215
American Water Works Association, 227; data of, 90, 91, 92
Americas, 5, 9, 60; health ministers conference for, 7
Anderson, Robert S., 142n
Aquatrol valve, 182
Aqueducts, 23
Argentina, 21, 64, 182; bonus incentive in, 155, 157; local committees in, 84; roof tanks in, 179
Arizona, 117, 208, 212, 213
Ascaris infestation, 206, 207, 208, 214
Asia, 35, 67, 181, 190, 235; construction costs in, 105, 108, 158–59; system supply capacity in, 139
Asian Institute of Technology, 134, 143

Asunción, 125, 126, 183
Athikomrungsarit, Charnvit, 143n
Azurín, J. C., 71n, 215

Bacolod City, *216, 218*
Bahl, Roy W., 66n
Balance of payments, 57, 59–61
Balantidium coli, 210, 212
Bangladesh, 158, 211
Bantu, 219
Barbosa, Frederico S., 217
Bartone, Carl R., 50n
Bassie, V. Lewis, 90n
Baumann, E. Robert, 90n
Bilharziasis. *See* Schistosomiasis
Birthrates, 74, 75
Block rate, 178, 179
Bobeda, Carlos M., 126n
Bonus incentive system, 157–58, 200
Borjesson, E. K. C., 126n
Boston, 207
Bradley, David J., 18n, 33n, 43n, 53n, 54n, 72n, 113n, 124n
Brazil, 160, 217, 220
Breast feeding, 38
Burton, Ian, 134n
Bush, J. W., 54n

Cairo, Tito H., 92n
Calcutta, 26
Cali, 220
California, 113, 206, 208
Calorie consumption, 77–78
Cameroon, 183
Canada, 108
Capital equipment, 60, 135, 162
Capital indivisibility, 166–68
Carruthers, I. D., 62n, 92n, 139n, 181n
Central America. *See* Latin America
Chemotherapy, in treatment of schistosomiasis, 42
Chico Romero, José A., 189
Childhood morbidity, 69, 70
Childhood mortality, 42, 68, 74–75; studies on, 220–21
Children, 74; and diseases, 40, 41, 46; nutritional state of, 39–40; as water carriers, 71, 73

Cholera, 33, 40–41, 71; in Bacolod City, *218;* life prognosis with, 222, *223;* relation to sanitation, *216;* studies on, 214–16
Cleasby, John L., 91n
Clustering, 97–98
Coelen, Stephen P., 66n
Colombia, 220
Committees, local, 84, 142, 143, 145, 181–82, 200
Community development, 83, 199
Community enthusiasm, 108–10, 128–29, 142, 199
Community facilities, construction of, *10,* 60, 83–84, 108–10, 141–42, 198; costs of, 167; financing of, 158–59, 175
Community water program promotion, 109, 129, 155, 199
Complementary programs. *See* Public sector investment (complementary)
Consumers, 122, 179, 182, 185; category of, 235, 237; costs to, 77–78, 123–28, 165–90, 201–02; current, 171–75; industrial, 170, 173, 177; new, 175–76; reaction to charges, 201–02; willingness to pay, 31, 47, 49, 111, 165, 175, 176, 184–90, 201. *See also* User charges
Contractors, 142
Control area, in disease studies, 37, 38
Cost-benefit analysis, 31, 52, 113–16, 126–27, 142, 164, 171–75; measuring in, 35, 46–47, 110–11, 132; in metering, 234–38; of public sector investment, 45, 200
Costa Rica, 160, 206
Costs, 22–26, 57–60, 75, *93,* 106, 190; averted 76–78; bonus, 157–58, 200; construction, 7, *10,* 18, 95–97, 105, 108, 123–28, 130–31, 141–42, 158–59, 167, 175; consumer, 77–78, 128–28, 165–90, 201–02; and cost effectiveness, 40–41, 42, 52–55, 226; disease, 34–35, 45–55, 69, 112–17, 196; economies of scale in, 82, 89–102, 138–40, 178, 198, 227–30, *231–33;* of operation and maintenance, 83–84, 90–92, 97, 98, 105, 108, 109, 110, 144, 159, 160, 161, 190; opportunity, 118, 129, 166–67, 170–71, 175; and service quality, 17–19, 45, 89–102, 119–21, 184; of sewage disposal, 9, *10, 14–16,* 40–41, 58, 98–102, 201, 235; sunk, 68, 165, 169, 178; and system size, 94–95; of UNDD targets, 7, 9, *11–13;* user participation in, *186–87;* WHO statistics on, 9, *10–16, 136, 186–87. See also* Marginal cost pricing; User charges
Coughlin, Robert E., 98n
Cvjetanović, B., 41n, 117

Dajani, Jarir S., 56n, 99n, 100
Dalton, G. E., 72n
deGreiff, Beatriz, 66n
deVlieger, C. A., 182n
Diarrheal disease, 33, 34, 46, 205–06; and nutrition, 40; reduction in, 113, 114; studies of, 39, 206–14

Dillon, Ann, 68n
Discounting earnings, 68, 75, 196
Diseases, 49–55; fecal disposal-related, 34 prevalence of, 53, 113; prognosis for, 223; rates of, 36–37, 52, 53, 113, 114, 196; reduction in spread of, 71; sources in rural areas, 35, 184; sufferers from, 54–55; water-based, 34, 41; waterborne, 33, 40, 41, 196; water-related, *32,* 34, 54, 114; water-washed, 34. *See also* specific diseases
Dominican Republic, 21, 22, 61; livestock watering in, 62–63; rural home values in, 65–66; system costs in, 92; underemployment in, 69
Donaldson, David, 18n, 22n, 127n
Downing, Paul B., 99n, 100
Drainage, 137, 182
Drinking water, 35; bacteriological examinations of, *120;* quality standards for, *121;* quality surveillance of, *120*
Dublin, Louis I., 51n

East Africa, 77, 143; diseases in, 114, 121, 212; water taxes in, 181
Economic development. *See* Economic growth
Economic efficiency, 165–66, 168–70, 171, 178
Economic growth, 57, 61–66, 74, 103, 126, 139, 147, 194
Economic output, 61–66, 70, 73–74; and health, 66–67, 69–70; women and, 72
Economies of scale, 138, 198; from developed countries, 90–92; from developing countries, 92–98; selected regressions in, *231–33;* and waste disposal, 99–102. *See also* Costs
Externalities, 184–85
Egypt, 211
Employment, 69, 70, 80, 129, 194, 195
Enke, Stephen, 75n
Environmental sanitation, 36, 208, 210, 214. *See also* Sanitation facilities
Epidemics, 77
Epidemiology, 117–18
Escherichia coli, 205, 209
Ethiopia, 57
Excreta disposal. *See* Sanitation facilities (for excreta disposal)

Fanshel, S., 54n
Farooq, M., 69n
Fein, Rashi, 51n
Fenwick, K. W. H., 62n, 70n, 214
Financial viability, 25; and economic efficiency, 168–70
Fish farming, 62
Flow-limiting device, 181, 182, 183
Ford, J. L., 230n

Fordilla valves, 125, 126, 182, 183
Frankel, Richard J., 134n
Frederiksen, Harald, 75n
Fresno County, 208

Gabon, 183
Gardens: irrigation of, 61, 174, 195, 200, 237
Gemmell, Robert S., 99n, 100
Georgia, 209
Germany, Federal Republic of, 81
Ghana, 72, 123, 160
Goodwin, Melvin H., 212
Gordon, J. E., 39n, 40n
Grab, B., 41n
Grants; conditional, 162–63
Grossman, Michael, 48n
Groundwater, 121, 167
Growth points, 102–03, 106, 107–08, 109, 137, 177, 194
Guatemala, 92, 139

Hand pumps, 22, 23, 25, 174, 184
Haines, T. W., 207
Harvey, Milton E., 79n, 80n
Health: calculation of better, 48, 49–50, 51–52; community, 35–36, 54; economic evaluation of better, 47–52; and economic output, 66–67, 69–70; and project costs, 112–17
Health changes: evaluation of, 49; monitoring of, 37
Health education, 39, 48; programs in, 44–45, 137, 188, 200, 215
Health improvement, 126–27, 184–85, 195, 196, 213; government programs in, 50, 155
Health insurance, 50
Health investment, 26, 117–18, 147; measurable benefits of, 35, 43, 46–47, 49, 222–26
Health ministries, 147, 153
Health services, 76; and program administration, 147, 153
Health state, 53, 54, 222–26; benefit vector in, 223, 224, 225; kinds of, 55, 225; weighting function in, 224, 225, 226
Health status index, 54–55, 224–25; and derivation of village water supply, *225*
Health studies, 36–43; cross-sectional, 36–37; problems of 38; sampling errors in, 38, 196; time series, 37
Heer, David M., 74n, 75n
Henderson, J. M., 17n
Herrara, Felipe, 81n

Herrick, Bruce, 75n
Hollister, Arthur C., Jr., 206
Honduras, 92, 132
Hoover, Edgar M., 108n
Hopi, 208
Horlacher, David E., 74n
House connections, 94–95, 123–25, 126, 176, 180, 181, 201; in Peru, *127*
House reservoirs, 179–80, 182
Human life: economic worth of, 49–50, 196

Ibadan, 217
Idelovitch, Emanuel, 134n
Illinois, 90
Imported material, 59, 60, 135; cost of, *136*
Income: distribution of, 49–97, 158–63; generation of, 196; redistribution of: 103–08, 147, 161, 162, 197; spent on water, 185–88
Index. *See* Health status index; Priority index
India, 127, 215; local contributions in, 159, 175; standpost tap in, 182; subsidy systems in, 160
Infrastructure investment, 57, 64, 102–03, 135–37, 194
Insects, 34
Instituto Nacional de Aguas Potables y Alcantarillados, 21, 63
Inter-American Development Bank, 94, 105, 107, 158, 159
Intermediate Technology Development Group, 134
International aid agencies, 21, 110, 158–59. *See also* specific agencies
International Development Research Centre, 134
Investment. *See* Public sector investment
Iran, 57, 211
Isard, Walter, 98n

Jarrett, Robert E., 221
Jordan, P., 122n, 219
Jordan, 62

Keeve, J. Phillip, 40n, 205n
Kentucky, 207
Kenya, 92, 174, 181, 190, 214
Kingston, 220
Kourany, Miguel, 209
Kpomkpo, 72

Labor, 60, 61, 195; free, 18, 129, 199; monetary value of, 130–31; and program administration, 141–42; scarcity of, 70, 72

Labor productivity, 42, 66–70; of women, 72–73
Lahore, 61
Land use: effects of pricing on, 177
Lane, Morton, 222n
Latin America, 35, 42, 67, 110, 142, 143, 179, 181, 189, 220; cost contribution of, villages in, 105, 108, 158, 175, 190; free labor in, 60, 129; growth centers in, 81; house connections in, 123, *127;* local committees in, 84, 181; program administration in, 145; revolving fund in, 159, 162; system capacity in, 139
Latrines, 100–01, 137, 215
Lauria, Donald T., 92n, 138n
Leibenstein, Harvey, 75n
Levy, Mildred B., 78n, 80n
Lima, 187
Little, Ian M. D., 131n
Little-Mirrlees method, 131–33
Livestock watering, 62–63, 174, 180, 181, 195, 200
Lowry, Ira S., 79n

McCabe, Leland J., 207
McJunkin, Frederick E., 22n
Mahler, Halfdan, 1n
Maintenance, system. *See* Operation and maintenance of systems
Malaria, 75
Malenbaum, Wilfred, 67n
Manila, 187
Manne, Alan S., 138n
Marginal cost pricing, 18, 159, 160, 165–68, 171–75, 179, 201, 236; externalities, 184–85; loss-making in, 1969; lumpiness in, 166–68, 169; problems of, 166, 167; rationale for, 165; second-best in, 170–71; shadow pricing in, 61, 131–34, 170,71, 195. *See also* Cost-benefit analysis; Metering; User charges
Marshall, Carter L., 46n
Massachusetts, 98
Mauritius, 209, 211
Maystre, Yves, 134n
Mendenhall, Ralph L., 62n
Metering, 65, 234–38; costs and benefits of, 171–75
Mexico, 21, 24, 69
Middleton, Richard, 93n
Milton, J. P., 46n
Mirrlees, James A., 131n
Mishan, Edward J., 47n
Monay, Venezuela, 210

Moore, Helen, 206
Moran, Ricardo, 75n
Morbidity rates, 213; reduction in, 69–70
Morocco, 5
Morse, R., 81n
Mortality rates, 67–69

Nairobi, 187
National resources, allocation of, 80, 82
Nepal, 127
New York City, 55
Nigeria, 183, 217
Nonprice allocation. *See* Water rationing
Norwegian Aid, 21

Operation and maintenance of systems, 25, 27, 142–44, 145, 198–99; costs of, 83–84, 90–92, 97, 98, 105, 108, 109, 110, 159, 160, 161, 190; technology in, 134–35; user charges for, 144, 159–62, 190
Opportunity cost, 118, 129, 166–67, 170–71, 175

Paddle wheel, 183
Pakistan, 61
Pakistan, East, 211. *See also* Bangladesh
Pan American Health Organization, 7, 23, 105, 159
Panama, 25, 209
Parker, R. N., 72n
Personnel: motivation of, 155–57; professional, 145, *154;* subprofessional, *156;* training of, 153–55, 200
Peru, 21, 109, 127, 160
Philippines, 40, 214–15
Philippines Cholera Committee, 214
Phoenix, 117
Pilferage of supplies, 158
Piped water, 23–24, 34, 123, 221, 234; and cholera, 216; and diarrheal disease, 206, 207, 211, 212, 213, 214; and schistosomiasis, 42
Pitchford, R. J., 217n, 219
Plastic pipe, 60, 135
Pompanito, 210
Population: growth, 73, 139, 140; in health studies, 37–39; location, 23, 82–84, 178, 194; migration, 22, 23, 64, 78–82, 139, 194; service targets, 5–13; size and programs, 20–21. *See also* Regional centers
Prest, A. R., 47n
Priority index, 105–06
Programs, complementary. *See* Public sector investment (complementary)

Project ranking, 110–11, 164, 202; worst first in, 103–08
Project planning. *See* Water supply programs (planning of)
Property values, 65–66
Public bathing facilities, 97
Public revenue, 57, 65–66, 103, 160, 161; collection of, 25, 26. *See also* Metering; User charges
Public sector investment, 13, 31, 45, 47, 57, 106–08, 109, 131, 133, 144; complementary, 102–03, 135–37, 167, 194; time frame for, 138–40
Public standposts. *See* Standposts
Puerto Rico, 113
Puffer, Ruth Rice, 68n, 220
Pump operator, 155
Pyatt, Edwin F., 51n, 113n

Quebec, 108

Recife, 220
Redford, Arthur, 79n
Rees, Judith, 134n
Regional centers, 79–80, 81, 102–03. *See also* Growth points
Reservoirs, 60, 62, 140, 179–80, 183
Resistencia, 220
Revolving funds, 159, 162
Rice, Dorothy, 47n, 51n
Richardson, Harry W., 81n
Riche Fond Valley, 42, 219
Riddell, Barry J., 79n, 80n
Robinson, Warren, C., 74n
Rockefeller Foundation, 41
Rogers, Peter P., 51n, 113n
Roof tanks. *See* House reservoirs
Rosser, R., 54n
Rubenstein, A., 208
Rural programs, 5–7, 13–20, 137; community enthusiasm for, 108–10, 128–29; defined, 20–26, 193; design period for, 138–39; problems of, 34–35. *See also* Sanitation facilities, rural

Safilios-Rothschild, Constantina, 79n
Saint Lucia: infection rates in, 121; rural water consumption in, 45, 183; schistosomiasis study on, 41, 42, 66, 219; water supply costs in, 125
Salmonella, 205, 209
San José, 160
San Salvador, 220
Sanitary education. *See* Health education

Sanitation facilities, rural: 5, 35, 42, 100, 214, 215, 217; and cholera, *216;* and enteric diseases, 207, 208, 209, 211; 212, 213; for excreta disposal, 39, 41, 46, 207; use of, 38, 46. *See also* Environmental sanitation; Sewage disposal
Santiago, 220
Santiago del Estero, 64
São Paulo, 187
Schistosoma, 217, 219
Schistosomiasis, 33, 41–42, 66, 222; control study of, 41; infection rates of, 121; life prognosis with, 222, *223;* studies on, 216–20
Schliessmann, D. J., 207
Scrimshaw, Nevin S., 39n, 40n
Seidel, Harris F., 90n, 91n
Semiarid regions, 195
Septic tanks, 101, 237
Serrano, Carlos V., 68n
Service access. *See* Access to service
Service, quality of, 17–19, 45, *96,* 110, 118–19, 198
Sewage disposal, 99–102, 147, 195, 235, 237; current status of, 5–7; in developing countries, *8, 9;* external assistance for, *58;* planning agencies for, *150*
— systems, operation and maintenance of: agencies responsible for, *152;* upgrading of, 127–28
— targets, 7–11; rural costs of, *13, 15;* urban costs of, *14, 15, 16*
Sewage treatment, 98–99, 101
Shadow pricing. *See* Marginal cost pricing
Shigella, 205, 207, 208, 209, 211, 212; elimination of, 113
Shipman, Harold, 94n, 101n, 119n
SIDA. See Swedish International Development Authority
Siegel, Francine M., 217
Simon, Julian, 75n
Skin diseases, 40; studies of, 213–14
Smith, Dean O., 74n
Snails, 41, 42, 216–17, 219
Snyder, John C., 74n
South Africa, 219
South America. *See* Latin America
Southeast Asia, 5, 7, 60
Sri Lanka, 75, 159, 211
Standard of living index, 50–51
Standposts, 123, 125, 174, 181, 182, 183, 201
Stewart, William H., 209
Subrahmanyan, K., 215
Sudan, 46, 210, 211

Index / 277

Sunk costs, 68, 165, 169, 178
Swedish International Development Authority, 21

Taghi Farvar, M. T., 46n
Tanzania, 72, 83, 124, 190; development project in, 92–93; specifications and cost estimates in, *93*
Tariffs. *See* User charges
Taylor, Carl E., 40n
Technical support, in maintenance, 22, 134–135, 143–44, 155, 198
Thailand, 21, 104, 143, 158
Trachoma, 46
Tropicale device, 182
Trypanosomiasis, transmission of, 123
Turkey, 5
Turvey, R., 47n
Tylor "waste not" valve, 182
Typhoid fever, 41, 71

Uemura, K., 41n
Ujàmaa, 83
Unakul, Somnuek, 18n
UNDD. *See* United Nations Development Decade
Unesco, 22
UNICEF. *See* United Nations Childrens Fund
UNIDO method, 132–33
Union of Soviet Socialist Republics, 22, 81
United Arab Republic, 211
United Nations Childrens Fund, 25
United Nations Development Decade, targets of, 7, 9, 13, 193
United Nations Research Institute, 50
United States, 81, 91, 229
Unrau, Gladwin O., 41n, 45n, 125n
Upper Volta, 77
Urban areas, 102; economic output of, 70; income in, 59; population migration to, 22, 78, 79; size of, 80, 81–82; slums in, 108, 179; subsidy systems in, 160–61; water supply needs of, 97, 197
Urban-rural subsidies, 160–63
User charges, 66, 84, 105, 110, 164, 197, 199; as flat rates, 180–81; geographically uniform, 176–79; for house connections, 123–25; negative effect of, 63; for operation and maintenance, 144, 159–62; 190; as percentage of income, *188;* and project evaluation, 164–90; for upgrading systems, 125–28; willingness to pay, 31, 45, 47, 49, 111, 165, 172, 175–76, 184–90, 201. *See also* Metering
Uttar Pradesh, 213

Vaccination programs, 76, 196
Vaccines: anticholera, 40; antityphoid, 41
Vandalism, 174–75
Vásquez, Manuel, 209
Venezuela, 113, 210, 211
Village industry: expansion of, 63–64
Village labor. *See* Labor
Villages, 22, 23, 24, 83–84, 102, 145, 157, 190, 195, 197; enthusiasm for water supply in, 108–10, 128–29, 142, 199; selection for water supply to, 104–08, 109, 128, 175–76, 194, 197; service costs to, 94–97, 105, 106, 178, 187–89; surveys in, 48, 189, 201. *See also* Committees, local
Virus fevers, 33

Wadycki, Walter, 78n, 80n
Wagner, Edmund G., 113n
Wall, John M., 40n, 205n
Wannoni, Luis, 113n
Warford, Jeremy J., 66n, 83n, 172n, 178n, 230n
Warner, Dennis, 18n, 43n, 56n, 72n
Wastewater, 61, 99, 108, 128, 174, 184
Water boards, 200; charging policy for, 176–77, 197
Water carriers, 71–72
Water charges. *See* Marginal cost pricing; Metering; User charges
Water consumption, 43–44, 49, 51–52, 57, 59, 75, 121, 166; from community supplies, *124;* and metering, 173, 235; reduction of, 77–78, 172–73, 201; regulating of, 171–72, 179–84; seasonal pattern of, 237–38. *See also* User charges
Water contamination, 108, 119–21, 184
Water meters. *See* Metering
Water quality, 42, 45, 119–21, 184
Water quantity, 39, 40, 42, 44, 121–28, 173
Water rationing, 171–72, 235
Water service: intermittent, 171, 184, 197
Water sources, 39, 64, 95–96, 97, 104, 106, 167
Water supply, 27, 40, 45, 47, 57–58, 83, 85, 188; access to, *4, 5, 6–13,* 18, 19, 25, 78–82, 97, 104, 185; capacity, 138, 167, 172; defined, 1; and health services, 76, 153; and nutrition, 39–40; priority index for, 105–06; subsidization of, 7, 9–13, 17–19, 21–26, 103, 105, 110, 160–63, 169, 174, 178, 185–90, 197; UNDD targets for, 7–10, *11–13,* 193; user participation in costs of, *186, 187. See also* Consumers; Costs; User charges
— policies, 26, 107–08, 165–66, 171, 193
— programs, 24, 137; administration of, 141–63, 199; central agency for, 144–45; external assistance for, 57, *58;* investment in, *16,* 18–19,

26–27, 45, 47–51, 52–53, 56–88, 116–18, 164, 167, 194, 195, 200, 202, 223–24; planning of, 27, 36, 61, 112–40, 144–45. *See also* Public sector investment.

— systems, 23, 72, 74, 82–84, 159; cost estimates of, 75, *93;* design of, 36, 118–27, 138–39, enthusiasm for, 108–10, 128–29, 199; expansion of, 159–60, 165, 179, 201; specifications for, *93;* in Tanzania, 92–94; technology in, 134–35, 182–84; upgrading of, 128–28. *See also* Operation and maintenance of systems; Urban areas; Villages

Water taps, 174; location of, 121, 123, 126, 180, 182–83

Water tariffs. *See* Marginal cost pricing; Metering; User charges

Water treatment, 97, 101, 135

Water troughs, 63

Water utilities data, 90–92, 227–33; regressions for, 228, 229–30, *231–33;* variables for, 227–29

Water vendors, 174–75

Water wastage, 45, 100, 173, 180, 181, 182, 183, 237

Watt, James, 113n, 208

Watts, V., 54n

Weir, John M., 41n, 216n

Weisbrod, Burton A., 42n, 51n, 66n

Wells, 22, 23, 25

West Africa, 181

Western Pacific, 60

White, Anne U., 18n, 33n, 54n, 72n, 113n

White, Gilbert, F., 18n, 33n, 54n, 72n, 77n, 113n, 212

WHO. *See* World Health Organization

Willingness to pay. *See* Consumers; User charges

Women, as water carriers, 71–72, 78

World Bank, 130

World Food Program, 129, 130

World Health Organization, 1, 117, 153; demonstration project with UNICEF, 21; disease studies by, 209, 210, 211, 214; survey data, 5, 9, 43, 60, 121, 147, 155, 185; water standards 19, 119

Zaina, 62, 70, 214

Zambia, 158, 190

Yap, Lorene Y. L., 78n

The full range of World Bank publications, both free and for sale, is described in the *World Bank Catalog of Publications,* and of the continuing research program of the World Bank, in *World Bank Research Program: Abstracts of Current Studies.* The most recent edition of each is available without charge from:

>PUBLICATIONS UNIT
>THE WORLD BANK
>1818 H STREET, N.W.
>WASHINGTON, D.C. 20433
>U.S.A.